# LEARNING TOGETHER

## A SOURCEBOOK ON

## JEWISH FAMILY EDUCATION

Janice P. Alper, Editor

Alternatives in Religious Education, Inc.
Denver, Colorado

Published by:
Alternatives in Religious Education, Inc.
Denver, Colorado


Library of Congress Number 87-70964
ISBN 0-86705-019-5

Printed in the United States of America

10  9  8  7  6  5  4  3  2  1

## Dedication

This book is dedicated to my mother, Gertrude Leichman Pearl-
stein, of blessed memory, who taught me the value of family,
and to her grandchildren, Steven, Louis, Julie, and Sharon Alper,
who are hopefully now learning that value through me.

# Table Of Contents

# Preface

**About This Book**   This book is written for Directors of Education, Rabbis, social workers in Jewish Family Service agencies, Jewish Center workers, teachers, Bureau of Jewish Education personnel, camp directors, program directors, indeed, all who work directly with or program for families in Jewish settings. It is also intended for people who work in an advisory capacity to Jewish agencies, such as members of school committees or members of agency boards.

The programs contained in this book were chosen as models which can be replicated in a variety of settings. Some are outlined in detail, while others contain only the framework of the program, allowing the facilitator to insert the content appropriate to the group with whom he/she is working. Almost all of the programs contain a bibliography/resource list. The programs which require full family participation contain interactional or parallel components; the generations blend together and adults never take the role of spectators to the activities. There are several programs, notably in the section on Family Life Education, which are designed strictly for adult participants, but serve to enhance family life as a result of their content.

**Contributors**   The contributors to this book come from all denominations of Jewish life and include classroom teachers and Directors of Education, social workers, Rabbis, college professors, Family Education Coordinators, program directors, and Bureau personnel. They work in synagogues, Jewish Family Service agencies, Bureaus of Jewish Education, and at day schools and colleges. All of them share a common desire to make a difference in the lives of the people with whom they are in contact. They engage their creativity, lobby, cajole, train, and direct family programs of all kinds in order to enhance Jewish family life today.

**Contents and Organization**   Each chapter begins with a title page which lists the title of the program, the contributor, the designer (if different from the contributor), the topic, target audience, time frame, and staff.

This book is divided into three parts. Part I, Family Education Programs, are those programs which were developed primarily in Jewish educational settings. They are organized according to time parameters. Ongoing programs continue over the course of a school or program year; multi-session programs involve two or more sessions, which occur over a given period of time; extended time programs are of longer duration than a normal school session of 2½ to 3 hours and include retreats. One-time programs are those which can be executed within the given hours of religious school without extending the day.

For purposes of this book, Family Education Programs are characterized by interactional activities which enrich and enhance family life and have learning as their goal. In some instances the line between a Family Education Program and a Family Life Education Program was blurry and an arbitrary decision was made as to the section in which the program would appear.

Part II contains Family Life Education programs. These programs were developed primarily at Jewish Family Service and at other communal agencies. The Family Life Education programs often require a facilitator trained in social work. Frequently the focus of these programs is one of intervention, with a Jewish component as an adjunct to them. An explanation of Family Life Education, written by Fradya Rembaum, the Assistant Director of the Council on Jewish Life, Jewish Federation Council of Greater Los Angeles, may be found on page 301.

Part III contains additional ideas in brief, an annotated bibliography, a list of contributors, and an index of chapters by subject. Additional Ideas In Brief are synopses of programs which have been used by schools, Jewish Family Service agencies, and the like. These brief program ideas are presented without detail. Yet, they are worthwhile for stimulating ideas for additional programmatic possibilities. The Annotated Bibliography, compiled by Barbara Eidelman Wachs, is divided into three sections: general background information about the family, curricular

materials, and program aids. The listing of Contributors is
arranged in alphabetical order, and includes their addresses. For
further information concerning any program, write directly to
the contributor. The Index Of Chapters By Subject is provided
to facilitate the accessing of programs by a particular subject.

Heading the list of contributors, you'll find my address. I look
forward to hearing from you and to learning about the personal
touches you have added to the programs which follow.

*"V'shinantam L'vanecha"* – teach diligently to your children so
that they may in turn teach diligently to theirs.

**Acknowledgments**   To all of the educators whose creative
efforts went into the making of this book, a thousand thanks.
It would not have been possible without each and every one
of those who shared their programs and ideas so generously
and willingly.

To the many librarians, secretaries, and clerks who helped me
to find the myriad of resources listed in this book, a special
thank you.

To my publishers at Alternatives in Religious Education, Inc.,
Audrey Friedman Marcus and Rabbi Raymond A. Zwerin, my
appreciation for the confidence shown me and for "nursing" me
along in this, my first effort for publication. It is a joy to work
with them and they have taught me much.

To the Coalition for Alternatives in Jewish Education, my gratitude
for supporting the idea of this project; to the CAJE Committee
on Family Education, my appreciation for the pioneering work
which has brought the issue of Family Education to the fore-
front; and to individual CAJE members who so willingly shared
their creative efforts in this volume, my special thanks.

To Joel Lurie Grishaver, *todah rabbah* for your encouragement
and support.

And finally, to Marvin, who gave up the theater, dinner out and dinner in, weekends and evenings, so that I could work on "my book." It certainly could not have come to fruition without his unshakable confidence in me, his love, his faith, and his devotion to our family.

# Introduction To
# Jewish Family Education

**The Way We Were**   As a child growing up in Brooklyn, New York, I assumed that my family was the norm. I thought everyone had parents, brothers and sisters, aunts, uncles, and cousins who came together every Sunday in their grandparents home to eat, to laugh, to argue, and to talk almost non-stop about everything from the latest movies to child rearing and business deals. For me all memories of childhood revolve around my family. The Jewish aspects of my life replay through my mind much as pictures on a screen.

I can still recall: Walking to *shul* on Saturday morning carrying the key to the house for my grandmother; the smell of simmering chicken soup, *gribenes*, and fresh baked *challah* on Friday afternoon, as I stepped gingerly on yesterday's newspaper which covered the freshly mopped floor to protect it. I remember my *zayda* leading the *Seders*, which grew larger every year with the addition of new cousins to the family. I still get a nervous shudder remembering the first time I said the *feir kashas* in Hebrew and Yiddish. Afterwards my *zayda* turned to his youngest son, who was probably 27 or 28 at the time, and humorously said in Yiddish, "Now it's your turn." I remember getting new clothes and shoes at Rosh Hashanah and Pesach, and Sukkot both at home and in *shul*, and carrying a flag with an apple and candle on top for Simchat Torah.

The very air I breathed when I was growing up was Jewish. Street after street in our neighborhood abounded with signs of the Jewish people — kosher butcher shops, delis, and other stores, *shuls*, *cheders*, and the like. My parents, my brother, and I lived in the same house with my mother's parents, and that environment has influenced my life as an adult.

I have, however, discovered that my childhood memories are different from those of many of my generation. When I tell my friends that we tore the toilet paper on Friday afternoon in order not to violate the Shabbos, or that we had a light burning all Friday night which was extinguished Saturday morning by a *Shabbos goy,* people stare at me openmouthed and unbelieving. But it is all true. Many of my contemporaries, though having had family structures similar to mine, had completely dissimilar experiences growing up. Their parents, like mine, were also children of immigrants, but wanting with all their hearts first and foremost to integrate into the general American society, they emphasized their religious and cultural heritage at home. Then came the post World War II years. Upward mobility became the dominant theme. The extended family was sacrificed on the altar of that mobility; the nuclear family was born in the tract homes of suburbia. For the thousands of Jewish families which moved to the suburbs, the synagogue became a surrogate for the extended Jewish family.

My own children, raised in suburbia, have an entirely different perspective about Judaism from me. My husband and I chose to raise our family in a community in Southern California where Jews were clearly in a minority. Very often, my now almost adult children, were the only Jewish kids in their public school classes. We made a conscious effort to provide our children with Jewish experiences. Yet, I have come to realize that their Jewish memories are vastly different from mine.

Family to me is a vast array of parents, siblings, aunts, uncles, cousins, grandparents, and relatives of relatives. Family to my children is the six of us as a single unit; other relatives are incidental. Holiday celebrations in my mind are strictly Jewish and family oriented. For my children, holidays represent vacations from school and the Jewish part is sometimes equated with separate children's programs at our synagogue. It is true that in our home there has always been a Sukkah, a *Seder,* and a weekly celebration of Shabbat, but the essence is different. Grandparents, aunts, uncles, and cousins are missing. In their places are close Jewish friends with similar interests, struggling to maintain and transmit the Jewish heritage yet still living fully in an essentially non-Jewish world.

The family I have raised is not unique; we may even be typical of the American Jewish family of today. My husband and I chose to raise our children away from the insular environment of our extended family. We tried to give them a sense of belonging to a people by providing them with a Jewish education in a synagogue religious school, by sending them to Jewish camps in the summer and on trips to Israel, and by observing Jewish traditions in our home. My children have strong positive identifications as Jews. Whether this identification will carry through into their adult lives remains to be seen. For, being Jewish is just one facet of my children's lives; it is not the entire, all-consuming way of life it has been for me. This to me is a frustration, but I know it is certainly not my frustration alone.

**Times Have Changed**    That the Jewish family has undergone radical changes of late is evident. Numerous books and journal articles point up these changes. Not only is the extended family of yesteryear with its many children and classic roles but a mere whisper of nostalgia today, even the nuclear family of the 50s and 60s is no longer typical. Steven M. Cohen, writing in the *American Jewish Yearbook* of 1982, provides one reason for these changes when he tells us that our demographic behavior tends to mirror that of the larger society in which we live.[1]

It is no surprise to note, then, that Jews are also experiencing a rising divorce rate (naturally leading to more single parent families); more intermarriage (in the early 1980s, nearly four out of ten Jews were intermarried with Christians[2]); changing roles for women (with most parents working, there is less time to nurture a Jewish environment in the home); marriages at a later age (Jews are single longer, thus becoming involved in creating Jewish family life at a later age); postponement of childbearing; and fewer children per family.[3]

At the same time that we are victimized by the negative aspects of the current sociology of the society at large and traumatized by the price it exacts, we are nevertheless blessed by its largesse. As Bernard Reisman so succinctly puts it, "The American Jewish community of today has essentially made it socially and materially. It is a well acculturated sub-community in America. In fact, it is the very success of the Jewish accommodation that has created a new set of needs for American Jews. They have so diluted their ties to Jewish culture and religion as to put in jeopardy the capacity of the Jewish community to survive as a distinctive entity. Thus, Jewish families today have to work at

Judaizing their lives just as their parents and grandparents had to work at Americanizing their lives."[4]

Certainly since Talmudic times, perhaps even since the days of Abraham, Judaism has been nurtured and sheltered in the home. "It is there that Jewish learning, commitment, sensitivity to values are cultivated and cherished."[5] Norman Linzer has noted that Jewish parents are expected to provide their children with the rudiments of life, to instill in them a curiosity about the world so that they are stable and productive individuals who possess a strong identification with their Jewish roots, historically, intellectually, and morally.[6]

Herein lies the rub. On the one hand, it is clear that the home should be the locus and focus of Jewish education. But, on the other hand, parents today either don't know enough about their heritage to educate their children, or they have abdicated this role to synagogues and Jewish agencies.[7]

It is not unusual that the Jewish community be called upon to assume a major role in Jewish education. For the past 2,000 years it is the community which has created and maintained the academy, the *yeshivah*, the *cheder*, the Talmud Torah, the day school, the Hebrew school, and the religious school. In fact, it *is* the responsiblity of every Jewish community to support its Jewish educational facilities. Indeed, as Gerald Bubis says, it is the responsibility of the community to strengthen the Jewish family not only by providing educational opportunities, but psychological, and sociological services as well.[8] Linzer, too, affirms this communal role, asserting that the primary interest of the Jewish community is "to buttress Jewish experience and identity in the face of rapid assimilation."[9]

Without doubt the community has responded to the perceived need. Federations have increased their allocations to Jewish education; central agencies for Jewish education are being strengthened and expanded; teacher training and support has become a high priority on the part of national and local institutions; new and innovative curricula and materials are available; and certainly more day schools, religious schools, and *yeshivot* open their doors to more students every year. But, just as the home alone cannot be the sole provider of Jewish education, so, too, the community alone cannot be the sole provider of Jewish education.

As Isa Aron so aptly puts it, there is a need to bridge the gap between school and home. Parents need to be educated themselves so that they can deepen their own Judaic knowledge.[10] Dr. Hertzel Fishman, writing in the *Pedagogic Reporter*, states: "Hebrew schools may teach about Judaism but even the best of them, by themselves, cannot mold Jewish character, forge values, internalize ideals, or sharpen Jewish commitments."[11] He goes on to say that for Jewish education to be lastingly significant, there has to be a qualitative school experience supplemented by the ambiance of home life and the personal examples of family members. Ongoing family reinforcement is needed even for the best of Hebrew schools in order to cope with the non-Jewish environment.[12]

There is evidence to suggest that involving families in Jewish education at an early stage of their children's life will have a positive effect on Jewish home practice.[13] Furthermore, it would appear that the fourth and (fifth) generation Jew is searching for answers and for models of acceptable Jewish behaviors.[14]

All of these findings and recommendations point surely to the urgent need for Family Education and Family Life Education in a Jewish setting. But how to go about it?

In recent years, leaders in the fields of Jewish education and Jewish communal service have called for a multi-disciplinary approach when dealing with the Jewish family. As long ago as 1968, Morton Teicher, writing in the *Journal Of Jewish Communal Service*, said that we need the involvement of institutions and agencies and professionals in Jewish education, including the synagogue, the Community Center, the Jewish Family Service agency, Rabbis, Jewish educators, social workers, and family members.[15]

It is true that our families need schools and agencies to nurture the seeds of Jewish knowledge and to provide moral and psychological succor during these tumultuous times. However, it is also clear that our schools and agencies need to be able to call upon and count on the home to implement, reinforce, and enhance the teachings, practices, and values of the Jewish heritage.

How do we as Jewish educators work with the home to foster the spirit of Judaism? How do we help people not born to Judaism, not raised with Jewish memories, not connected to Israel, to prayer, or to the Hebrew language, identify with the history, values, and practices of Judaism? And how do we help those who, though born into a Jewish home, yet not having a sufficient Jewish education, want to develop and maintain and transmit to their children a Jewish life style and mind set? To link home and community in one united educational effort, a variety of high quality programs are needed. Bernard Reisman, among many others in the field, has outlined what some of those programs might be. He called for programs that involve parents in the study of Jewish content parallel with their children's study, programs in Jewish literacy which deal with skills connected with Jewish holidays and life cycle events, programs which introduce participants to Jewish texts and resources, and workshops which help people clarify their ties to the Jewish community.[16]

Bringing programs of this nature into being presents an enormous challenge. But the challenge has not been without its champions. Talented Jewish educators/agency personnel have devoted themselves to the task of creating and implementing just such programs. The best of these programs and program ideas have been carefully sought out for presentation in this sourcebook.

This book is but a beginning in the work of bringing schools/agencies and the home together to participate in Jewish activities, to share Jewish experiences, to create Jewish memories, and to make being Jewish an active, dynamic aspect of life. When the home, once again, becomes the main focus of Jewish life, then the family education in which we are all involved will have fulfilled its purpose. Each program we facilitate brings us one step closer to this goal.

**Jewish Family Education**  In this book we have delineated two types of education for the family. One is Jewish Family Education, the other is Jewish Family Life Education. The latter includes programs and workshops related to life cycle or contemporary family situations, among which are: Marriage preparation, childbirth preparation, support groups for Jews by Choice and intermarried couples, parenting issues, mid-life and aging crises, etc. In concept and technique, Family Life Education is a combination of group or family therapy and adult education. For a full discussion of Jewish Family Life Education, see the Introduction To Jewish Family Life Education by Fradya Rembaum, on page 301.

The former, Jewish Family Education, does not involve intervention or crises of transition. When both a student and his/her family come together for Jewish learning on any topic, it is called Jewish Family Education.[17] Such programs are specifically geared to provide participants with the knowledge, skills, and tools for enhanced Jewish experiences which can be transferred to their homes and integrated into their lives. These programs provide an intergenerational learning component for all participants. The learning may be interactive (generations learn together) or parallel (generations learning the same material separately) depending on the nature of the material, the size of the group, and the ages of the participants.

A Jewish Family Education program may be a means of enhancing the school or class curriculum by introducing new materials, reinforcing what has been learned, or culminating a unit of study. It may be constructed in a variety of ways. It may be part of the school curriculum or it may be a program completely independent of the school curriculum. In either case it is designed to bring families together to focus on a specific Jewish part of their lives. It is important to have programs that are equally worthwhile for all family members, taking into account their diverse ages, as well as their intellectual levels, varied educational backgrounds, and personal Jewish histories.

### Guidelines for Implementing Jewish Family Education Programs
In a note to the editor of this volume, Rabbi Jeffrey Schein states, ". . . the importance of Jewish Family Education is self-evident. However, there is no simple recipe for it. Good Family Education is more than just fine programs. The best offerings in Family Education reflect a careful assessment of the needs of Jewish families within a given community." With

this statement in mind, we looked at "Family Education" by Sherry Bissell Blumberg in *The Jewish Principals Handbook*, edited by Audrey Friedman Marcus and Raymond A. Zwerin. Many of her suggestions regarding choosing and organizing a Family Education program have been adapted below.

**How to Begin: Choosing An Appropriate Family Education Program**   The following suggestions will help you as you begin to choose an appropriate Family Education program:

1. Work Together With Others – Enlist the cooperation of parents, Rabbi, School Committee, teachers, and other professional staff for the initial planning stages.

2. Define the Need – Be prepared to demonstrate to your colleagues and lay boards or committees how such a program will be of benefit to your community or agency. It is helpful to consult current literature and to cite existing programs which support your position. Write a rationale which clearly indicates how everyone will benefit from Family Education.

3. Target Audience – Focus on one group in your community, e.g., families with children in specific grade levels, single parent families, intermarrieds, senior adults, etc.

4. Personnel – The staff should serve as role models. Seek out individuals who have rich Jewish backgrounds and observe Jewish practices and traditions in their homes. In addition, they should be individuals who have good group skills and can work with parents and children together. Beth Kellman suggests arranging a workshop which enables the staff to focus on the exact skills needed in order to work with mixed age groups.[18]

5. Budget – Ascertain if there is sufficient money in the budget to underwrite the first family program. If not, arrange for a special allocation for this project. Most school and curriculum related programs can be implemented with minimal expense. A classroom teacher can be expected to be involved in a one or two session program or an all-school program as part of his/her teaching obligation. Money should be budgeted, however, for special needs, such as film rentals, refreshments,

a baby sitter, a substitute teacher if it is a long-term program, buses, and the like. Charging minimal fees to offset some of the expenses may be helpful, as well as asking parents to provide materials and refreshments or to drive on field trips.

6. Program Content – Develop a list of programs that will be suitable to your setting and your specific population. This list can cover the spectrum from one-time holiday workshops to a multi-session series on dealing with aging parents. Programs such as the latter fall under the fabric of Jewish Family Life Education and are covered in the introduction to Part II by Fradya Rembaum on page 301. The parameters of the program will be defined by the target audience and the budgetary considerations. Consider how the program fits in with the synagogue or agency philosophy. Decide whether it complements other congregational or agency programs.

7. Facilities – Be sure that adequate space is available for a variety of activities. Consider seating, movement of people, and acoustics.

## Organizing a Family Education Program

The following represent an overview of the steps necessary for organizing a Family Education program.

1. Choosing the Program – Choose the kind of program you would like to initiate in your setting — *Shabbaton*, class program, retreat, etc. Take into consideration the factors outlined above.

2. Planning – Call a planning meeting with the appropriate committee, the synagogue or agency professional staff, the teacher or facilitator, and other individuals who may be interested in providing a leadership role.

3. Selecting a Theme – Select a theme or subject which complements or enriches the curriculum or program and/or responds to the needs of your community.

4. Finding a Date – Set a date and clear it with the staff and coordinate it with the appropriate community, agency, and/or synagogue calendars.

5. Locating the Appropriate Setting – Look over the physical facility to determine how it can lend itself to your program.

This will help you decide whether or not you can have an active program with several things happening at once, or whether only a discussion group can be held, or whether or not you can show a film.

6. Structuring the Program – The structure or format of Family Education and Family Life Education programs and workshops may vary from formal lectures and lecture-discussions to large scale interactional activities. Some things to consider when deciding on a structure are:
   a. The nature of the target audience
   b. Objectives – what you would like the end result to be
   c. A variety of formats, such as separate or parallel sessions for parents and children and interactional sessions with parents and children together
   d. Appropriateness of the content
   e. Abilities and talents of staff

7. Content – Clearly state the goals and objectives of the program. Limit the program to one specific issue, topic, or theme, even it if is a multi-session program.

8. Preparation of Materials — It is vital to outline the schedule in detail in writing and to prepare the necessary materials in advance. The following is a suggestion of how to proceed:
   a. First make an outline of the program. If you are conducting a one-time program, be sure to provide a plan for the day. Everyone likes to know what he/she will be doing. If it is a multi-session program, prepare an agenda for each session.
   b. Prepare materials for participants, such as handouts, background reading, bibliographies. No matter what the subject or format, it is essential to provide participants with a bibliography and a resource list. Have books on display and available for check out at the time of your program.
   c. Obtain appropriate visual aids and mediated materials. Be sure to preview films, videotapes, and filmstrips.
   d. Prepare instructions for participants and staff.
   e. Purchase supplies, refreshments.
   f. Draw up a plan for the physical facility and review it with custodial personnel.
   g. Invite and brief guest speakers, guest staff, and entertainers.

9. Staff Orientation – Review the program with the staff. Go over details of the program as you see it, but be sure to allow for creativity and constructive diversions on the part of the facilitators. Clearly delineate the role of the facilitator.

10. Publicity – A well planned publicity campaign will assure a large attendance and keep your constituency sensitized to the availability of Family Education programs. Some ideas for publicizing school programs and communal programs are as follows:

    a. School programs – Inform everyone who is supposed to participate in your program through letters, phone calls, and school or synagogue bulletins. Be sure that publicity includes time, date, location, dress, theme, activities, what to bring and any fees, as well as deadlines by which to register.

    b. Communal programs – Utilize agency mailing lists, press releases to the secular and Anglo-Jewish newspapers, and public service announcements on radio and television. Prepare attractive flyers and posters which can be placed in strategic places – synagogue or agency lobbies, Judaica stores, bagel bakeries, kosher meat markets, etc. Inform colleagues and include your program in your agency brochure.

11. Evaluation – In advance, decide on how you will evaluate and assess your program, i.e., simple questionnaire, feedback sheet, discussion, etc. Have the necessary materials ready for the participants' reactions before the program adjourns.

**School-Wide Family Programs**    Two examples follow of different types of school-wide programs:

1. Grade Level Programs – These are Family Education programs which are developed to coincide with and complement the curriculum of one or more grade levels in the school. These programs are usually specific to the content studied in class. If your school is small, you may need to have several grades come together for the programs.

After several offerings parents come to expect family programs such as these every year. In a non-threatening manner, this helps them to integrate Jewish practices into their lives, particularly if the curriculum spirals conceptually.

2. Special Days – Another way to have school-wide programs is to set aside special days during the school year specifically for Family Education (see Chapter 18, "Pesach Fair," and Chapter 31, "Tzedakah Encounter"). On special days classes are cancelled in favor of the program. In order to ensure maximum attendance, it is necessary to have families invested in the program. Do this by assigning each family a specific responsibility for the day. In addition, review the program with key families so that they can call others to encourage their attendance.

**Weekend and Extended Time Programs**   Weekend and extended time programs run longer than a regular class period and require even more exacting planning than other types of programs. You will want to arrange an adequate facility, plan an engrossing and varied program, enlist an enthusiastic and knowledgeable staff, and have all the necessary materials and supplies on hand.

1. The Facility – Retreat weekends should take place at a facility where there are comfortable accommodations for couples and additional sleeping facilities for children. You will also need several meeting rooms, a safe play area if there are young children, and safe hiking trails if you are in the mountains or near the sea. Determine who does the cooking for the group if food is not provided by the facility.

2. Program – Select a theme or subject that will be of interest to all of the age groups involved. Consider having parallel discussion (adults and children separately) if there is a wide age span. Divide program responsibilities between the professional staff and the adult and teen participants. Prepare a variety of back-up activities in case a change in the weather would affect programming. Include a variety of activities, both cognitive and affective, and be sure to allow some free time.

3. Staff – The staff should include an overall coordinator or director whose task it is to develop the program, prepare pub

licity, recruit participants, administer the program on site, oversee the finances, and train and hire staff. The teaching staff may be teachers or facilitators from the school or agency, volunteers from the congregation or community, or the agency or synagogue professional staff. Additional staff might include bunk counselors, a craft specialist, a music specialist, a dance specialist, and a doctor or nurse. Teen aides should have specific program and personnel responsibilities. Review these in advance.

4. Special Supplies – Materials and supplies should be gathered in advance and be available nearby when needed. Some items to include are:
   a. A well stocked first aid kit
   b. *Siddurim, Chumashim, Sefer Torah, kipot, tallitot*
   c. Films, videotapes, projectors, VCR, TV, and other audio-visual equipment
   d. Sports equipment and board games
   e. Pencils, paper, scissors, glue, masking tape, markers, and crayons
   f. Costumes or dress up clothes for fun

**Some Other Considerations When Planning Programs** Helpful suggestions are always welcome. Here are a few that will prove to be especially useful as you embark on a program of Family Education.

1. Relax. Let the participants be your guide. No matter how carefully you have planned, there will always be elements of surprise. These, however, usually enrich a program . . . if you don't let them destroy it or you.

2. Review and evaluate each program with the staff involved, sharing the reactions of the participants. Conversely, sharing the results of the evaluation with participants may also be beneficial.

3. Before relegating the program to the file drawer, indicate what did and did not succeed and what suggestions and changes should be made for the future.

4. Start small. There is no need to involve everyone in your community the first time around. Don't play the numbers game.

How many participants is less important than how those who did participate enjoyed and learned from the program. It is always advisable to run a program twice before deciding whether or not it should be part of a regular cycle of programs.

5. Once you have established Jewish Family Education programs in your community, plan them on an ongoing basis. Include program details in publicity and enter dates on all pertinent calendars.

Jewish education on any level is an act of *tikkun*. When Jewish education involves students of all ages and agencies of all types, then even the Holy One, Blessed be the Name, must *(kive-yachol)* smile.

## Endnotes

1. Steven Martin Cohen, "The American Jewish Family Today," *American Jewish Yearbook, 1982* (New York, American Jewish Committee, 1982), 136-37.

2. Egon Mayer, *Love and Tradition: Marriage Between Jews and Christians* (New York, Plenum Press, 1985), 7.

3. Gerald B. Bubis, "Strengthening the Jewish Family As An Instrument Of Jewish Continuity," *Journal of Jewish Communal Service* 58 (Summer 1983): 306-17.

4. Bernard Reisman, "Jewish Family Education," *Pedagogic Reporter* 28 (Spring 1977): 5.

5. Abraham Joshua Heschel, "Celebration and Exaltation," *Jewish Heritage* (Summer 1972): 7.

6. Norman Linzer, "The Future Of the Jewish Family: Personal and Communal Responsibility," *Jewish Education* 52 (Spring 1984): 13.

7. Gerald Bubis, "The Modern Jewish Family," *Journal of Jewish Communal Service* 47 (Spring 1971): 239.

8. Bubis, "The Modern Jewish Family, 246."

9. Linzer, "The Future Of the Jewish Family," 13.

10. Isa Aron, "The Jewish Education Gap," *Reform Judaism* (Spring 1985): 21.

11. Hertzel Fishman, "Raising Children Jewishly," *Pedagogic Reporter* 37, no. 1 (February 1986): 1.

12. Ibid., 2.

13. Ruth Ravid, "The Effect Of Jewish Early Childhood Education On Jewish Home Practices," *Jewish Education* 53 (Fall 1985): 12-15.

14. Michael Wolf, "Perspectives In Jewish Family Education," *Pedagogic Reporter* 35 (June 1984): 28.

15. Morton I. Teicher, "How Should Jewish Communal Agencies Relate To the Jewish Family Now and In the Future?" *Journal of Jewish Communal Service* 44 (Summer 1968): 320-29.

16. Reisman, "Jewish Family Education, 6-7."

17. Sherry Bissell Blumberg, "Family Education," In *The Jewish Principals Handbook* (Denver, Alternatives in Religious Education, Inc., 1983), 461.

18. Kellman, Beth, "Family Days and Family Jewish Education," In *Creative Jewish Education: A Reconstructionist Perspective*, Jeffrey L. Schein and Jacob J. Staub, eds. (New York, Reconstructionist Rabbinical College Press and Rossel Books, 1985), 57-58.

# Chapter 1

 **TITLE:** P.A.C.E. — Parents and Children for Education

 **CONTRIBUTED BY:** Jo Kay and Ira Schweitzer

 **DESIGNED BY:** Irma Moskowitz, then principal at Temple Emanu-El, East Meadow, New York and Jo Kay, the teacher of the P.A.C.E. program, conceptualized the curriculum; Jo Kay then wrote the original curriculum as the year progressed.

 **TOPIC:** Integrating parents into school activities with parallel education programs

 **TARGET AUDIENCE:** Initially, families with children in 4th Grade; eventually, families with children in 4th Grade and above.

 **TIME FRAME:** Grades 4-5 twice a month during school year, once with adults and children and once with parents alone; Grades 6 up once a month

 **STAFF:** Classroom teacher, substitute teacher, workshop facilitators

**Overview**   The P.A.C.E. program was developed at Temple Emanu-El in East Meadow, New York. It is an optional program for families with children in Grades 4 to 12. There are adult level classes, student classes, and family classes. The content is parallel to the school curriculum. In order to implement a P.A.C.E. program, the synagogue community must endorse it wholeheartedly, carefully nurturing parents and teachers and making a financial commitment as well.

**Purpose**   The purpose of the program is to bring parents and students together for mutual study and learning experiences. The ultimate goal is to create a bridge between the religious school and the home.

Chapter

# 1

**Preparation**   When beginning a P.A.C.E. program, the factors to consider are curriculum, staff, budget, calendar, and the size of the school.

**Curriculum**   Review the school curriculum and select an appropriate grade at which to start the program. It is best to begin with children in Grades 4 and 5. At 10 or 11 years old, children are able to study cognitive material together with their parents in a meaningful way, and they feel comfortable having their parents in school with them. At Temple Emanu-El the program begins in the fourth grade. Since parents will have fewer classes than do the students, it may not be possible for them to cover the entire curriculum for that grade; therefore, it is necessary to be selective about the materials prepared for adult study.

**Staff**   The personnel for this program should have experience in group dynamics and non-judgmental facilitating. It is beneficial to offer an in-service program for teachers who want to develop these skills in order for them to phase into the program. It is essential to have staff development workshops and seminars on a regular basis so that teachers have the opportunity to process the experience of teaching both child and parent in the same classroom and teaching just the adult at other times. In addition, a person with a masters degree in social work should be available to team teach with the regular teacher when called upon.

**Budget**  The P.A.C.E. teachers at Temple Emanu-El are given a bonus for teaching in this program. Other fiscal factors include hiring substitutes to teach the regular classes when family classes are held. There are field trips, additional supplies, additional books and materials for class sessions and workshops. Funds also need to be available for support personnel, such as a social worker.

**Calendar**  Prepare a P.A.C.E. calendar which coincides with the religious school and synagogue calendar. Be sure to plan field trips and to be cognizant of special holidays and special events at the synagogue. Classes should meet during normal religious school hours.

Chapter

1

**Program Description**  At Temple Emanu-El the level of parent participation varies from year to year. In the fourth and fifth grades, parents come to school twice a month, once for a family class and once for an adult class. In the sixth grade the joint classes continue once a month, and there are five or six separate adult classes over the course of the year (depending on the calendar). In the seventh through twelfth grades there is a joint class once a month and students come to regular classes at all other times.

Family classes run the gamut from arts and crafts workshops and gaming to in-depth text study, guest speakers, films, field trips, music, and cooking — all activities which promote interaction within the framework of the curriculum. When there are large groups present, it is helpful to subdivide the class into smaller units with adults and children together. This allows for greater interaction, especially when dealing with issues of concern.

After each class, families are given response cards and asked to react to the lesson anonymously. These are a good check on the progress of the program.

**Sample Lesson**  The following is a sample lesson on the Holocaust for students in Grade 6 and their families:

## FAMILY CLASS

I. Administration: Attendance, Field Trip, Other Class Business

II. Torah Study

III. Class Lesson

A. What does it mean to be moral (a moral person)? Put answers on the board.

B. How do we make choices? What comes into play? What factors or considerations do we weigh? When faced with value decisions, do people always make the *moral choice?* What might be the consequences when we don't make the moral choice? Read the statement on Jewish responsibility from *To Live As a Jew* by Samuel Rosenbaum, pp.23-24).

C. Show film: *The Hangman.*

1. How does what is going on in the world, at school, at work, at the synagogue, relate to this movie? To the Holocaust?

2. Do you speak out? Why stick your neck out? Why not? What's the best way to speak out?

D. Show second film: *Joseph Schultz.*

1. Introduce film — a dramatization (not real footage) of things that happened during the Holocaust. Joseph Schultz is faced with a situation which forces him to make a particular choice. As you watch, see if you can relate Schultz's dilemma to situations faced by the *Judenrat.*

2. Show film.

3. After the film: Should the *Judenrat* have responded as Schultz did? Maimonides would have said yes — all die rather than deliver one Jew. But Rambam's statement was debated by many Rabbis. How do you feel about it?

4. Schultz responded as an individual. Does an individual's response differ, perhaps, from the response of a person in a position of leadership or authority? As a communal leader, a member of the *Judenrat,* do the choices change? How? How would you have responded in the role of the *Judenrat* official? Discuss these questions in small groups and report back.

Chapter

1

E. Summary — brief reading from textbook.
Finally: There is a Talmudic saying: "Judge not thy neighbor until thou art come into his place" or "No one should judge unless, in absolute honesty, in a similar situation, he or she might not have done the same."

**Sample Family Assignment**    The following is a letter describing a family assignment:

Dear P.A.C.E. Family,

Next week is Tu B'Shevat and our class will be having a special creative "*Seder*" with fruits and wine and flowers and songs. It should be a wonderful experience for us all.

Chapter

1

In Judaism, the tree has come to represent *life, knowledge*, and the *oneness of the Jewish people*. When we plant a tree, we make an investment in the future. By the same token, choosing to marry and have children is stating a belief in the future.

Your assignment is to be done as a family. You are to write a four to six line response to the question below. Your response should reflect the thoughts and feelings of both parents and children, and will be an integral part of our Tu B'Shevat *Seder* next week.

Question to consider:
How is the growth of our family like the growth of a tree? Try to think of other things the family and the tree might mean. If you have any questions, call me. Have fun! See you all at the *Seder.*

P.S. Bring your response to class next week.

**Editor's Comments**    At Temple Emanu-El about one-third of the families opt for P.A.C.E.. In the school there are two and three classes per grade level, so P.A.C.E. can be instituted for each grade level of the program. In smaller schools where there may be only one class per grade level, you may want to consider combining grades to implement P.A.C.E.. You may also wish to entertain the idea of joining with another school.

P.A.C.E., as presented here, is a program for one school. It may also be instituted as a communal program with several synagogues joining together to have classes for families with children in specific grade levels. A cooperative effort among synagogues will reduce some of the cost of hiring the extra staff. Involving the Rabbi and/or Director of Education as part of the teaching staff will also cut down on the expense of an extra teacher or substitute.

**Chapter**

**1**

At Temple Emanu-El P.A.C.E. is a year long program. The format may be altered by making P.A.C.E. a part of the school program for a limited time during the school year — e.g., five weeks, ten weeks, etc. Such an abbreviated format will mean parents are not required to make a commitment for a long period of time and that the subject matter will be focused on a specific aspect of the curriculum. As an example, if the curriculum is life cycle, parents could come to class for four or five sessions which deal with birth and naming. Students can learn about the birth of Isaac and then parents can tell their child about his/her birth. Together they can talk about names, for whom the child was named, family name, etc. This can be followed by a craft activity, such as the making of wimpels or birth certificates decorated with Jewish motifs. A local *mohel* could be invited to speak about *Brit Milah*.

A segment of the history curriculum sequence is another ideal topic for a shorter version of P.A.C.E. Students and parents can study about a specific period of history at their own levels and then become involved together in activities. These might include planning campaigns for heroes and heroines of the period, making parallel time lines for Jewish and world history, or reading the literature of the time. Similar short term programs can be set up for studying Jewish values, anti-Semitism, the Holocaust, modern Israel, prayer, community, etc. The key is to begin at one grade level and then to add a grade every year. Eventually, the program will blossom into a full range program like the one that exists at Temple Emanu-El.

## Bibliography/Resources

Kay, Jo. "Family Education P.A.C.E." *Compass* (Spring 1980).

_____. "P.A.C.E. Parents and Children for Education." *Pedagogic Reporter* (April 1985).

Rosenbaum, Samuel. *To Live As a Jew*. New York: KTAV, 1969.

**Mediated Materials**
*The Hangman*. McGraw-Hill Training Systems, P.O. Box 641, Del Mar, CA 92014, 1964. (film, 12 min.)

*Joseph Schultz*. Anti-Defamation League, 823 United Nations Plaza, New York, NY 10017, 1973. (film, 14 min.)

Chapter

1

# Chapter 2

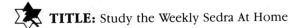 **TITLE:** Study the Weekly Sedra At Home

**CONTRIBUTED BY:** Dr. Michael Korman

**TOPIC:** Torah study

**TARGET AUDIENCE:** Families with children of all ages

**TIME FRAME:** Weekly sessions of 30-90 minutes, depending on the ages of the children involved

**STAFF:** Facilitator, interested volunteers

**Overview**  For the People of the Book, ongoing study is mandated. In our synagogues, we read the *Sedra* each week, but many Jews do not actually take time to study the portion. Educator Michael Korman has compiled a book for congregational families which gives an overview of each *Sedra*, along with suggested discussion topics. The book is the catalyst for continuous study of Torah by the congregational families.

**Purpose**  The purpose of this program is to extend Jewish education beyond the classroom by encouraging family study of Torah at home.

Chapter

2

**Preparation/Procedure**  Those who express an interest in being involved in such a program should attend a workshop to learn how to use the materials. The workshop should include a model discussion and resource materials. Some time should be spent on how to approach Torah study in settings with children of varying ages. For example, with younger children, the *Sedra* can be told as an ongoing story of the history of our people. Or, a flannel board or some type of costume may be used each week. For older children a question may be selected based on the text and children can listen for the answer as the text is read. Children who read can be asked to read over the portion ahead of time and tell in their own words what they have read. More advanced students can be asked to formulate their own questions. Dr. Korman's study guide includes questions for discussion. The book *Torah for the Family* by Philip L. Lipis and Louis Katzoff contains questions for younger children (ages 4-8), for intermediate ages (8-12), and for adults.

A well conceived publicity campaign can be of help in maintaining enthusiasm for this ongoing program. The facilitator, or person in charge of the program, should stay in touch with the families. He/she should make the congregation aware of the progress of the program through bulletin articles and word of mouth.

**Program Description**  The discussion of the weekly *Sedra* should take place around the family Shabbat table. Dr. Korman suggests that it follow the Shabbat meal; however, it may also be done earlier in the evening as well. The summary of each portion is limited to one page, so the book does not necessarily cover all details of each *Sedra*. Only one or two important aspects are discussed. It is recommended that each week a different family member prepare for the discussion by reading the entire *Sedra* in advance and recapitulating it at the Shabbat table. Following this the weekly summary should be read and discussed. An example of a summary follows:

PORTION OF THE WEEK – 41 — PINCHAS
Numbers 25:10-30:1

Moses was disappointed because he was not allowed to enter the Promised Land. But this did not weaken his faith in God. Moses divided the land among 12 tribes as he was instructed, and then he devoted his attention to his successor.

Chapter

2

Moses knew the difficulties facing a leader. He knew the people are never of one mind and that they must be guided toward unity. The leader must be capable of the special tasks that lay ahead when conquering and settling the Promised Land.

Moses turned to God for help, and God named Joshua as the man who possessed the necessary spirit and qualities of leadership. He further told Moses how the leadership is to be transmitted.

In the presence of the High Priest Eleazer and all the people, Moses was to place his hands on Joshua's head and outline Joshua's duties. Moses placed both hands on Joshua to show that he was giving his leadership over without anger or jealousy and with high hopes for Joshua's success.

A limitation was placed on Joshua's authority. Before deciding upon any course of action, he was to consult God's will through Eleazer, who alone was entrusted with the interpretation of the Torah. This act ensured that the democratic way would be continued. All, including kings, were subject to the laws of Torah. The real and final ruler is, therefore, God.

Discussion Topics:
1. How important is it for a leader to find a suitable successor?

2. Is the synagogue a democratic institution?

3. Does our Jewish community function in accordance with democratic principles?

**Editor's Comments**   The program as presented is suitable for families with children who are able to read at a third grade level or above. It is easily replicated when the appropriate materials are acquired.

For families of younger children, it is suggested that the more traditional stories be used. These may be Bible stories or folk tales — whatever sustains the interest of younger children. Books that are beautifully illustrated work best. Once a habit is formed to include these stories at the Shabbat table, it is easy to move into the Torah as reading and interest levels become more sophisticated. Harlene Winnick Appelman has designed a variation of this program to accommodate younger families called the "Table Top Series." (See Contributors list for her address.)

Chapter
2

## Bibliography/Resources

Beiner, Stan J. *Sedra Scenes*. Denver: Alternatives in Religious Education, Inc., 1982.

Blank, Barbara Trainen. "Talking Torah." *Hadassah Magazine* (January 1987): 32-33.

Chill, Arthur A. *A Guide To Sidarot and Haftarot*. New York: KTAV, 1971.

Edwards, Anne. *A Child's Bible*. New York: Paulist Press, 1967-73.

Epstein, David, and Stutman, Suzanne Singer. *Torah With Love: A Guide for Strengthening Jewish Values Within the Family*. Englewood Cliffs, NJ: Prentice-Hall, 1986.

Grishaver, Joel Lurie. *Being Torah: A First Book Of Torah Texts*. Los Angeles: Torah Aura Productions, 1985.

Hertz, Dr. J. H. *The Pentateuch and Haftorahs*. London: Soncino Press, 1972.

Hollender, Betty R. *Bible Stories for Little Children*. New York: Union of American Hebrew Congregations, 1986.

Korman, Dr. Michael. *Family Mitzvah Education Program I: Study the Weekly Sidra At Home*. Houston, TX: The William S. Malev Schools for Religious Studies, Congregation Beth Yeshurun, 1983.

Lipis, Philip L., and Katzoff, Louis. *Torah for the Family*. Jerusalem: World Jewish Bible Society, 1977.

Loeb, Sorel Goldberg, and Kadden, Barbara Binder. *Teaching Torah: A Treasury Of Insights and Activities*. Denver: Alternatives in Religious Education, Inc., 1984.

Newman, Shirley. *A Child's Introduction To Torah*. New York: Behrman House, 1972.

Plaut, W. Gunther; Bamberger, Bernard J.; and Hallo, William W. *The Torah: A Modern Commentary*. New York: Union of American Hebrew Congregations, 1981.

*The Torah: The Five Books Of Moses*. Philadelphia: Jewish Publication Society of America, 1978.

Chapter

2

# Chapter 3

 **TITLE:** Stepping Stones — To a Jewish Me

 **CONTRIBUTED BY:** Saundra Heller

 **TOPIC:** Basic Jewish content courses - synagogue, synagogue symbols, family, symbols of the Jewish home, Torah, Shabbat, holidays, life cycle

 **TARGET AUDIENCE:** Interfaith families (children and parents) unaffiliated with the Jewish community

 **TIME FRAME:** Two year program; weekly 2 hour and 20 minute classes for students during the school year; weekly 2 hour and 20 minute classes for parents January through May; additional bi-monthly programs and activities

 **STAFF:** Teachers for each class who are willing to meet weekly for staff sessions and once a month for in-service training; guest speakers

**History**   Rabbi Steven E. Foster of Congregation Emanuel, Denver, and Chairperson of the Joint Commission on Outreach for the Union of American Hebrew Congregations, has, for many years, felt the importance of outreach programming. He has made it a point to convey both to his synagogue Board and to his congregation statistics about the interfaith population and their needs.

Because of the Board's heightened awareness, an outreach professional was hired in 1983. Rabbi Foster personally committed himself to raise outside money for funding outreach programs, and Temple Emanuel provided in-kind services. The outreach professional, Saundra Heller, works with the congregation's Outreach Committee to program for the congregation, to provide support groups for mixed married couples and those in serious relationships, to provide support groups for Jewish parents of mixed married couples, and to provide community education programs addressing the needs of the interfaith population.

Rabbi Foster was also eager to bring into being a separate and special Jewish educational program for children of unaffiliated mixed married families who were not exposed to Judaism. He envisioned the program as tuition free and limited to two years for any child.

During the same period of time, the Allied Jewish Federation of Denver was learning the results of a new demographic study of Denver. The Federation was interested in establishing programs which met the needs pointed up by the study. To accomplish this, it set aside a $100,000 grant and established a Long-Range Planning Committee, with representatives from all branches of the community, whose task it was to plan for needed communal services in the 80s and to test their feasibility. The Long-Range Planning Committee prepared rigorous guidelines, structures, and evaluations for the purpose of serving five different identified groups. Among these groups were mixed marrieds. "Stepping Stones - To a Jewish Me" was one of six proposals to receive grant money.

To meet the additional financial needs of the project, funds were raised from private sources, and Congregation Emanuel

Chapter

3

provided in-kind services. At the Federation's request, an Advisory Committee was formed, with membership from Federation, Temple Emanuel, and the community, to serve as a liaison between "Stepping Stones" and the community at large.

**Overview**   "Stepping Stones — To a Jewish Me" is a religious school program for children of unaffiliated interfaith families. It involves a series of classes for the children, along with several interactional programs which require parental involvement. During the first year of the program (1985-86), there were five classes, kindergarten through junior high school, accommodating 65 children. The second year of the program (1986-87), there were 68 children representing 45 families, and a weekly track was added specifically for parents.

Chapter

3

This program represents a partnership between parents and children. Parents are therefore encouraged to discuss participation in the program with their children and to involve them in the decision to attend. Parents are also asked to be supportive of material covered in classes and to reinforce it at home. Ongoing feedback from parents is an integral part of the program.

**Purpose**   The purpose of the program is to enable a child and his/her family to establish, in a gradual way, ties to and identification with the Jewish heritage and the Jewish community. It is hoped that participants will get in touch with their personal world views and come to understand the relationship between what they learn in the "Stepping Stones" classes and their everyday lives.

**Preparation/Procedure**   The program is publicized in both the local press and the Anglo-Jewish press, and a phone number listed for people to call for further information. Fliers are posted at libraries, Jewish Community Center, hospitals, and businesses. Brochures are sent to the Federation mailing list.

It is important to develop the school calendar in conjunction with the community calendar so that participants can be involved in special communal events. Participants are made aware of events taking place in the Jewish community.

Teachers are professionals who are highly invested in the success of the program. Several "Stepping Stones" teachers are partners in interfaith marriages and others are Jews by Choice. Throughout the course of the year, teachers contribute to the building of the curriculum and participate in evaluation of it. During weekly meetings and monthly in-service sessions, teachers have an opportunity to get in touch with their own attitudes about their Judaism and about the population they are teaching, and to develop professionally. They are encouraged to create a classroom environment that promotes trust, communication, warmth, and comfort.

Chapter

3

Prior to launching the program, Rabbi Howard Bogot, National Education Director for the Joint Commission on Jewish Education of the Union of American Hebrew Congregations and Central Conference of American Rabbis facilitated two workshops — one for the community and one specifically for the "Stepping Stones" teachers. The Central Agency for Jewish Education in Denver provided an additional teacher training workshop which included hands-on demonstrations on home holiday celebrations. The Central Agency is available to teachers throughout the year, providing guidance on appropriate resources and answers to a variety of questions.

Applicants for the program are first interviewed on the telephone. Then, if it seems that the program would be appropriate and if they are interested, the parents attend an orientation and registration session. A Parent Questionnaire is sent out to parents in September and May, asking why the parents are enrolling in the "Stepping Stones" program, whether or not the child has been exposed so far to any elements of Judaism or to faiths and traditions other than Judaism, and inquiring of their expectations vis-a-vis the program.

**Program Description**  Classes meet weekly on Sunday afternoons from 1:00-3:20 over the course of the school year from September to May or June. Lessons include presentation of cognitive material, along with creative experiential activities designed to help students internalize and synthesize the lessons. The modeling of rituals and ceremonies for parents and children is considered of utmost importance.

The curriculum utilizes *To See the World Through Jewish Eyes*, developed by the Union of American Hebrew Congregations, as well as a variety of other excellent Jewish books and material. Each student receives age appropriate books which are used as resources in the classroom. These are sent home at the end of the year so that children may begin to build their own Jewish libraries.

The units of study for the classes include: synagogue symbols, services and Torah; family home symbols, Shabbat, *mitzvot*, *tzedakah*, life cycle. The holidays are studied as they occur during the course of the year. The "Chanukah Event," a 2½ hour experiential activity involving parents, is described in brief below.

Chapter

3

At the "Chanukah Event," families are given the opportunity, through a values clarification exercise, to talk about the December holiday symbols found in their homes. They learn the Chanukah blessings and some of the background of the holiday, make a *chanukiah* for home use, participate in a brief reading, and enjoy *latkes* together.

"Stepping Stones" families also prepare a Pesach meal for all the "Stepping Stones" children and parents (about 200 people), and participate in a model *Seder*. Among field trips are those to the community book fair, the Jewish Center, and the Federation building.

Parents are required to attend sessions during which an overview of the program and the curriculum is presented. They are expected to come to all of the experiential activities and field trips. Parents also receive study guides and background material for the curriculum areas in which their children are involved.

Parents may also opt for a special track which consists of ten Sunday sessions of basic Jewish education, four sessions of Jewish community visitation, and eight meetings of a support group. The Sunday education sessions, covering such subjects as theology, philosophy, history, and Peoplehood are taught by different Rabbis in the community. The sessions on the Jewish community educate the participants about, and help them become familiar with, the structure of the Denver Jewish community. The support group sessions address such issues as child rearing, thoughts and feelings about being in an interfaith marriage, and other subjects of mutual interest.

**Editor's Comments**   "Stepping Stones" has specific goals and a particular way of reaching out to the target population. Others who wish to implement such a program might want to think about various other possibilities. For instance, both parents and children might be involved together in all of the sessions. Study materials would be read at home between sessions, so that when families come to school together, they have some knowledge of the subject. Such a program can be structured with segments for parents to interact with children, followed by a time for parents and children to meet separately with a teacher. In their session parents can ask questions or get clarification; in theirs, the students can have a cognitive lesson.

**Chapter 3**

This program also lends itself to a series of retreat weekends. Four weekends could be offered, each one focusing on a different unit of the curriculum. Families could sign up for one or all of the retreats. In addition to the weekly classes that would take place between weekends, families could participate in the kind of special programs provided by "Stepping Stones."

Once families make a commitment to such an outreach program, they could be assigned mentor families who would assist them in personalizing the content of the curriculum. A mentor family could invite their participant family for Shabbat and holiday celebrations, share life cycle events with them, and be available for support. Together the two families might make a commitment to a community project, such as visiting a home for the aged on a regular basis, writing to Soviet Jews, or collecting food for the needy.

Travel to Israel should be encouraged for all participants. One unit of the curriculum might be devoted to the study of Israel, its meaning for Jews religiously, culturally, and historically.

Integrated into this unit could be information about travel to Israel, family programs in Israel, and financial assistance available from the community and private sources.

If possible, youth groups, such as USY, NFTY, NCSY, Hashachar, BBYO, etc., can provide a one year complimentary membership. Likewise, to help them connect to the larger Jewish community, parents can be given a one year gift of membership in a Jewish organization, such as Hadassah, B'nai B'rith, ORT, etc.

## Bibliography/Resources

Benson, Paulette, and Altschuler, Joanne. *The Jewish Family: Past, Present and Future*. Denver: Alternatives in Religious Education, Inc., 1979.

Bogot, Howard, and Syme, Daniel. *I Learn About God*. New York: Union of American Hebrew Congregations, 1986.

Brin, Ruth F. *The Shabbat Catalogue*. Hoboken, NJ: KTAV, 1978.

Cedarbaum, Sophia N. *A First Book Of Jewish Holidays*. New York: Union of American Hebrew Congregations, 1984.

Cone, Molly. *Hear, O Israel*. Book 4, *About God*. New York: Union of American Hebrew Congregations, 1973.

Eban, Abba, and Bamberger, David. *My People*. Vol. 1. New York: Behrman House, Inc., 1978.

Eban, Abba, and Bamberger, David. *My People*. Vol. 2. New York: Behrman House, Inc., 1979.

Fischman, Joyce. *Bible Work and Play*. Book One. New York: Union of American Hebrew Congregations, 1985.

_____. *Holiday Work and Play*. New York: Union of American Hebrew Congregations, 1986.

_____. *Let's Learn About Jewish Symbols*. New York: Union of American Hebrew Congregations, 1969.

Chapter

3

Garvey, Robert. *Let's Learn About the Jewish Holidays*. Hoboken, NJ: KTAV Publishing House, Inc., 1980.

Gersh, Harry. *When a Jew Celebrates*. New York: Behrman House, Inc., 1971.

Grishaver, Joel Lurie. *Bible People Book One*. Denver: Alternatives in Religious Education, Inc., 1980.

_____. *Bible People Book Two*. Denver: Alternatives in Religious Education, Inc., 1981.

_____. *The Life Cycle Workbook*. Denver: Alternatives in Religious Education, Inc., 1983.

Jacobs, Louis. *The Book Of Jewish Belief*. New York: Behrman House, Inc. 1984.

Karp, Laura. *Student's Encounter Book for When a Jew Prays*. New York: Behrman House, Inc., 1975.

Karp, Laura. *Student's Encounter Book for When a Jew Seeks Wisdom*. New York: Behrman House, Inc., 1976.

Kipper, Lenore C., and Bogot, Howard I. *The Alef-Bet Of Jewish Values*. New York: Union of American Hebrew Congregations, 1985.

Kripke, Dorothy K. *Let's Talk About Being Jewish*. Hoboken, NJ: KTAV, 1981.

Kurinsky, Miriam. *Student Activity Book for My People*. Vol. 1. New York: Behrman House, Inc., 1980.

Kurzweil, Arthur, and Strauss, Ruby. *My Generations: A Course In Jewish Family History*. New York: Behrman House, Inc., 1984.

Lorber, Miriam, and Shamir, Judith. *Let's Learn Torah*. Hoboken, NJ: KTAV, 1983.

Resnick, Anita. *Meet the Stickmans*. Hoboken, NJ: KTAV, 1974.

Chapter

3

Rosenberg, Amye. *Mitzvot*. New York: Behrman House, Inc., 1984.

_____. *Tzedakah*. New York: Behrman House, Inc., 1979.

Rossel, Seymour. *When a Jew Prays*. New York: Behrman House, Inc., 1973.

_____. *When a Jew Seeks Wisdom*. New York: Behrman House, Inc., 1976.

Sugarman, Joan G., and Freeman, Grace R. *Inside the Synagogue*. New York: Union of American Hebrew Congregations, 1984.

Sugarman, Morris J. *Student Activity Book for My People*. Vol. 2. New York: Behrman House, Inc., 1981.

Sugarman, Morris J. *When a Jew Celebrates Student Activity Book*. New York: Behrman House, Inc., 1986.

Weisser, Michael Cantor. *My Synagogue*. New York: Behrman House, Inc., 1984.

Chapter

3

# Chapter 4

**TITLE:** How to Start a Synagogue Havurah Program

**CONTRIBUTED BY:** Sally Weber

**TOPIC:** Havurot as a means of strengthening Jewish family life

**TARGET AUDIENCE:** Anyone in the community

**TIME FRAME:** Ongoing

**STAFF:** Chairperson or coordinator or program director

**Overview**  The *havurah* movement has become a mainstay of many congregations across the country. It provides congregants with a sense of community and an opportunity to share life cycle and holiday experiences within a small group. In her role as Program Director at Adat Ari-El Congregation, North Hollywood, California, Sally Weber has been actively involved in the national *havurah* movement and in establishing and strengthening *havurot* in her own congregation.

Following are excerpts from Ms. Weber's manual, *How to Start a Synagogue Havurah*. Included here are her overview (above), the rationale for *havurot*, a description of how they benefit synagogues, as well as step-by-step instructions and guidelines on how to form *havurot* — including policies, applications, placing people, addressing special needs, planning meetings, and selecting programs. (The headings in this chapter will follow this outline and, from here on, will differ from the headings found in the other chapters in this book.)

Chapter

4

**Rationale**  In our grandparents' and great-grandparents' generations, the sanctuary was the focus of the synagogue. One entered by that door or not at all.

Our parents found another door — the synagogue as an organization. Synagogue affiliation and involvement meant joining the Men's Club, the Sisterhood, the Board of Directors, the PTA.

By the mid-1970s, a new generation of Jews was looking to see what doors existed for *them*. They were often new to the community, generally well educated in the secular world, but only minimally educated Jewishly. These "families," be they couples or singles, with or without children, turned to the synagogue to find a unique community — a Jewish place where one could do Jewish things — an intimate Jewish setting where the demands for expertise would not be great, but the possibility for sharing and growing together with other Jewish families would be open.

The synagogue *havurah* program, first articulated by Rabbi Harold Schulweis at Valley Beth Shalom Congregation, Encino, California, was a response to this need. Schulweis described *havurot* as a way to break down the walls of the synagogue, to create a community within the synagogue community.

Since the mid-1970s, the notion of synagogue *havurot* has spread across the country. *Most* Conservative and Reform congregations either have had or are considering starting a *havurah* program. Some of the programs are enormously successful, with more than 50% of the congregation joining. Some remain small, with only a small percentage of congregants involved, but with those *havurot* lasting literally through generations. (One, in fact, has gone from parents to their children, and is now being visited by the grandchildren!)

**What Is a Synagogue Havurah and What Can It Do For Your Congregation?**    A synagogue *havurah* is a group of 15-20 members — couples and/or families, sometimes couples and singles, sometimes all singles — who meet regularly for Jewish celebration, learning, and socializing. The *havurah* offers a unique opportunity for Jews to get together and plan programs which meet their unique Jewish needs. Although the social "chemistry" in a *havurah* is important, a *havurah's* ability to plan a meaningful agenda is even more so.

Chapter

4

People come to the *havurah* experience with a variety of expectations. Many find themselves in large, impersonal congregations where it is difficult to reach out and make new friends. Others have relocated from other cities and lack the extended family with whom they have celebrated Jewish holidays and life cycle events. Some are eager to find a place to increase their Jewish skills, e.g., making Shabbat, leading a *Seder*, or discovering more about synagogue life. Others are eager to find a place to share Jewish study and look to *havurot* as study groups. They then begin developing the characteristics of a *havurah* as members start sharing Shabbat, holidays, and life cycle events together.

Significantly, *havurot* provide a unique opportunity to bind congregants to the congregation. *Havurah* members tend to involve one another in synagogue activities. Thus, for example, if one family decides to volunteer to staff a game booth at the Purim Carnival, several other *havurah* members are likely to be involved. *Havurot* often participate in social action activities. In one synagogue, a *havurah* volunteered to take over the synagogue's "Food Pantry" program for the hungry and homeless.

As a result of sharing Jewish life together, *havurot* are quite receptive to specific kinds of adult learning environments. It is not unusual to find either an entire *havurah* or several *havurah* members armed with tape recorders attending holiday workshop classes in preparation for the *havurah* celebration of that holiday. Likewise, *havurot* are eager to invite the Rabbi, Cantor, and Director of Education to meetings to discuss in more detail Shabbat and holiday liturgy, music, texts, etc.

**How to Begin**   A strong synagogue *havurah* program requires a working committee and solid Rabbinic backing. This is a program which is very easy to market. However, staff support and the administrative and programmatic talents of a committed Steering Committee are indispensable.

Chapter

4

The committee's task includes designing publicity, preparing an application process, screening applications, placing families in compatible *havurot*, providing programming resources, and helping with interpersonal dilemmas which inevitably develop in groups.

An ideal Steering Committee will include:

1. A congregant willing to chair the committee, ideally for two years (one year to learn the job, one year to model leadership for the next chairperson).

2. A congregant who has good knowledge of the congregation — e.g., Who is friends with whom? Who doesn't speak to whom? Which families have shared interests, children who are friends, special talents, etc.

3. A congregant who has good interpersonal skills and the ability to help other people problem solve. Inevitably, there will be someone in a *havurah* who is stubborn, rigid, negative, or misplaced in that particular group (maybe all of the above!). *Havurot* often need a "consultant" available to them to vent frustrations and develop methods for dealing with these situations without tearing the group apart.

4. A congregant willing to serve as a program resource person. The task of this person might include collecting information on upcoming community events, such as lectures and film

series, to share with *havurot*; collecting and/or preparing study or discussion guides; finding community resources for programming, such as Federation speakers, professors at local colleges, Jewish professionals and congregants who are willing to share their expertise with *havurot*, etc.

5. One or two additional members. There will be other tasks, such as helping with placement, setting up *havurot*, planning *havurah* Shabbat dinners, and other special programs.

**Policies**   The *Havurah* Steering Committee needs to address several policy issues. First, most synagogue *havurah* programs require membership in the synagogue in order to belong to a *havurah*. Some synagogues have experimented with publicizing the program to the community-at-large, but making it clear that this is a program sponsored by the synagogue for the purpose of enhancing the quality of synagogue life.

Chapter

4

When a program is open to the community, non-affiliated members are usually limited to two couples or a small percentage of singles in each *havurah*. Such policies should be presented to the synagogue Board of Directors for approval after being accepted by the Steering Committee. It is important to have a clear synagogue policy from the beginning.

Second, the committee must determine standards regarding Shabbat programming and *kashrut*. This will, of course, correspond to the policy of the synagogue. Many synagogues request that *havurot* schedule only Shabbat-related activities on Friday night and Saturday. Many congregations recommend that all meals be dairy in order to avoid problems for members who observe *kashrut*. A member of a *havurah* should never feel excluded from an activity because of his/her personal level of observance.

**Havurah Applications**   *Havurah* applications can be as simple or as complicated as you please. They can be short answer or check list formats. The essentials are: Name, address, phone, ages, ages of children (if any), interests, special needs. (Do not suggest anything you're not ready to offer, such as a camping *havurah* if you have no idea how to organize group camping trips.)

Ideally, *havurah* applications should be sent to members with their new member or membership renewal packets. This assures that most applications will be returned within the same general time period, and that your committee will have the largest pool possible from which to draw.

**Placing People In a Havurah**   When placing people, consideration must be given to the applicant's requests: Young families often want to be with other young families, parents of teen-agers often want other teen-agers in the group, etc. Special requests need to be handled individually and a member of the Steering Committee should call anyone whose application indicates special needs (i.e., do parents in their 50s with young school age children want to be with adults their ages or in a group with children their children's ages?).

Chapter

4

Many synagogues have experimented with intergenerational *havurot*. This format is more popular with seniors, singles and single parents, and less popular with couples with school age children. People at different life stages appear to have very different needs in terms of peer groups. However, if a *havurah* is task oriented — i.e., if it is primarily a study group or primarily a social action group — the task itself can help bind together members of disparate ages and family composition. This format should be taken into consideration when developing a *havurah* program which meets the needs of your specific congregation.

It is also important to pay particular attention to the applicant's interests. Most people indicate an interest in making new friends, celebrating holidays, and learning more about Jewish life. Sometimes, however, there are more particularistic needs, some of which fall within the purview of *havurot* and some of which do not.

**Special Havurot**
**Singles Havurot**   Singles *havurot* are a unique and uniquely Jewish answer to the problem of where to go as adults to make

Jewish friends. These groups take a bit more coordination and assistance from the Steering Committee or from a staff member than couples and family *havurot*, but are important additions to synagogue life.

Singles *havurot* should be grouped by age, usually with an age span of no more than 10-12 years. It is very important to screen applicants. Since the purpose is to create a group which will make an ongoing commitment to meet together, do not place singles who only express the need to find someone to date.

**Camping Havurot**   Yes, it is possible! A committed camper is needed to coordinate this group. A camping *havurah* is not always a traditional *havurah*. Often, it is a more open and fluid collection of congregants who plan retreats to the mountains, deserts, beaches, in campers, with tents, etc. Synagogue policies regarding Shabbat observance and *kashrut* guidelines should be stated from the beginning.

Chapter

4

**Guidelines for Setting Up a Havurah**   In setting up a *havurah*, the first task is to help people share what they feel is important about themselves — something they want others to know about them. Stress the democratic nature of a *havurah* and the need, therefore, to develop a common agenda which reflects the interests and needs of all the members.

There are various ways to encourage this kind of interaction at a first meeting. It is important to understand that the first meeting will help set the tone for the new *havurah* and that stimulation of discussion and sharing of ideas will help create the atmosphere for the *havurah's* later meetings.

**Before the First Meeting**
1. The first meeting should be held in the home of one of the new *havurah* members. Generally, people are very eager for a *havurah* to begin and it is relatively easy to find a host couple. The representative from the Steering Committee who is going to attend the first meeting should call members of the group to inform them of the time and place of the meeting.

2. In addition to the phone call, invitations can be sent out to the members notifying them of the time and place.

3. Since the first meeting has a partly social function, some kind of refreshment is desirable. However, tell the host couple that they need not be fancy — cake and coffee arc sufficient. No one should feel that having a *havurah* meeting will require extensive social (or financial) preparations.

## At the First Meeting

1. Introductory Activities – The most important aspect of *havurah* is the members. Spend time helping everyone to get to know each other and to share a little about why they are there and what they hope to experience in a *havurah*. Possible ice-breakers include:

   a. Why I joined: The host begins by stating why their family joined the *havurah* and by offering personal background information on occupation, general and Jewish schooling, and other Jewish activities. Then each person, in turn, shares similar personal background information.

   b. Most important Jewish experience: The facilitator asks members to share their names, their most important Jewish experience, and what they want from the *havurah* experience. Presentations should be somewhat brief, but long enough to encourage people to share information fully.

   c. Personal odyssey: How did you come to live in this community? What were the personal and family factors which resulted in your now being a resident of this community? People can take turns sharing their personal histories and go back as many generations as necessary to explain why their family settled where they did.

   Note to the facilitator: It is very important that each member speak for himself/herself (NOT: "Well, my wife will tell you what we want . . ."). Some members will be more reticent to speak than others — encourage everyone to share something about themselves, or come back to them after the other members have concluded to see if they have anything to add. Presentations should be brief. If one person seems to be speaking too long, suggest that there will be many meetings in the future to share more with each other. Say that it is important, at the first meeting, that everyone have the opportunity to speak. (This can provide a model for the group for how to handle a too-talkative member!)

2. Agenda Setting – Summarize some of the stated interests and needs — e.g., activities for children, need to learn more about Judaism, celebrating holidays, etc. In some groups there will be obvious common interests; in others, the needs may be very diverse. Note that the *havurah* is rarely only one thing, such as all study sessions and speakers. It may also be the Shabbat dinner and the *Oneg Shabbat* after services, interspersed with attending lectures, having a discussion, family activities, etc. It is important that everyone's interest be represented, but unlikely that any one person's interest will be represented all the time.

3. Discussion Of the Nature Of *Havurah*
   Explain that the word *havurah* derives from the Hebrew word for friend. The *havurah* is comprised of "families" who have agreed to meet together in each other's homes to study, socialize, celebrate Jewish life, and hopefully to form some surrogate for the extended family. As the members involve themselves in Jewish programs and activities, they transform from a friendship unit seeking personal gratification to a fellowship pursuing purposes which move beyond individual needs. Each group develops its own activities and discovers its own essence. The emphasis is on the group, with responsibility being as equally divided as possible. *Havurah* coordinators are not leaders or chairpersons, but rather "guides" who help the *havurah* interact with the synagogue through coordinator meetings with the Steering Committee.

Chapter

4

4. Tasks Of a First Meeting
   a. Choosing a coordinator – This should be a rotating position. The coordinator is the liaison from the *havurah* to the Steering Committee. Responsibilities include sharing information distributed by the Steering Committee relating to programming, community resources, special synagogue activities, and attending periodic coordinator meetings. The coordinator also encourages *havurah* members to participate actively in program planning and in helping to carrying out planned activities.
   b. Setting time and place for a second meeting – Suggest that the agenda for the second meeting might be asking each member to bring to the meeting two or three suggested *havurah* activities. The host can ask each member to share a personal goal for the *havurah*, then list the suggestions

on a blackboard or piece of paper. After each member has participated, the group can then select specific shared goals and program ideas which might lead to achieving those goals.

c. *Havurah* Roster – Ask a volunteer to prepare a roster to distribute to all members at the next meeting.

## How Programs Are Chosen

1. Usually meetings are held once a month. It is preferable to set the date at the first meeting — e.g., the third Saturday of each month, the first Sunday of each month. In this way, members can note *havurah* meeting dates on their calendars well in advance. Meetings can be either all adult or family activities.

2. Meetings are usually held in the members' homes on an alphabetical rotating basis.

3. Ideally, program planning should be done by the *havurah* as a whole. However, planning can also be done by a small group of *havurah* members who have volunteered to plan several months of programming based on interests previously expressed by *havurah* members.

The host family should be responsible for calling or sending notices to all members reminding them of the meeting. Yet another family should have responsibility for the program — facilitating a discussion, bringing a speaker, organizing a holiday craft activity. The more people you have involved in planning a *havurah* event, the greater your guaranteed attendance and the greater the participation.

4. *Havurot* should plan at least one meeting a year to review goals and programs, to be certain that everyone's interests are still being met. New coordinators can also be chosen at these meetings.

**Choosing a Name**     Encourage the *havurah* to choose a name which represents its interest or identity — e.g., *Chevrah* (Association), *Kadimah* (Forward), one of the Tribes of Israel, etc. It is very important also that the Steering Committee have some way of identifying each *havurah* for the purpose of disseminating information, contacting them about special programs, and arranging seating at a *Havurah* Shabbat dinner.

## After a Meeting

1. Contact members who missed a meeting and bring them up to date. Inform them of the next meeting.

2. Contact the coordinator after a couple of months to see how things are going, if they need resources for program planning, and any other assistance.

**Additional Programs**   An important programming vehicle is the periodic Coordinators' meeting. These meetings, planned by the *Havurah* Steering Committee and held two, three, or four times per year, are attended by the coordinator of each *havurah* and his/her representative. The purpose of the meeting is to share program ideas, provide new programming resources, help the Steering Committee learn directly from *havurot* about their needs, successes, and failures, and provide an opportunity for all the *havurot* to meet one another and to feel part of a unified synagogue program.

Chapter

4

*Havurot* can be incorporated into general synagogue programming in a variety of ways. At one synagogue, the *Havurah* Steering Committee takes responsibility for providing *havurot* to staff the game booths at the annual Purim carnival. One *Havurah* Steering Committee has organized *havurot* to usher at Friday evening worship services. Many have annual *havurah* Shabbat dinners at the synagogue and special Shabbat services which highlight the achievements of the *havurah* program.

Some *havurot* can be encouraged to take on major service programs at their synagogues. There are *havurot* which have assumed responsibility for the congregational Food Bank, *havurot* which have taken leadership of the synagogue-wide adult education program, *havurot* which have created works of art to adorn their sanctuaries.

The purpose of these programs is to encourage and promote the sense that the synagogue *havurah* is an integral part of synagogue life, not an entity left to fend for itself. The sense of community should always be foremost, in the mind of the Rabbi, the Steering Committee, and the *havurah*.

**Editor's Comments**  Ms. Weber facilitates a *havurah* news-letter which contains news of the congregation's *havurot* and information about community resources, program suggestions, and educational pieces. Such a newsletter, published three or four times a year, can be a valuable vehicle for information. It can also be used to boost morale, smooth communication, and foster community. If a separate newsletter is not feasible, include news of the *havurot* in the congregational bulletin.

*Havurah* Coordinators' Committee meetings should be held two to four times a year. A member from each *havurah* should be invited to report at each of these meetings. In addition, the *Havurah* Steering Committee should introduce program ideas, resources, and other vehicles for enhancing *havurah* program-ming. These meetings are also a good setting for problem solv-ing, as many *havurot* may have worked through problems which another *havurah* is experiencing.

*Havurah* Steering Committee meetings are ideally held monthly, for the purpose of working on *havurah* placements, planning-major events (i.e., a *Havurah* Shabbat dinner, *Havurah* Shabbat service, or scholar-in-residence program, planning Coordinator meetings, etc.).

With the increase in interfaith marriages, it is important to inte-grate such couples into *havurot*. In some instances it may be more valuable to have them involved with families of mixed backgrounds than with a group in which everyone is a Jew by Choice or is intermarried.

The synagogue facilities need to be available for the *havurot*. If several *havurot* want to use the *sukkah* on the same evening or have a Passover *Seder* at the same time, the efforts should be coordinated through the *Havurah* Steering Committee. It can be arranged in such a way that two or three *havurot* get together and share the celebration as an even greater "extended family."

Abigail Gumbiner has written a chapter entitled "Havurah" in *The Jewish Principals Handbook*, edited by Audrey Friedman Marcus and Raymond A. Zwerin. In it she provides cogent infor-mation on how to form *havurot*. A valuable series of appendixes include samples of a *havurah* invitation, ideas for "getting

acquainted" activities, expectations, new member policy, workshops for *Havurah* Coordinators, and achieving consensus.
That chapter, along with Ms. Weber's recommendations, provide
all the necessary tools for successfully integrating *havurot* into
the congregation.

## Bibliography/Resources

Bubis, Gerald, and Wasserman, Harry, with Lert, Alan. *Syna-
    gogue Havurot: A Comparative Study*. Lanham, MD:
    University Press of America, Inc., 1983.

Gumbiner, Abigail. "Havurah." In *The Jewish Principals Hand-
    book*. Audrey Friedman Marcus and Raymond A. Zwerin,
    eds. Denver: Alternatives in Religious Education, Inc.,
    1983.

Kushner, Lawrence; Wolf, Arnold Jacob; and Gendler, Everett.
    "Communities Within Synagogues." In *The Third Jewish
    Catalog*. Sharon Strassfeld and Michael Strassfeld, eds.
    Philadelphia: Jewish Publication Society, 1980.

Neusner, Jacob, ed. *Contemporary Judaic Fellowship In Theory
    and Practice*. New York: KTAV, 1972.

Novak, William. "From Somerville To Savannah . . . and Los
    Angeles and Dayton." *Moment* (January/February 1981).

Reisman, Bernard. *The Havurah: A Contemporary Jewish
    Experience*. New York: Union of American Hebrew Con-
    gregations, 1977.

_____. *The Jewish Experiential Book: The Quest for Jewish
    Identity*. New York: KTAV, 1979.

_____. "Professional Leadership for the Havurah." *Journal of
    Reform Judaism* (Winter 1977): 51-63.

Sawin, Margaret A. *Hope for Families*. New York: Sadlier, 1982.

Stein, Jonathan. "In Defense Of the Congregational Havurah."
    *Journal of Reform Judaism* (Summer 1983): 43-49.

Chapter

4

Weltner, Linda. "Communities Without Synagogues." In *The Third Jewish Catalog*. Sharon Strassfeld and Michael Strassfeld, eds. Philadelphia: Jewish Publication Society, 1980.

Chapter
4

# Chapter 5

 **TITLE:** Bridging the Gap

 **CONTRIBUTED BY:** Melissa Coopersmith and Maureen Carey-Back

 **DESIGNED BY:** Melissa Coopersmith and Maureen Carey-Back at the Philadelphia Geriatric Center in cooperation with the Solomon Schechter/Forman Day School

 **TOPIC:** Acquainting children with the aging process; bringing senior adults and children together

 **TARGET AUDIENCE:** Children in Grade 3 and PGC nursing home residents (patients)

 **TIME FRAME:** Four month ongoing program; monthly inter-generational programs of varying lengths; bi-monthly 2 hour educational classroom programs for students; weekly 2 hour educational programs for the PGC participants

 **STAFF:** 2 facilitators for PGC participants; 4 classroom teachers for the children

**Overview**   "Bridging the Gap" is an intergenerational program coordinated by the staff of Philadelphia Geriatric Center and the Solomon Schechter/Forman Day School. It is designed to bring old and young Jewish people together to talk about issues they have in common and to get to know each other. It takes careful preparation and orientation for students and for participating senior adults, so that both groups know what to expect from each other.

**Purpose**   The purpose of this communication between generations is to encourage the opportunity for both groups to share feelings and gain a greater appreciation and awareness of each other's personal heritage and backgrounds.

Chapter

5

**Preparation/Procedure**   The Solomon Schechter/Forman Day School selected the entire third grade class (33 children, 4 teachers) to participate in this unique experience. Philadelphia Geriatric Center participants were chosen on the basis of: high cognitive functioning, experiencing isolation, or requesting to be a part of this particular group. Physical limitations do not prevent residents from participating in the program. The idea of commitment was necessary from all participants and staff involved. Two children were assigned to each resident. Parent and family member involvement was encouraged on an ongoing basis, and invitations were sent out to family members for the final student/resident interaction.

Prior to the first interaction, each generation went through extensive sensitivity exercises. Educational tools used were a homemade video exchange of brief personal introductions and an instant aging lesson emphasizing the physical limitations associated with aging.

Instant aging involved the use of props to simulate disabilities associated with the elderly. The children experienced limited eyesight which emulated the cataracts which many older adults encounter. This was done by putting vaseline on eye glasses and then trying to read the newspaper. They also experienced arthritis through trying to button a shirt wearing rubber gloves. Like the residents, students expressed feelings of frustration and dependency.

The residents send personal messages to their special friend and show them any special aspect of nursing home living (e.g., their room, activity room, synagogue, etc.). Each student is then sensitized through seeing what his/her special friend looks like and whether or not the special friend uses a wheelchair or walker for ambulatory purposes. The children also made a videotape of themselves in school. They tell their special friends who they are, what they like to do, and any other pertinent information about themselves. Both groups become more sensitive to each other's needs and, most importantly, break any barriers for the first visit.

Chapter

5

**Program Description**    Each program usually lasts from 2-3 hours with several interactional activities. The following is an outline of a Purim Encounter.

**Purim Encounter**
Meeting and greeting of special friends with nametags

Sing-along – Purim, Hebrew, and Yiddish songs with enlarged print

Armchair exercises – the idea of exercising in a chair is likely to provoke curiosity for both students and residents. Senior adults and children are involved in a series of armchair exercises which improve physical mobility and coordination, decrease tension and anxiety, increase physical contact, and are fun.

*Jewish Jeopardy* – children and PGC residents act as teams to explore with each other their own Jewish heritage.

Making *hamantaschen* – *hamantaschen* are made together and secret recipes and baking techniques are revealed.

Lunch – *hamantaschen* for dessert.

Discussion – quiet time for children and residents to review and share the day's events with each other.

Gifts – both children and residents exchange handmade Purim gifts. Additional programs were: a Passover *Seder*, Shabbat celebrations, Israel Independence Day Parade. Children and residents are encouraged to write, telephone, and visit each other.

**Evaluation**  In evaluating "Bridging the Gap," the following observations were made by the facilitators:

1. The group cohesiveness created a strong and lasting relationship. Many children remained in contact after the last formal activity. This exchange is ongoing and, in some cases, continues up until the death of the resident.

2. The program created a mutual respect for each generation's similarities and differences.

3. Both groups experienced "grandparent-hood" or "grandchild-hood."

4. Staff gained insight into the life cycle of young and old.

Chapter
5

**Editor's Comments**   Philadelphia has the advantage of having a day school and a geriatric population in the same community. However, one does not need to have these exact two elements in order to implement this program. Identify a group of senior adults which meets regularly in a local community center or synagogue. These should be adults who are physically well, and who would enjoy a program with young children. Contact the appropriate group worker who acts as coordinator to schedule a visit with them. There are many possible activities for such a program. Cooking is always fun, but there may not be a kitchen facility available. If that is the case, assign children to bring items for sandwiches, sodas, and dips, which they can make together with the senior adults.Plan craft activities which will allow both groups to use their creativity — collages for the holidays, Sukkah decorations, Purim masks, *mizrach* plaques, or mobiles of any kind. Making clay objects is a mutually beneficial project. Be sure to arrange to have the items fired in a kiln and presented to the creators when they are complete.

An excellent activity for senior adults and students in sixth grade and above is the recording of oral histories. In advance plan a class lesson on family history and the questions to be asked so as to obtain the needed information. At the same time, inform the seniors that they will be asked to talk about their backgrounds with the children when they visit. On the day of the program, come prepared with portable tape recorders, portable video cameras (if possible), and cameras. Have students record the history of their friends on the tapes by asking directed questions. Take pictures together. The recordings can be transcribed or copied so that both students and seniors have a permanent record of the event.

A class can prepare a presentation (musical or dramatic) which is presented at the time of the visit. Once this presentation is over, involve the seniors in some creative dramatics with the children (improvisation, assigned role plays, or paper bag dramatics). Ask children to bring costumes in order to enhance the spontaneity of the drama. Also, there are many senior adult groups that have choirs and dramatics clubs. They can prepare a program for the students.

Chapter

5

Creative writing is a good way to involve senior adults and school age children interactively. They can write group poems, respond to an object or picture shown them, or write an ending to a story. Good resources for the writing of group poems are the books of Kenneth Koch, particularly *Wishes, Lies, and Dreams*.

The telling of an ongoing story is another way to stimulate creative writing. To begin an ongoing story, have everyone sit in a circle with each person adding something to the story. Using this as a catalyst, ask senior adults and students to write their own stories. Compile them in a booklet and send it to the seniors when it is completed.

When a group of senior adults meets regularly (weekly, monthly, etc.), schedule several classes to meet with them one at a time. The interactional activities will vary, depending on the ages of the children. However, some things may remain constant, such as sharing a meal or food together. If it is not practical to take students to a geriatric facility or community center, invite the seniors to the synagogue or school.

## Bibliography/Resources

Blue, Rose. *Grandma Didn't Wave Back*. New York: Dell, 1972.

Fassler, Joan. *My Grandma Died Today*. New York: Human Sciences Press, 1971.

Koch, Kenneth. *Wishes, Lies, and Dreams*. New York: Vintage Books, 1970.

Myerhoff, Barbara. *Number Our Days*. New York: Dutton, 1978.

Pomerantz, Barbara. *Bubby, Me, and Memories*. New York: Union of American Hebrew Congregations, 1983.

Chapter

5

# Chapter 6

 **TITLE:** Preschool Holiday Workshops

 **CONTRIBUTED BY:** Rabbi Nathan H. Rose

 **TOPIC:** Shabbat, Chanukah, Purim, Pesach

 **TARGET AUDIENCE:** Parents of preschool age children (3-4 year olds)

 **TIME FRAME:** Four 90 minute workshops

 **STAFF:** One facilitator well versed in preschool education and Judaica

**Overview** "Preschool Holiday Workshops" feature total family involvement for families with three and four-year-old children. The program consists of four 90 minute holiday workshops, during which families join together to learn about the holidays through songs, stories, crafts, and other activites. These workshops, sponsored by Temple Beth El in Rochester, New York, are open to everyone in the community.

**Purpose** The purpose of the program is to increase awareness and observance of holidays in the home. The program also serves to introduce the religious school and the synagogue to young families, in order to encourage enrollment in the early grades of religious school.

Chapter

6

**Preparation/Procedure** The content of the four workshops is basically the same: families use a "discovery bag" containing ritual objects for each holiday; they hear a story and sing a song; they complete two craft projects, one of which is a ritual object which may then be used in the home; they participate in a reinforcement activity. In some cases there are parallel activities for parents and children (see Passover below). In addition, other ritual objects, such as Chanukah candles, Shabbat candles and candlesticks, *mishloach manot*, and kits for *bedikat chametz* are sent home to encourage additional observance. A booklet is also available for each holiday which includes a guide to observance, a glossary, a story, songs, crafts, recipes, and a bibliography.

It is the responsibility of the facilitator to determine age appropriate craft activities, the story, and the song for each holiday workshop. If the facilitator has limited experience with preschoolers, he/she should consult with a knowledgeable early childhood specialist who can be of assistance in this area. All supplies, materials, and food items should be readied in advance.

The facilitator also prepares an evaluation form in advance, a sample of which follows:

EVALUATION

Dear Parents:

We would appreciate your taking a few minutes to fill in the following form. *DO NOT* sign your name. Your answers will be of tremendous help to us.

Please check the appropriate boxes.

I. We attended the following workshops:  Chanukah _____
                                         Shabbat   _____
                                         Purim     _____
                                         Passover  _____

II.

| | We did these in our household before attending the Workshop | We did these things as a result of the Workshop |
|---|---|---|
| *Chanukah* | | |
| Light Candles | _____ | _____ |
| Say Blessings | _____ | _____ |
| Play *Dreidel* | _____ | _____ |
| Cook Holiday Foods | _____ | _____ |
| Other (specify) | _____ | _____ |
| | | |
| *Shabbat* | | |
| Light Candles | _____ | _____ |
| Say *Kiddush* | _____ | _____ |
| Attend Services | _____ | _____ |
| Have Shabbat Dinner | _____ | _____ |
| Other (specify) | _____ | _____ |
| | | |
| *Purim* | | |
| Attend Services | _____ | _____ |
| *Mishloach Manot* | _____ | _____ |
| Have Purim Meal | _____ | _____ |
| Bring Children in Costume | _____ | _____ |
| Other (specify) | _____ | _____ |

Chapter

6

*Passover*
Buy Passover Foods      _____    _____
Change Dishes            _____    _____
Search for *Chametz*      _____    _____
Sell *Chametz*            _____    _____
Burn *Chametz*            _____    _____
Have a *Seder*            _____    _____
Attend Services          _____    _____
Other (specify)          _____    _____

III. Booklets – We used the booklets for:
Blessings                                    _____
Guideline for observing holiday              _____
Crafts and activities                        _____
Other (please specify)                       _____
We did not use the booklets                  _____

IV. We felt the Workshops were:    Good     _____
                                   Average  _____
                                   Poor     _____

We would like to recommend the following:

_____
_____
_____
_____

We did not like the following about the Workshops:

_____
_____
_____
_____

V. What is the age of your *OLDEST* child? _____

## Program Description
### Shabbat
1. Introductory Activities
   a. Sit in a circle and talk about Shabbat as a special day.
   b. Pass around the Shabbat discovery bag. As each item is

taken from the bag, discuss its purpose and add it to the Shabbat table. (A tablecloth or white butcher paper should be placed in advance over the Shabbat table.) Bag contains: candles, candlesticks, wine, *Kiddush* cup, *challah*, *challah* platter, *challah* cover, *tzedakah* box.

c. Distribute booklets and teach "Shabbat Shalom."

d. Read *The Seven Days Of Creation* by Leonard E. Fisher.

2. Craft Activities

a. Prepare *challah* dough in advance. Have each family braid a *challah*, coat it with egg, and put it in the oven to bake.

b. Make *challah* covers (see *Let's Celebrate!* by Ruth Esrig Brinn, p. 9).

3. Reinforcement Activities.

a. Read another Shabbat book — *Shabbat Can Be* by Raymond A. Zwerin and Audrey Friedman Marcus or *Good Shabbos Everybody* by Robert Garvey.

b. Families set tables for Shabbat.
Light the candles and say the blessings.
Recite *Kiddush*.
Say *HaMotzi*.
Sing *"Shabbat Shalom."*

c. Share thoughts and feelings about Shabbat.

d. Distribute the booklets.

Chapter

6

## Chanukah

1. Introduction

a. Pass around the Chanukah bag and as each item is taken from the bag, discuss its purpose. Bag contains: *chanukiah*, potato, *dreidel, gelt*.

2. Craft Activities (see *Let's Celebrate!* by Ruth Esrig Brinn, p. 35)

a. Make wrapping paper.

b. Make a spinning *dreidel*.

3. Reinforcement Activities (in a circle)

a. Sing "I Have a Little Dreidel." Use spinning *dreidel*.

b. Read *Hanukkah ABC* by Lillian Abramson.

c. Light the *chanukiah* and sing blessings. Serve jelly doughnuts and teach the blessing to be recited over them. Before everyone goes home, distribute *dreidel*, candles, *gelt*, small toys, and Chanukah booklets.

**Purim**

1. Introduction

    a. Pass around the Purim discovery bag. As each item is taken from the bag, discuss its purpose. Bag contains: *Gragger*, *hamentaschen*, costume, *shalach manot* box, crown, *megillah*, mask.

    b. Teach the song "When You Hear the Name Of Haman Clap Your Hands."

2. Craft Activities

    a. Make *hamentaschen*. Each family can cut dough with a cup, add filling, then bake.

    b. Make *graggers*. (See *Let's Celebrate!* by Ruth Esrig Brinn, pp. 48-49.)

Chapter

6

3. Reinforcement

    a. Read another Purim story — *Happy Purim Night* by Norma Simon or *A Purim Album* by Raymond A. Zwerin and Audrey Friedman Marcus.

    b. Sing "When You Hear the Name Of Haman Clap Your Hands" again. This time use *graggers*.

    c. Sing "Chag Purim." Encourage children to sing "*rash, rash, rash*" and use *graggers*.

    d. Distribute *hamantaschen* and Purim booklets.

    e. Discuss how families will celebrate Purim this year.

**Passover**

1. Introduction

    a. Pass around the Passover discovery bag. As each item is taken from the bag discuss its purpose and add it to the Passover table. (Have a table to set in advance.) Bag contains: *Kiddush* cup, *maror*, shank bone, *charoset*, egg, parsley, feather, candle, spoon, *Haggadah*, *Seder* plate.

    b. Sing "*Dayenu*."

    c. Read *But This Night Is Different: A Seder Experience* by Audrey Friedman Marcus and Raymond A. Zwerin or *Pesach Is Coming* by Hyman and Alice Chanover.

2. Crafts (see *Let's Celebrate!* by Ruth Esrig Brinn, pp. 56, 57, 59, 61)

    a. Make a *Kiddush* cup.

    b. Make a *Seder* plate.

c. Make a *matzah* cover.

d. Make *charoset*.

3. Parallel Activities

    a. Children go on a *chametz* hunt. They may throw the *chametz* to the birds or wash it down the sink. ·

    b. Parents discuss *hilchot* Pesach with Rabbi or Director of Education.

4. Reinforcement

    a. Read *Where Is the Afikomen?* by Judy Groner and Madeline Wikler or *Pesach Is Here* by Hyman Chanover.

    b. Sing "One Morning" and the order of the *Seder — Kadesh, Urchatz,* etc.

    c. Quickly review the order of the *Seder,* encouraging children to ask questions.

    d. Distribute the booklets.

Chapter

6

**Editor's Comments**   These workshops follow a two year cycle and much of the same audience participates each time. For this reason, Temple Beth El uses different craft activities each year. The booklets, however, remain the same. The focus is also on a different *mitzvah* each year. This program can be expanded to include other holidays and observances — e.g., Sukkot, Tu B'Shevat, *Havdalah.* A celebration of Yom HaAtzma'ut may be added as well, even though there are no specific *mitzvot* or *halachot* for this occasion.

Each workshop, with the exception of Pesach, is designed so that parents and children are together at all times. At the Passover workshop, the parents have a brief session during which they discuss *hilchot* Pesach with the Rabbi. A session of this type for parents would be a valuable addition to each workshop, as it allows parents an opportunity to explore the *mitzvot* of the holiday in more depth and to learn some important background material. Parents who are repeating the program have an opportunity to expand their knowledge and also to share their experiences with those who are new to the program.

Another way to vary the program is to ask each family to bring to the workshop a ritual object pertaining to the holiday and to share it with the group. The facilitator can assure that all appropriate artifacts are presented by having a duplicate set of items displayed on a table and talking about those which may not have been brought by the families. It is also important to have, as they do at Temple Beth El, a display of books and mediated materials for parents to peruse. The display should include both children's books and adult reference materials. If at all possible, provide order forms to assist families to purchase the materials.

Each of the programs contains songs and stories. If desired, creative movement can be added — i.e., Chasidic dancing to *niggunim* for Shabbat, marching like the Macabbees for Chanukah, walking like a king or queen or hero/heroine at Purim, escaping to freedom or acting like Moses, the leader for Pesach. Stories may be told using puppets or flannel boards or with accompanying actions. For Shabbat assign each family a story and have them retell it to the group using one of these methods.

An additional useful handout is a home inventory of Jewish objects. Explain to parents that while they may not have all of the items and books listed, this inventory serves as a checklist of what they have now and what they may strive to have in years to come.

Since one purpose of the program is to increase home observance of each holiday, Rabbi Rose suggests that the synagogue provide a vehicle to facilitate this. For instance, if there is a *havurah* program, encourage existing *havurot* to adopt one of the participating preschool families for a celebration. Or, encourage the preschool families to form a *havurah* themselves. However this is done, encourage participating families to celebrate together. They can use the skills they have learned in the workshops and can use the ritual objects they have made.

Chapter

6

## Bibliography/Resources
### Holidays In General
Brinn, Ruth Esrig. *Let's Celebrate!* Rockville, MD: Kar-Ben Copies, 1977.

*Encyclopaedia Judaica*. Jerusalem: Keter Publishing House, 1972.

*The Five Megillot and Jonah: A New Translation*. Philadelphia: Jewish Publication Society, 1974.

Gersh, Harry. *When a Jew Celebrates*. New York: Behrman House, 1971.

Goodman, Philip. *The Hanukkah Anthology*. Philadelphia: Jewish Publication Society, 1976.

_____. *The Passover Anthology*. Philadelphia: Jewish Publication Society, 1961.

_____. *The Purim Anthology*. Philadelphia: Jewish Publication Society, 1949.

Goodman, Robert. *A Teachers Guide To Jewish Holidays*. Denver: Alternatives in Religious Education, Inc., 1983.

Heschel, Abraham Joshua. *The Sabbath: Its Meaning for Modern Man*. New York: Farrar, Straus & Giroux, 1978.

Kaplan, Aryeh. *Shabbos: Day of Eternity*. New York: National Conference of Synagogue Youth, Union of Orthodox Congregations, 1947.

Millgram, Abraham E. *Sabbath: Day Of Delight*. Philadelphia: Jewish Publication Society, 1965.

Renberg, Dalia Hardof. *The Complete Guide To Jewish Holidays*. New York: Adama Books, 1985.

*The Shabbat Manual*. New York: Central Conference of American Rabbis, 1972.

Siegel, Richard; Strassfeld, Michael; and Strassfeld, Sharon, eds. *The First Jewish Catalog*. Philadelphia: Jewish Publication Society, 1973.

Strassfeld, Michael. *The Jewish Holidays: A Guide and Commentary*. New York: Harper & Row, 1985.

Waskow, Arthur. *Seasons Of Our Joy*. Toronto: Bantam Books, 1982.

Chapter

6

**For Children**
**Shabbat**
Cedarbaum, Sophia. *The Sabbath*. New York: Union of American Hebrew Congregations, 1960.

Fisher, Leonard. *The Seven Days Of Creation*. New York: Holiday House, 1981.

Garvey, Robert. *Good Shabbos, Everybody*. New York: United Synagogue Commission on Jewish Education, 1951.

Garvey, Robert. *Holidays Are Nice*. New York: KTAV Publishing Co., 1960.

Gellman, Ellie. *Shai's Shabbat Walk*. Rockville, MD: Kar-Ben Copies, 1985.

Levy, Sara G. *Mother Goose Rhymes for Jewish Children*. New York: Bloch Publishing, 1945.

Salop, Byrd. *The Kiddush Cup Who Hated Wine*. New York: Jonathan David Publishers, 1957.

Saypol, Judyth Robbins, and Wikler, Madeline. *Come, Let Us Welcome Shabbat*. Rockville, MD: Kar-Ben Copies, 1978.

Schlein, Miriam. *Shabbat*. New York: Behrman House, 1983.

Silverman, Althea O. *Habibi and Yow*. New York: Bloch Publishing Co., 1946.

Simon, Norma. *Every Friday Night*. New York: United Synagogue Commission on Jewish Education, 1961.

Sol, Robert. *A Wonderful Shabbat*. New York: KTAV, 1954.

Weilerstein, Sadie Rose. *Molly and the Sabbath Queen*. New York: Behrman House, 1949.

————. *What Danny Did*. New York: Bloch Publishing Co., 1944.

Chapter 6

_____. *What the Moon Brought*. Philadelphia: Jewish Publication Society of America, 1942.

Zwerin, Raymond A., and Marcus, Audrey Friedman. *Shabbat Can Be*. New York: Union of American Hebrew Congregations, 1979.

**Chanukah**
Abramson, Lillian. *Jeremy's & Judy's Hanukah*. New York: Behrman House, 1956.

_____. *Hanukkah ABC*. New York: Shulsinger Brothers, 1968.

Adler, David. *A Picture Book Of Hanukkah*. New York: Holiday House, 1982.

Bearman, Jane. *Eight Nights: A Chanukah Counting Book*. New York: Union of American Hebrew Congregations, 1978.

Behrens, June. *Hanukkah*. Chicago: Children's Press, 1983.

Drucker, Malka. *Hanukkah: Eight Nights, Eight Lights*. New York: Holiday House, 1980.

Garvey, Robert. *A First Chanukah Word Book*. New York: KTAV, 1952.

Hirsh, Marilyn. *I Love Hanukkah*. New York: Holiday House, 1984.

_____. *The Hanukkah Story*. New York: Bonim Books, 1977.

Saypol, Judyth Robbins, and Wikler, Madeline. *My Very Own Chanukah Book*. Rockville, MD: Kar-Ben Copies, 1977.

Scharfstein, Sol. *Chanukah Fun and Story Book*. New York: KTAV, 1952.

_____. *Draydel, Draydel, Draydel*. New York: KTAV, 1969.

Schlein, Miriam. *Hanukkah*. New York: Behrman House, 1983.

Chapter

6

Shostak, Myra. *Rainbow Candles: A Chanukah Counting Book*. Rockville, MD: Kar-Ben Copies, 1986.

Sol, Robert. *The First Book Of Chanukah*. New York: KTAV, 1956.

**Purim**

Cedarbaum, Sophia. *Purim: A Joyous Holiday*. New York: Union of American Hebrew Congregations, 1960.

Cohen, Barbara. *Here Come the Purim Players*. New York: Lothrop, 1984.

Cone, Molly. *Purim*. New York: Crowell, 1967.

Saypol, Judyth R., and Wikler, Madeline. *My Very Own Megillah*. Rockville, MD: Kar-Ben Copies, 1976.

Schlein, Miriam. *Purim*. New York: Behrman House, 1983.

Simon, Norma. *Happy Purim Night*. New York: United Synagogue Commission on Jewish Education, 1959.

————. *The Purim Party*. New York: United Synagogue Commission on Jewish Education, 1959.

Wikler, Madeline. *The Purim Parade*. Rockville, MD: Kar-Ben Copies, 1986.

Zwerin, Raymond A., and Marcus, Audrey Friedman. *A Purim Album*. New York: Union of American Hebrew Congregations, 1981.

**Passover**

Adler, David A. *A Picture Book Of Passover*. New York: Holiday House, 1982.

Auerbach, Julie Jaslow. *Everything's Changing — It's Pesach!* Rockville, MD: Kar-Ben Copies, 1986.

Bial, Morrison D. *The Passover Story*. New York: Behrman House, 1952.

Chapter

6

Cedarbaum, Sophia N. *Passover: The Festival Of Freedom*. New York: Union of American Hebrew Congregations, 1960.

Chanover, Hyman. *Pesah Is Coming*. New York: United Synagogue Commission on Jewish Education, 1956.

_____. *Pesah Is Here!*. New York: United Synagogue Commission on Jewish Education, 1956.

Drucker, Malka. *Passover: A Season Of Freedom*. New York: Holiday House, 1981.

Engel, Rose C. *My Passover Haggadah*. Cedarhurst, NY: Tara Publications, 1971.

Groner, Judy, and Wikler, Madeline. *Where Is the Afikomen?* Rockville, MD: Kar-Ben Copies, 1985.

Marcus, Audrey Friedman, and Zwerin, Raymond A. *But This Night Is Different: A Seder Experience*. New York: Union of American Hebrew Congregations, 1980.

Rosen, Anne. *A Family Passover*. Philadelphia: Jewish Publication Society, 1980.

Saypol, Judyth, and Wikler, Madeline. *My Very Own Haggadah*. Silver Spring, MD: Kar-Ben Copies, 1974.

Scharfstein, Edythe. *The Book Of Passover*. New York: KTAV, 1953.

Schlein, Miriam. *Passover*. New York: Behrman House, 1983.

Simon, Norma. *My Family Seder*. New York: United Synagogue Commission on Jewish Education, 1961.

Wikler, Madeline. *My First Seder*. Rockville, MD: Kar-Ben Copies, 1986.

Chapter

6

# Chapter 7

 **TITLE:** The Joy Of Shabbat

 **CONTRIBUTED BY:** Dorothy C. Herman

 **TOPIC:** Making Shabbat part of one's life

 **TARGET AUDIENCE:** Families with students in Grades 4-6

 **TIME FRAME:** Six 2½ hour sessions for students, two or three 2 hour workshops for parents; time frame can be flexible

 **STAFF:** Coordinator, Rabbi, classroom teacher, art, music specialist

**Overview**   "The Joy Of Shabbat" is a curriculum piece for 4th, 5th, and 6th Grade students with parallel workshops for parents. The students participate in six 2½ hour sessions and the parents in three workshops of 2 hours each. The parent workshops are held separately from student sessions.

Prior to developing the program, the author did a survey of several 5th Grade children in neighboring congregations in the community. Both Reform and Conservative congregations were included in the survey. The results of the survey suggested that children had the skills to participate in Shabbat rituals. However, while many owned Shabbat objects, few students ever used them. This program provides a model for including Shabbat observance regularly in one's life and has been published by the Central Agency for Jewish Education of Miami.

Chapter

7

**Purpose**   The purpose of this program is to encourage participants to make Shabbat a part of their lives. The goals for students and parents are to:

1. Develop basic knowledge about Shabbat — its observances, rituals and history.

2. Develop basic skills in reciting and using Shabbat prayers, blessings, and songs.

3. Prepare, serve, and participate in a Shabbat dinner.

4. Attend Shabbat services.

5. Observe Shabbat together on a regular basis.

**Preparation/Procedure**   In all publicity for this program, emphasize that its success depends on parallel participation by parents.

Acquaint the classroom teacher(s), Rabbi, and the music and art specialists with the program. Reserve dates and arrange for appropriate facilities and custodial help. Be sensitive especially to the needs of children from single parent homes.

The aforementioned booklet contains worksheets, book and story lists, recipes, music and craft projects, and has details for

each of the class sessions, sample letters, and invitations. Obtain
the booklet if you are planning to implement this program.

Have someone in the congregation take pictures of all sessions
to show during the last session. A video recorder may be set up
on a tripod to record the proceedings as they occur. Edit the
tape before showing it to the participants. Also, arrange for a few
parents to help with the cooking sessions. Meet with the staff to
share and evaluate progress.

**Program Description**   The following is an outline of the
six sessions for students, each lasting 2½ hours. Be sure to allow
time for record keeping and *tzedakah* projects when necessary.

**Student Sessions**

Session I
> 1. Introduction of Unit:
>    Holiday Chart
>    "Bible Search-a-Quote"
>    Shabbat Traditions
> 2. Cooking: *Matzah* Balls
> 3. Music: Gift of Shabbat

Session II
> 1. Review Blessings — Shabbat Discussion
> 2. Cooking: Kugel
> 3. Music: *Birkat Hamazon* — Songs

Session III
> 1. Parent/Grandparent Worksheet and Discussion
> 2. Shabbat Is . . . Poetry
> 3. Cooking: Mock derma
> 4. Shabbat Music In the Synagogue

Session IV
> 1. Ritual Museum
> 2. Art: *Challah* covers, table decorations, or centerpieces
> 3. Shabbat Dinner Preparation

Session V
> 1. Committee Sign-ups and Invitations
> 2. Reading and Discussion Of Shabbat Stories

Chapter

7

Session VI
    1. Evaluations: Verbal and written
    2. Slide Presentation Of Class Sessions, Parents Workshops, and Shabbat Dinner

**Outline of Session I**   As an example, an outline of Session I follows. (All of the sessions have the same three components — Class Input, Cooking, and Music.)

Class Input
1. Objectives
    a. Using the Holiday Chart, the students will list basic information about Shabbat.
    b. Students will read and discuss the Shabbat sayings posted on the bulletin boards.
    c. Students will play "Bible Search-a-Quote" to discover what the Bible says about Shabbat.
    d. Students will listen to a talk about Shabbat traditions.

2. Set-up
    a. Post Shabbat sayings and pictures of Shabbat ritual objects on the bulletin boards. Some examples of such sayings are:

"There is no Judaism without the Sabbath." (Leo Baeck)

"If a battle has commenced previous to the Sabbath, Jews are permitted to continue fighting on the Sabbath whether in attack or defense." (*Shabbat* 75)

"Danger to life takes precedence over the sanctity of the Sabbath." (*Shabbat* 75)

"More than Israel has kept the Sabbath, the Sabbath has kept Israel." (Ahad Ha'am)

"The Sabbath is the day for rehearsing the world to come, the ideal world." (Mordecai Kaplan)

    b. Display ten gift wrapped boxes on a long table at the front of the room.

    c. Post a reproduction of the Holiday Chart on poster board on the front board. This chart is divided into six categories, each descriptive of Shabbat: When Celebrated, Biblical

Chapter

7

Reference, Why Celebrated, How Celebrated In Home, How Celebrated In Synagogue, and Food-Symbols.

3. Procedures – Suggested Activities

   a. Introduce the subject of Shabbat, explaining that Shabbat comes every week and that it is the focal point of the week for Jewish people.

   b. Give students five minutes to fill in the appropriate columns on a blank Holiday Chart. (Through the charts the teacher will be able to ascertain what the students know about Shabbat.) The answers will be discussed later in the lesson.

   c. Fill out the second column on the Holiday Chart (Biblical Reference). Ask what the students wrote here. List the responses on the master Holiday Chart. Distribute the Bibles. Play "Bible Quote Search" (see below for rules) to discover what the Bible says about Shabbat. Add the biblical citations to the master chart and have the students do the same on their charts.

Chapter

7

### BIBLE SEARCH-A-QUOTE

1. Divide the class into teams of four or five.

2. Give each person a Bible.

3. The teacher says, "Attention." All students stand.

4. The teacher says, "Search-a-Quote." Students put one hand on top of the Bible.

5. The teacher writes a biblical reference on the board and says, "Begin." Use any of the following: Genesis 2:1-3, Exodus 20:8, Exodus 31:16-17, Deuteronomy 5:12, Numbers 15:17-21, and Psalm 104:14.

6. Students look up the reference and raise a hand upon finding it. When one team has all hands raised, one member is chosen to read the page number and quote. If it is correct, the team receives one point. If it is incorrect, the team which finished next has the opportunity to give the correct quote. Each quote is then discussed.

Cooking
1. Objectives
   a. Students will describe the significance of Shabbat dinner.
   b. Students will prepare *matzah* balls.

2. Procedures and Suggested Activities
   a. Explain that the students will be responsible for cooking the family Shabbat Dinner and that parents will be involved with students in an evening of learning and preparation.
   b. Post the rules for the kitchen and have students read them and discuss their responsibilities.
   c. Assign students to a group and a station and distribute recipes. Each station, set up in advance, includes ingredients, utensils, and materials to complete the dish.
   d. The teacher reads and discusses the recipe with special emphasis on measuring spoons and cups.
   e. The students will follow the recipe, prepare and cook *matzah* balls, and clean their area.

Chapter

7

Music Of the Rituals
This lesson is presented to the students in the religious school and to the parents on their study evening.

1. Objectives
   The students/parents will:
   a. Set a Shabbat table with ritual objects.
   b. Recite/sing/chant the blessings in Hebrew and English over candles, wine, and *challah*.
   c. Light the candles, drink grape juice/wine, and eat *challah*.
   d. Hear a talk about the ritual objects, their use, and meaning.
2. Procedures and Activities – This section of the lesson should be taught by a person with a rich feeling for Shabbat. As an introduction that person shares his/her early memories, perhaps describing the excitement that grew within the home as sundown neared. The descriptions should be vivid so that the participants might almost smell and taste Shabbat. It is necessary to create a mood of expectancy.
   a. The teacher calls attention to the ten gift wrapped packages on the front table and gives one out to each of ten participants. The teacher explains that these are all gifts of Shabbat. Each is needed to create the mood and flavor of this special day. Excitement will build as the session

progresses and as participants guess the contents of each
package. Give a prayer sheet to each person.

b. Using word descriptions, the table is described as being in
the dining room, large enough for the whole family.

c. One by one, the gift holders are asked to come to the front,
open their box, and place the object on the table. The
boxes are numbered so that they can be called up in the
following order:

Tablecloth
*Tzedakah* box
Candlesticks
Candles
Matches
*Kiddush* cup
Grape juice/wine
*Challah* board
*Challah*
*Challah* cover

Chapter

7

d. After calling up those who hold the first five gifts, choose
someone to light the candles. Describe the customs
associated with lighting the candles, why we light them,
who may light them, when they are lit, and the meaning of
the blessing. Next teach or review the blessing and chant
it in Hebrew and English over the lighted candles.

e. Now call on students with the next two boxes —*Kiddush*
cup and grape juice/wine. Chooose someone to make *Kiddush*, then comment on what the word *Kiddush* means,
why we recite it, who recites it, why wine is used, and the
kind of wine used on Shabbat. Using the song sheets, teach
or review the *Kiddush*. A participant distributes grape
juice/wine to each person which is sipped after each time
the *Kiddush* is chanted.

f. Finally, call on students with the last three boxes — *challah* board, *challah*, and *challah* cover. Choose a participant
to bless the *challah*, then comment on why a blessing is
said over the *challah* and why there are two *challot*. Each
participant receives a piece of *challah* and eats it after
*HaMotzi*.

g. The blessings are added to the holiday chart under the
heading "Foods and Symbols."

Extra credit for students
Choose one of the Shabbat sayings from the bulletin board and write what it means to you.

**Parent Workshops**   Parent workshops last 2 hours each and take place on three separate evenings. A schedule of the workshops follow:

Parent Workshop I
  1. Introduction Of the Unit

  2. The Spirit Of Shabbat

  3. The Gift Of Shabbat (parallel with student lesson)

  4. The Sharing Of Shabbat

Chapter

7

Parent Workshop II
  1. Review, Update, Sharing Of Personal Experiences

  2. Music Of Shabbat (parallel with student lesson)

  3. Shabbat Is . . . Poetry (parallel with student session)

  4. Committee Sign-Ups for Shabbat Dinner

Parent Workshop III (after the Shabbat Dinner)
  1. Review and Sharing Of Personal Experiences

  2. Slide Presentation Of the Children's Class Sessions, Parent Workshop, and Shabbat Dinner

  3. Evaluation

  4. Creating Jewish Memories

  5. Future Directions

An outline of one 2 hour parent workshop follows:

Goals
  1. Parents will continue to develop a sense of community.

  2. Parents will review Shabbat rituals.

  3. Parents will sing Shabbat songs.

  4. Parents will write Shabbat poetry.

  5. Parents will volunteer for positions at the Shabbat dinner.

Procedure
1. Welcome and Introductions

2. Update: Parents share their reactions to the program and to the activities they experienced with their children.

3. Music Of Shabbat: The Shabbat table is set in advance. The music teacher reviews the blessings. (Provide a song sheet and a copy of *Birkat HaMazon*.) The parents learn the *Birkat HaMazon* and the same Shabbat songs that the students learned in class.

4. Shabbat Is . . . . Parents create poetry just as their children did. (This exercise gives the parents an opportunity to interact with each other.)

**Editor's Comments**   This model may be adapted as a spiral curriculum beginning in the earliest grades of religious school. Each year families learn about a different aspect of Shabbat and begin to practice what they have learned. Ideally, by the time the family has a sixth grade student, the Shabbat as a whole day experience is a part of their lives. The program as presented here focuses on *Erev Shabbat*. The same format may also be used to teach about Saturday observances and rituals. Parent workshops can center around Torah study, the Shabbat worship services, and *Havdalah*. Student sessions can also include Torah study, along with presentations about the portion of the week. The meal can be a Shabbat luncheon or *Seudah Shleesheet*. Many of the other content areas presented in this program are valid as well, such as the music of Shabbat, poetry, stories for Shabbat, interviews with grandparents, and creating Jewish memories.

Chapter

7

One suggestion for a follow-up activity is for families to make a Jewish family photo album. Families are encouraged to take pictures of Jewish events in their lives, caption the pictures and place them in an album. At one synagogue this was turned into a photo contest with judges selecting the winning album. The criteria for judging included content, captions, neatness, and interest. All entries were awarded a certificate of merit and the winners received *challah* covers. Instead of a contest, you might have a Jewish photo album display in the school or Jewish Community Center as a year-end activity. Everyone can share their Jewish memories for that year.

The format of "The Joy Of Shabbat" may be adapted for holiday celebrations. Focus on a different holiday each school year with in-depth class lessons and a parallel parent session. Such programming will provide families with additional perspectives on those days which have special religious or historical significance.

## Bibliography/Resources

Beiner, Stan J. *Sedra Scenes: Skits for Every Torah Portion.* Denver: Alternatives in Religious Education, Inc., 1982.

Bial, Morrison David. *Liberal Judaism At Home.* New York: Union of American Hebrew Congregations, 1971.

Brin, Ruth. *Shabbat Catalogue.* New York: KTAV, 1978.

Cardozo, Arlene Rossen. *Jewish Family Celebrations: The Sabbath, Festivals and Ceremonies.* New York: St. Martin's Press, 1982.

Efron, Benjamin. *Pathways Through the Prayerbook.* New York: KTAV, 1962.

Epstein, Morris. *All About Jewish Holidays and Customs.* New York: KTAV, 1970.

*Gates Of the House: The New Union Home Prayerbook.* New York: Central Conference of American Rabbis, 1977.

Goodman, Robert. *A Teachers Guide To Jewish Holidays.* Denver: Alternatives in Religious Education, Inc., 1983.

Herman, Dorothy C. *The Joy Of Shabbat: An Experiential Approach To the Teaching Of Shabbat.* Miami: Central Agency for Jewish Education and Temple Beth Am Religious School, 1982.

Hertz. J.H. *The Pentateuch and Haftorahs.* London: Soncino Press, 1972.

Heschel, Abraham Joshua. *The Sabbath: Its Meaning for Modern Man.* New York: Farrar, Straus & Giroux, 1978.

Chapter

7

Katz, Michael, and Freedman, Joseph L. *Seder Shabbat: A Guide To Shabbat Observance*. New York: Leaders Training Fellowship, 1978.

Klein, Isaac. *A Guide To Jewish Religious Practice*. New York: The Jewish Theological Seminary of America, 1979.

Levy, Deborah, and Marcus, Audrey Friedman. *The Learning Center Book Of Jewish Holidays and Symbols Grades 1-3*. Denver: Alternatives in Religious Education, Inc., 1977.

Loeb, Sorel Goldberg, and Kadden, Barbara Binder. *Teaching Torah: A Treasury Of Insights and Activities*. Denver: Alternatives in Religious Education, Inc., 1984.

Millgram, Abraham E. *Sabbath: The Day Of Delight*. Philadelphia: Jewish Publication Society, 1944.

Plaut, W. Gunther; Bamberger, Bernard J.; and Hallo, William W. *The Torah: A Modern Commentary*. New York: Union of American Hebrew Congregations, 1981.

Ross, Lillian. *The Fourth Commandment — A Sabbath Manual*. Miami: Central Agency for Jewish Education, 1979.

Saypol, Judyth Robbins, and Wikler, Madeline. *Come, Let Us Welcome the Sabbath*. Silver Spring, MD: Kar-Ben Copies, 1978.

Schauss, Hayyim. *The Jewish Festivals, History and Observance*. New York: Schocken Books, 1978.

*A Shabbat Manual*. New York: Central Conference of American Rabbis, 1972.

Siegel, Richard; Strassfeld, Michael; and Strassfeld, Sharon, eds. *The First Jewish Catalog*. Philadelphia: Jewish Publication Society, 1973.

Syme, Rabbi Daniel. *The Jewish Home — Book I*. New York: Union of American Hebrew Congregations, 1976.

Chapter

7

*There Is a Season: A Values Clarification Approach To Jewish Holidays.* Denver: Alternatives in Religious Education, Inc., 1978.

Waskow, Arthur. *Seasons Of Our Joy.* Toronto: Bantam Books, 1982.

Wolfson, Ron. *The Art Of Jewish Living: The Shabbat Seder.* New York: The Federation of Jewish Men's Clubs and The University of Judaism, 1985. (475 Riverside Dr., Suite 244, New York, NY 10115)

*World Over* 42, no. 2 (October 10, 1980).

Zisenwine, David, and Abramowitz, Karen. *The Sabbath: Time & Existence.* Tel Aviv, Israel: Everyman's University Publishing House, 1982; distributed by Alternatives in Religious Education, Inc., Denver, Colorado.

Chapter

7

**Mediated Materials**

*Torah Toons* I and II. Los Angeles: Torah Aura Productions, 4423 Fruitland Ave., Los Angeles, CA 90058, 1982, 1983. (slide-tape presentations, 5-7 min. each)

# Chapter 8

 **TITLE:** The Melton Bar/Bat Mitzvah Program

 **CONTRIBUTED BY:** Carol K. Ingall

 **TOPIC:** Integrating B'nai Mitzvah students into the community

 **TARGET AUDIENCE:** Families with children in Grades 6 or 7

 **TIME FRAME:** 1 to 2 school years; 2 hour weekly sessions; 1 hour of weekly consultation time; workshops of 2-3 hours; field trips of 3-4 hours

 **STAFF:** Coordinator, librarian, Rabbi, art specialist, song leader, Cantor

**Overview**   The Bar/Bat Mitzvah Program described here was originally developed at Temple Emanu-El, Providence, Rhode Island. It is published and distributed by the Melton Research Center of The Jewish Theological Seminary of America. The packet consists of 33 color coded cards which fall into four general categories: cognitive learning, rituals and life cycle, the synagogue, and the Jewish people. The program is designed to begin in the sixth grade and takes anywhere from 14 months to two years to complete. The structure of the program provides for ongoing interaction between parents and student.

**Purpose**   The program emphasizes the behavioral aspects of being a Jewish adult and prepares the student to enter the Jewish community with a level of commitment to it.

Chapter

**8**

**Preparation/Procedure**   Since this is a voluntary program, it is essential to plan a preliminary meeting for students and parents. Parents should also be invited to a separate meeting without children present. There they are oriented to the program, their role is explained, and they are made aware of the resources and opportunities available to them as they go through the program.

The program coordinator should be a person who is sensitive to the needs of the group and can motivate the students. It is the coordinator's responsibility to assist students on an individual basis when necessary and to maintain group cohesiveness.

A tentative calendar should be prepared in advance, as well as the reward for completing the program or parts of the program.

**Program Description**
1. Project cards — There are 33 color-coded project cards divided into four categories:

> White — Cognitive material (see XXVII. below)
>
> Blue — Rituals and Life Cycle (see V.)
>
> Yellow — The Synagogue (see III.)
>
> Pink — The Jewish People (see XXIV.)

There is also a record book in which to record completed projects. When a student completes a project it is turned in to the facilitator, who reads it and records it in the student's record book if it is acceptable.

Examples of the project cards follow:

---

### XXVIII. TALMUD

A. Name the six books of the *Mishnah* and tell briefly the contents of each book. Who were the Tanaim?
B. What is the Gemara? Who were the Amoraim?
C. What is *Midrash*?
D. What is *Halachah*?
E. What is *Aggadah*?
F. Look carefully at a page of the Babylonian Talmud. The page is subdivided through the use of separate columns and different print. What do these subdivisions stand for?

---

### V. HOME RITUALS

Participate as reader in the following home ceremonies:

A. *HaMotzi*
B. *Kiddush*
C. *Birkat HaMazon*
D. Portions of the Passover *Seder*
E. Blessing Shabbat/*Yom Tov* candles
F. *Havdalah*
G. Lighting Chanukah candles

---

### III. SHABBAT MORNING SERVICES

Attend Shabbat morning services with your family. Try to follow the prayers carefully. What are the main divisions of the service? Which prayer of that service was most meaningful to you? Quote the part that was most important to you. Discuss with your parents. Write up your discussion.

---

### XXIV. LATE MEDIEVAL PERSONALITIES

Identify the following great personalities who lived during the later Middle Ages:

A. Joseph Caro (Karo)
B. Gluckel of Hameln
C. Sabbatai Zevi
D. Israel ben Eliezer, the Ba'al Shem Tov
E. Elijah ben Solomon, the Vilna Gaon

---

Chapter

# 8

The cards may be completed in sequence. However, given the time limitation, some cards may be set aside as special projects, and some may be combined into one project. The coordinator should use discretion and assign the projects according to the needs of the students and their families.

2. Discussion – The program as presented encourages Shabbat discussion groups which provide students with opportunities

to complete the projects. The discussions may be focused each time on one particular project, or the coordinator has the option of having students plan presentations. The Teacher's Guide contains several suggestions on how to do this.

3. Library Time – Set aside at least one hour a week for library work. Set up a special reserve shelf or corner with the specific books necessary for the research. A list of resource material is contained in the Teacher's Guide.

4. Workshops – Many of the projects lend themselves to workshops which can be held Sunday afternoons, evenings, and during school vacations. Among those suggested are holiday cooking projects, *tallit* making, calligraphy, and stained glass.

5. Field Trips – Field trips to Jewish communal agencies, local synagogues, kosher butchers, Jewish bookstores, and a Jewish funeral home help to broaden the participant's knowledge of the community and give credence to some of the projects. Parents are expected to go on the trips with their children.

6. Rewards – Give some recognition for completion of the program. Certificates are significant. At Temple Emanu-El, graduates are given a specially commissioned silk-screened poster. A special Shabbat should be set aside to honor the graduates.

**Editor's Comments**   Enlisting the aid of Jewish community leaders, Rabbis, scholars, and artists will greatly enhance this program. In congregations or areas where there are a limited number of students, be sure to make provision for students to enter the program at different times. The project cards allow for great flexibility. The coordinator may select them for each individual student. He/she may also decide which cards will be earmarked for classroom discussions, workshops, and field trips. In some instances it may be necessary to make revisions on the cards to suit individual needs. For instance, there is one card designating a trip to Jewish New York. Since this is not feasible for many congregations, it can be revised as a local tour.

**Bibliography/Resources**
Appelman, Harlene Winnick. *CAJE Network Newsletter for Family Educators*, February 1987.

Chapter

8

Becker, Joyce. *Jewish Holiday Crafts*. New York: Bonim Books, 1978.

Beiner, Stan J. *Sedra Scenes: Skits for Every Torah Portion*. Denver: Alternatives in Religious Education, Inc., 1982.

Brown, Steven G. *Higher and Higher: Making Jewish Prayer Part Of Us*. New York: United Synagogue of America, Department of Youth Activities, 1979.

Goodman, Hannah Grad. *The Story Of Prophecy*. New York: Behrman House, 1965.

Grishaver, Joel Lurie. *The Life Cycle Workbook*. Denver: Alternatives in Religious Education, Inc., 1979.

Hertz, J.H. *The Pentateuch and Haftarahs*. London: Soncino Press, 1972.

Ingall, Carol K. *Bar/Bat Mitzvah Program*. New York: Melton Research Center, 1984.

Klein, Isaac. *A Guide To Jewish Religious Practice*. New York: The Jewish Theological Seminary of America, 1979.

Lewit, Jane, and Epstein, Ellen Robinson. *The Bar/Bat Mitzvah Planbook*. New York: Stein and Day, 1982.

Loeb, Sorel Goldberg, and Kadden, Barbara Binder. *Teaching Torah: A Treasury Of Insights and Activities*. Denver: Alternatives in Religious Education, Inc., 1984.

Marcus, Audrey Friedman, et al. *Bar and Bat Mitzvah: A Family Education Unit*. Denver: Alternatives in Religious Education, Inc., 1977.

Moskowitz, Nachama Skolnik. *The Jewish Life Cycle Game*. Denver: Alternatives in Religious Education, Inc., 1984.

Plaut, W. Gunther; Bamberger, Bernard J., and Hallo, William W. *The Torah: A Modern Commentary*. New York: Union of American Hebrew Congregations, 1981.

Chapter

8

Reisman, Bernard. *The Jewish Experiential Book: The Quest for Jewish Identity*. New York: KTAV, 1979.

Strassfeld, Sharon, and Strassfeld, Michael, eds. *The Second Jewish Catalog*. Philadelphia: Jewish Publication Society, 1976.

Trepp, Leo. *The Complete Book Of Jewish Observance*. New York: Behrman House/Summit Books, 1980.

Ungerleider-Mayerson, Joy. *Jewish Folk Art: From Biblical Days To Modern Times*. New York: Summit Books, 1980.

*Value Prompters*. Denver: Alternatives in Religious Education, Inc., 1973.

Zwerin, Raymond A., and Marcus, Audrey Friedman. *Shabbat Can Be*. New York: Union of American Hebrew Congregations, 1979.

Chapter

8

**Mediated Materials**
*Bar Mitzvah*. Yeshiva University, Audio Visual Center, 500 West 185th St., New York, NY 10033. (film, 15 min.)

*Secret Space*. Roberta Hodes, 420 E. 23rd St., New York, NY 10010. (film, 78 min.)

*Thirteen Years*. Bernard Timberg, 52 President St., Brooklyn, NY 11231. (film, 11 min.)

**Information on Twinning**
National Conference on Soviet Jewry
10 East 40th Street
New York, NY 10016

Your local committee for Soviet Jewry

# Chapter 9

 **TITLE:** Bar/Bat Mitzvah Family Education

 **CONTRIBUTED BY:** Maralee Gordon

 **DESIGNED BY:** Maralee Gordon and Sharon Morton

 **TOPIC:** Family preparation for Bar/Bat Mitzvah service

 **TARGET AUDIENCE:** B'nai Mitzvah students and parents

 **TIME FRAME:** Four 75 minute classes and one Shabbat dinner and worship service

 **STAFF:** B'nai Mitzvah coordinator, Rabbi, Director of Education, Cantor, special guests

**Overview**   This is a five session Bar/Bat Mitzvah program developed at Congregation Am Shalom in Glencoe, Illinois. It involves the congregation's professional staff, community representatives, as well as some families in the congregation whose children have already become Bar or Bat Mitzvah. It is offered twice a year and is mandatory for all families and students who become B'nai Mitzvah at Am Shalom. The program consists of four 75 minute class sessions and a family Shabbat dinner and service. Families attend sessions the semester before the Bar/Bat Mitzvah. This gives them enough time to incorporate ideas they glean from the classes, to establish correspondence with a Soviet twin, to study further, and to compile readings for their service should they so desire. Classes are held early in the semester before the Bar/Bat Mitzvah. As part of the program, parents receive a booklet guiding them through the process of Bar or Bat Mitzvah.

Chapter

9

**Purpose**   The goals of the program are to increase the meaning of Bar/Bat Mitzvah for the whole family; to increase family communication regarding expectations of each other; for the Bar/Bat Mitzvah to clarify his/her expectations of the event itself; to broaden family knowledge in specific areas relating to Bar/Bat Mitzvah: the service, the Torah, the Jewish calendar, *mitzvot*, and *tzedakah*.

**Preparation**   Letters are sent to families in the Bar/Bat Mitzvah class. The letters contain information about the Bar/Bat Mitzvah class in general and the dates of the family sessions in particular. A second letter is sent home six weeks prior to the first family session reminding them of the program and reinforcing the student's presence, even if the parents cannot attend.

The staff meets together to review the curriculum and prepare the materials. At Am Shalom the Bar/Bar Mitzvah coordinator and the Director of Education serve as facilitators. The congregtional Rabbi, Cantor, volunteers from the Soviet Jewry Twinning Program, and congregational members are all invited to specific sessions to share their expertise.

It is essential to coordinate the curriculum of the religious school and Hebrew school with the Bar/Bat Mitzvah program. This assures that a child entering the Bar/Bat Mitzvah year will already have a familiarity with the service, the Torah, the prayers and blessings, and with the concept of Bar/Bat Mitzvah as a communal experience with historical significance.

**Program Description**    A Suggested schedule for the program follows:

**Suggested Schedule**
Week One
  1. Introductions
  2. *Tzedakah*
  3. What is Torah?
  4. "Nitty-Gritty" Of Bar/Bat Mitzvah
  5. Family Classwork: Thoughts on Bar/Bat Mitzvah
  6. Homework: Responsibilities/privileges (see below for hand-out sheet)

Chapter

9

Week Two
  1. Sharing of homework
  2. *Haftarah* Readings
  3. *Mitzvot* — What Are They?
     "B'mitzvotav Project." (Students are asked to fulfill 20 *mitzvot*.)
  4. What Is Prayer?
  5. Classwork: Prayer writing
  6. Homework: Bar/Bat Mitzvah Interviews (see below for handout sheet); pass out readings for *The Prophet Game* in Week Four.
  7. Shabbat Dinner
     a. Potluck Shabbat Dinner for Bar/Bat Mitzvah families
     b. Shabbat Service with student participation and prayers written by parents and students

Week Three
  1. The Am Shalom Bar/Bat Mitzvah – the Rabbi
  2. Discussion on results of Bar/Bat Mitzvah Interviews
  3. Haftarah Readings

  4. Let's Talk About the Prophets
  5. Homework: Write an introduction to your *Haftarah* reading.

Week Four
  1. Bible Search
  2. Prophet Sharing (see *The Prophet Game* below)
  3. Preparation for writing a personalized service
  4. *Haftarah* Readings
  5. Twinning
  6. Class Evaluation

As an example of the materials used in this course, the homework assignments for Weeks One and Two and the handout for *The Prophet Game* from Week Four follow:

Chapter

9

RESPONSIBILITIES & PRIVILEGES
Homework Week One

The age of thirteen is the time when a person becomes a full member of the Jewish community. This means both privileges and responsibilities are received and accepted by the Bar or Bat Mitzvah (Bar and Bat Mitzvah are actually terms for the *individual* reaching the age of thirteen). The responsibilities of being a full member of the Jewish community include that of *participation* and that of *observance* of the *mitzvot*. Privileges include being allowed to receive the honor of an *aliyah* (called to the Torah), the privilege to study at a higher level, the privilege of full *participation* in ritual events, in decision making processes, and in opportunities to help others.

At all stages of our lives we have various responsibilities and privileges. These change over time as we mature. Discuss as a family and list below the responsibilities and privileges that come with each stage of life:

| Age/Stage | Responsibilities | Privileges |
|---|---|---|
| 0-5 | | |
| | | |
| | | |
| | | |

6-12

_____    _____
_____    _____
_____    _____
_____    _____
_____    _____

13-18

_____    _____
_____    _____
_____    _____
_____    _____
_____    _____

young adulthood

_____    _____
_____    _____

Chapter

# 9

_____    _____
_____    _____

parenthood

_____    _____
_____    _____
_____    _____
_____    _____
_____    _____

As a family discuss what would be an appropriate new responsibility and an appropriate new privilege for a thirteen-year-old.

## BAR/BAT MITZVAH INTERVIEWS
### Homework Week Two

As a family find three persons to interview who have experienced the celebration of Bar or Bat Mitzvah. You may interview either the individual or, if it is possible, the individual with his/her family. One of these individuals may be someone who has experienced an Am Shalom Bar or Bat Mitzvah, but this cannot be a brother or sister of the current Bar or Bat Mitzvah candidate. You may interview parents or grandparents, friends at other congregations, either in this geographical area or not.

1. How was the family involved in the preparation for or service of Bar/Bat Mitzvah?

   _____

   _____

2. How did the party reflect the religious significance of the occasion?

   _____

   _____

3. What did the Bar/Bat Mitzvah student do during the service? (What was his/her part?)

   _____

   _____

4. Describe your (the Bar/Bat Mitzvah student's) feelings before, during, and after the service.

   _____

   _____

5. What was the most exciting part of your Bar/Bat Mitzvah?

   _____

   _____

6. What happened at your Bar/Bat Mitzvah to make the world a better place (the giving of *tzedakah*, twinning with a Soviet youngster, volunteer work, etc.)?

   _____

   _____

(Use additional sheets of paper if there is not enough space for you to record your answers.)

### THE PROPHET GAME
Week Four

Gathered in this room are experts on 10 different prophets or leaders found in the second section of the Bible, *Nevi'im* (Prophets). Each expert is wearing a badge with the name of the prophet or leader on which he/she is well versed. To answer the questions below, locate an expert for each prophet and ask your question. Then write down the answer you receive in the space provided. Happy hunting!

1. What was the national crisis and test of faith that inspired the prophecies and writings of *Joel*?

2. Describe *Jeremiah's* foreign policy.

3. *Hosea's* description of the relationship between God and Israel was based on what situation from his own life?

4. On what issue(s) did the prophet *Nathan* advise King David in the Book of *Samuel*?

5. *Amos* was a prophet by calling, but what was his vocation? What was his concept of the Chosenness of the Israelites?

6. How did *Saul* become first king of Israel? How did he abuse his kingship?

7. What were the *Judges*? What was the nature of *Samson's* leadership?

Chapter

9

8. What were two important characteristics of *Joshua's* leadership?

9. Where did *Ezekiel* prophesy and to whom? In what way was he unique among the prophets?

10. Chapters 40 to 55 of the Book of *Isaiah* is called Second Isaiah (Deutero-Isaiah). Why?
The prophecies of Deutero-Isaiah are uttered from what geographical locale?
What was Deutero-Isaiah's main message to the exiled Israelites?

**Editor's Comments**   In this program, as in the other B'nai Mitzvah programs described in this book, the Bar/Bat Mitzvah ceremony is regarded as a culmination of a particular period of study. We know that many students drop out of religious school after this event, so it is essential to develop a mechanism for families to continue Jewish study together. One session, or part of one session, should be devoted to future directions and ongoing meaningful family study. Using the knowledge gained through the Bar/Bat Mitzvah experience, families should be encouraged to continue to come to weekly or monthly sessions during which they can study specific Jewish texts. Eventually, the participants can become group leaders for others who come into the program.

**Bibliography/Resources**   See the bibliography for Chapter 8, "The Melton Bar/Bat Mitzvah Program."

Chapter

9

# Chapter 10

 **TITLE:** Bar/Bat Mitzvah Parent Workshops and Support Groups

 **CONTRIBUTED BY:** Robin Eisenberg

 **TOPIC:** Making a Bar/Bat Mitzvah meaningful for families; creating community

 **TARGET AUDIENCE:** Parents of potential B'nai Mitzvah

 **TIME FRAME:** Workshops – four 1 hour programs; Support Groups – two 1½ or four 1 hour programs

 **STAFF:** Rabbi, Cantor, Director of Education

**Overview**   The "Bar/Bat Mitzvah Workshops and Parent Support Groups" at Temple Beth El in Boca Raton, Florida, involve families whose children will become Bar or Bat Mitzvah within the next six to twelve months. They are offered twice a year — in the spring and in the fall.

At an introductory session, parents and students hear about the logistics of the Bar/Bat Mitzvah ceremony, administrative details, and the order of the service. This session is followed by a series of family Workshops, each held on a Sunday morning during religious school hours. Resources compiled from the Workshops are made available in a resource center for use by families. These range from explanations of the worship service to sample invitations to creative services and personal prayers. In addition, there are four monthly meetings attended by both parents and students which focus on the service. The cycle of programs is arranged so that all Workshops and classes are completed three months prior to Bar or Bat Mitzvah.

Chapter

# 10

**Purpose**   The purpose of this program is to provide a support network for families whose children will become B'nai Mitzvah in the coming year. It is designed to help them create community and to integrate into the larger Jewish community. It is also designed to provide a variety of resources for the participating families which pertains to Bar/Bat Mitzvah.

**Preparation/Procedure**   In preparing this program it is necessary to develop a schedule which coincides with the religious school calendar and the Bar/Bat Mitzvah schedule for the coming year. Once this is done, the schedule should be sent to participating families along with a letter explaining the program. This can be done over a period of time, allowing each group of participating families to contribute something to the resource center. As a start include a synopsis of each Torah portion with a list of bibliographic references, a variety of prayer books and creative services and resources which include Jewish poetry, stories, and quotations. If at all possible, set aside a library shelf with the appropriate books and articles.

**Program Description**   The program consists of Sunday morning family Workshops which meet for a period of 6 months, as well as small classes (called Support Groups) which meet once a month. The Workshops begin 12 to 18 months prior to the Bar/Bat Mitzvah ceremony, while the Support Groups meet 6 to 12 months prior.

**Sample Schedules**   A sample schedule for both the Workshops and the Support Groups follows:

Sunday Morning Family Workshops
Session I: Introductory Session On Overview and Administration
    A. Introductions

Chapter

# 10

    B. Ice Breaker
        1. Sharing memories and special feelings about parent's own Bar or Bat Mitzvah preparation and service
        2. Discussion of what parents are looking forward to most about their child's Bar or Bat Mitzvah celebration

    C. Logistics and administrative details
        1. Fees and use of the building
        2. Student's training, prerequisites
        3. Times for ceremony
        4. Invitations
        5. *Tzedakah* projects

    D. The service itself
        1. Twinning
        2. Torah/*Haftarah* portions
        3. *Aliyot*
        4. Family participation
        5. *Tallit/tefillin*

    E. Culminating Activity
        1. In the sanctuary the *Sefer Torah* is passed from one family to the other.

Session II: Making Your Child's Bar/Bat Mitzvah Special Through
  A. Family Projects
    1. The value of family projects
    2. Creative approaches to the Bar/Bat Mitzvah
      ceremony

Session III. Making Your Child's Bar/Bat Mitzvah Special
Through Participation
  A. Friday night — candles/*Kiddush*

  B. Saturday
    1. Parents' prayer
    2. Involvement of siblings and other family members

  C. Who, what, where, when, and how of the worship
    service

**Chapter**

**10**

Session IV: Making Your Child's Bar/Bat Mitzvah Special —
Helping Your Child Learn and Feel Good About Studying
  A. How to guide writing of speeches
    1. How to help with Hebrew even if you can't read it

  B. How effectively to monitor your child's progress

Session V: Making Your Child's Bar/Bat Mitzvah Special – A
Religious, Historical Experience, and a Celebration Of Coming
Of Age
  A. The history of Bar/Bat Mitzvah and its significance in
    Jewish life

  B. Brainstorm creative ways to celebrate.


Monthly Support Groups for Students and Parents Together
Session I: Review the order of the service, *tallit*, and *aliyot*.

Session II: Review Bar/Bat Mitzvah Torah portion, its meaning,
where it fits into the cycle of readings, why B'nai Mitzvah read
from the Torah.

Session III: Review *Haftarah*, how it ties in with the Torah pro-
tion, the purpose of the *Haftarah*, the source of the *Haftarah*.

Session IV: Service rehearsal – choreography of the service, assignment of *aliyot* and other honors, review of the blessings for the *aliyot*, special prayers and blessings

**Editor's Comments**   Since this program is designed to create a community within a community, a means should be developed to have participating families assist each other with Bar/Bat Mitzvah preparations. It is wise to encourage mutual invitations to all the B'nai Mitzvah ceremonies. Other ways to assist are by hosting Shabbat dinners, *Ongei Shabbat*, or a *Kiddush* on the Bar/Bat Mitzvah weekend.

The area of family projects should be expanded to reach out to the community at large. Families can opt to make or buy a gift for the synagogue, such as a *tallit* or Torah stand, prayer books, *chumashim*, etc. They can also engage in a specific *tzedakah* or social action project outside the synagogue community, such as a food or clothing collection for a local shelter, or raising money for a specific organization, such as the American Association for Ethiopian Jews. Each family should also decide what it will contribute to the resource center, such as a personal prayer, a personal interpretation of the Torah portion, invitations, pictures, etc.

Chapter

10

**Bibliography/Resources**   See the bibliography for Chapter 8, "The Melton Bar/Bat Mitzvah Program."

# Chapter 11

 **TITLE:** The Mitzvah Of Bar/Bat Mitzvah

 **CONTRIBUTED BY:** Rabbi David Lieb

 **TOPIC:** *Mitzvot* in relation to Bar/Bat Mitzvah

 **TARGET AUDIENCE:** Families with children of Bar/Bat Mitzvah age

 **TIME FRAME:** Four 2 hour sessions which take place 6-8 months prior to the Bar/Bat Mitzvah

 **STAFF:** Rabbi or B'nai Mitzvah Coordinator

**Overview**   These classes are held at Temple Beth El in San Pedro,.California, for all families who have children becoming B'nai Mitzvah. Children and parents attend the classes together. The classes, as well as individual sessions with the Rabbi and Cantor, are an integral part of each student's Bar/Bat Mitzvah preparation. The emphasis of the program is on the term "commandment" and the issue of Jews and divine authority. Integrated into the sessions are three examples of commandment — *tefillin*, *tzedakah*, and *tzitzit*.

**Purpose**   The purpose of this program is to emphasize the *"mitzvah"* aspect of the Bar and Bat Mitzvah. Through an understanding of the traditions of *tefillin*, *tzedakah*, and *tzitzit*, participants become connected with Jewish history and with the Jewish community.

Chapter

**11**

**Preparation/Procedure**   The "Family B'nai Mitzvah Class" is scheduled for families which have children who will become Bar or Bat Mitzvah within 6 to 8 months of the beginning of the program. The classes are offered two or three times a year, depending on the number of children in this age group.

A letter is sent to parents about eight months prior to the Bar/Bat Mitzvah ceremony reconfirming the date of the ceremony and inviting the parents to an orientation session. At that session students are given their Torah and *Haftarah* assignments. They read from the prayer book for the Rabbi and Cantor in order to ascertain whether additional sessions or tutoring are necessary.

Parents are given the schedule for the family classes and a timetable so that they may help their children with preparation. At Temple Beth El, the Cantor begins to work with a student about 4 to 6 months in advance, and the Rabbi works directly with each student about 2-3 months in advance.

**Program Description**   A sample schedule of the program follows:

## Schedule
Session I
- A . General introduction
- B. Purposes and expectations
- C. Administrivia
- D. Lesson
    1. The history and meaning of becoming Bar/Bat Mitzvah
    2. Commandment in Reform Judaism
    3. Assignment: Torah portion summaries

Session II
- A. Lesson
    1. The Torah and *Haftarah*
    2. Looking at *Sifrei Torah* (Assignment: The *Haftarah* Connection)
    3. Writing a speech (Assignment: Main idea of speech, speech outline)
    4. *Tefillin*: A sample commandment

Chapter

# 11

Session III
- A. Lesson
    1. The Jewish worship service (Assignment: Parents' Prayer)
    2. The music of the service
    3. *Tzedakah*: Another sample commandment (Assignment: A family *tzedakah* project)

Session IV
- A. Lesson
    1. *Tzitzit*: A third sample commandment
    2. Tying *tzitzit*
    3. Why 13 — *Midrash* and the psychology of adolescence
    4. Review and evaluation

**Editor's Comments**   The program described here covers a wide range of Jewish content, including history, Jewish religious practice, the liturgy, and Torah study. Its main focus is on *mitzvot* and the Bar/Bat Mitzvah ceremony itself. An enhancement to the program as it presently exists would be to make *tallitot*, *kipot,* or prayer book covers for the Bar or Bat Mitzvah worship service. Instructions for these projects may be found in Chapter 33, "Bar/Bat Mitzvah Family Retreat."

The families involved in this program should be urged to continue actively to pursue *mitzvot* and *tzedakah.* Recruit them to become a part of a "Mitzvah Corps" for the congregation. Provide opportunities for them to visit the sick, assist families in transition or crisis, staff a help line for victims of physical abuse or addictive behavior. They can also form a "Simcha Corps," assisting families before a *Brit Milah,* Bar/Bat Mitzvah, or a wedding, etc.

Chapter

11

The program can be expanded by adding more intense study sessions over the course of the year. These additions can be structured as three mini-courses, each with a separate emphasis. Each mini-course would consist of 3 or 4 two hour sessions. One mini-course might focus on the prophetic literature. Families study selected readings from the Prophets and discuss the readings in relation to their Torah portions. Another mini-course might focus on the music of the service and a study of trope. Both parents and students would learn the appropriate Torah and *Haftarah* trope, as well as the melodies sung at the worship service. The third mini-course might be the "Family B'nai Mitzvah" class as it is described above.

**Bibliography/Resources**   See the bibliography for Chapter 8, "The Melton Bar/Bat Mitzvah Program."

# Chapter 12

 **TITLE:** Jewish Family Month

 **CONTRIBUTED BY:** Susan Rachlin

 **TOPIC:** Providing a wide variety of Jewish cultural, social, and educational activities for Jewish families throughout the community

 **TARGET AUDIENCE:** Everyone in the community

 **TIME FRAME:** One month; 6-9 months initial preparation.

 **STAFF:** Coordinator, administrative assistant, facilitators for the various programs

**Overview**   "Jewish Family Month" is a community-wide program that was developed by Susan Rachlin of the Board of Jewish Education of Greater New York. It is an intensive program with a variety of educational, social, and cultural activities designed to appeal to those with differing affiliation levels in the Jewish community, and to the Jewish family in particular. Many individuals are needed to assist with planning, coordination, and implementation of the program. It requires the support of a central agency to help ensure its success.

**Purpose**   The main purpose of the program is to raise Jewish family consciousness. The areas of commonality that evolve among the participants can lead to an improvement in family communication. Other purposes are to coordinate existing programs within the community to appeal to the Jewish family, to help agencies and services to network among themselves to provide integrated services to the Jewish family, and to assist the Jewish family in making further commitments to Jewish education and community involvement.

Chapter

# 12

**Preparation/Procedure**   This program is geared to a community which has social service agencies, synagogues, and a Federation. Form a committee to work together to formulate and execute the program. It should consist of lay and professional people who are responsible for specific tasks and functions. It is also necessary to set a time frame for the program.

**Program Description**   The following represents an outline of mass community events, organizational events, and small group activities which can take place during Jewish Family Month.

### Mass Community Events

1. Concerts featuring choir groups, Jewish soloists, composers, instrumentalists, and Cantors.

2. Cultural happenings – a "fair like" atmosphere with crafts, book sales, records, Judaic art objects, all displayed in rented booths.

3. Tzedakah fair featuring booths or displays about Jewish organizations and agencies and their work. Included in this event could be workshops led by local educators teaching about *tzedakah*.

4. Children's conference, geared to children ages 11-15, who will have an opportunity to explore issues particular to them and their personal Jewish experience.

5. Film festival featuring movies based on Jewish themes and/or films from Israel.

### Organizational Events

1. Local organizations are encouraged to sponsor events on an ongoing basis, such as: Family *Shabbatot*, *Havdalah* services, Mini-retreats, Scholar-in-residence.

### Small Group Activities

These activities are geared to individuals in specific age groups and should be scheduled several times a week during a month-long period. Examples include:

Chapter

# 12

1. Youth group discussing the Jewish view of illness, death, and dying.

2. Senior adults discussing "Who is a Jew?"

3. Newly married couples talking about Jewish identity and self-awareness.

4. Parents of preschool children involved in a discussion about effective Jewish parenting.

5. Individual families who join together to discuss life cycle events or holiday related activities.

**Editor's Comments**  The program described here took place over the course of one month in a community with a large Jewish population. It can be replicated on a smaller scale for one week or even for a weekend and should be considered as a yearly event.

This program requires an extensive public relations campaign jointly created and carried out by the sponsoring agencies and cooperating organizations. A program guidebook which describes all of the activities for the month can be distributed to the community through the mail, by local merchants, and at the various agency offices. Each sponsoring organization can be responsible for one program. Such programs might include worship services for families, speakers after services or during the week to talk on issues of personal relationships, films, book reviews, live theater, or an art exhibit. Additional suggestions for publicizing the events include a poster project or contest and/or a paid advertising campaign.

A smaller community might adapt the program by including a Jewish home tour and inviting non-Jews to participate. The homes selected can focus on different Jewish events in the life of a Jew — e.g., birth and naming, Bar/Bat Mitzvah, Shabbat, or the holidays. At each home, be sure to have an interactive program so that guests can participate as families in a naming, make a *mizrach* or *Seder* plate, look up significant dates in their lives according to the Jewish calendar, trace their family history and write a letter back home as if they were still in the country of their family's origin. Supply each visitor with a "Passport," and have families collect a stamp representing each stop on the tour. Another way to end the program is to give each family a piece of fabric with which to design a patch for a wall hanging which reflects their personal connection with their tradition.

The format for a weekend may include the following: Shabbat dinner (or several Shabbat dinners) for intergenerational groupings of families; activities at the *Oneg Shabbat*, such as music, storytelling, and discussion groups. On Shabbat morning families gather for *minyanim*. Those with young children attend a service where Torah study is less formal. Families with older children attend services for which other families have prepared the Torah study. Some family members can lead the service and others can read from the Torah. A luncheon can follow services. Afternoon activities can include family communication sessions, book reviews, and lectures on art, as well as more storytelling and discussions. Later, text study can be followed by *Havdalah*.

*Motza'ay Shabbat* and Sunday activities may revolve around an organizational fair, during which each participating Jewish

Chapter

12

organization plans a family activity and publicizes its organization; films; theater, both spectator and participatory; and dance.
The Jewish Family Home Tour can take place on Sunday at the
same time as the other activities. Conclude the weekend with a
box supper and family concert.

Chapter
# 12

# Chapter 13

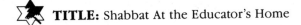 **TITLE:** Shabbat At the Educator's Home

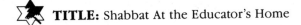 **CONTRIBUTED BY:** Sherry Bissell Blumberg

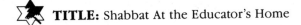 **DESIGNED BY:** Sherry and David Blumberg

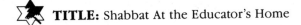 **TOPIC:** Shabbat in the home

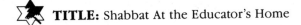 **TARGET AUDIENCE:** Congregational families who want to begin to integrate Shabbat into their lives

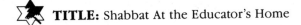 **TIME FRAME:** Ongoing throughout the year; requires two years for optimal success

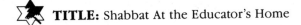 **STAFF:** Coordinator

**Overview**   Many Jews have been raised in an environment in which Shabbat has minimal significance or meaning. Weekends are often regarded as a time to relax and unwind. The concept of Shabbat as a time apart from ordinary activities, even those of the weekend, needs to be developed before Shabbat can become a part of one's life. The program cited here is designed to encourage *Erev Shabbat* home celebrations in a manner that is comfortable with the life styles of the families involved. The program allows participants to be a part of a network of people who support each other in this effort. It is expected that the first group of families will recreate the Shabbat celebration in their homes for others. A period of one or two years is necessary for the program to reach its optimum goals.

Chapter

# 13

**Purpose**   The goal of this program is to encourage home celebrations of Shabbat on a regular basis.

**Preparation/Procedure**   Send out publicity announcing the Shabbat home celebrations program. Enable participants to specify whether they would like to be hosts or guests. With this model the initial numbers may be limited, because it involves ongoing outreach to the community at large. The model by Nachama Moskowitz, which is discussed in the Editor's Comments, provides for a *shadchan* (matchmaking) service.

It is suggested that dinners be limited to three or four families per household. Providing hosts and guests with a book such as *The Art Of Jewish Living: The Shabbat Seder* by Ron Wolfson, or *A Shabbat Manual*, published by the Central Conference of American Rabbis, will enable them to perform the required *mitzvot* and recite the appropriate blessings. Give hosts a list of places where they can purchase kosher food.

**Program Description**   The synagogue professionals or agency professionals host the first set of Shabbat dinners in their own homes. One week later the families which participate in the first set of dinners meet to discuss and process their experiences. Be sensitive to families for whom this was a new experience. Help all families focus on their feelings and on how they can best transmit their positive experiences to others. This first processing session should include the following content:

1. A discussion about the Shabbat experience.

2. Study about Shabbat using such texts as *The Sabbath* by Abraham Joshua Heschel, Exodus 20:8-11, Deuteronomy 5:12-15.

3. Future directions of program (ongoing Shabbat dinners; extended time programs, including Shabbat afternoon *Kiddush*, *Seudah Shleesheet*, and *Havdalah*; dinners with study sessions at the table [see Chapter 2, "Study the Weekly Sedra At Home"], etc.). Before the session is over, each participating family is given the names of three or four families to invite to Shabbat dinner.

Chapter

# 13

Prior to the next set of dinners, it is important to have a workshop which assists the hosts in learning the skills necessary for implementing the Shabbat table service. Practice reciting or singing the *Kiddush* and various other blessings. Help the hosts learn how to teach the blessings to others. Allow time for people to share what they will be doing in their homes and to exchange ideas.

**Editor's Comments** Nachama Skolnik Moskowitz has adapted this program at Temple Israel in Tulsa, Oklahoma as a once a year event. The focus of the evening is to have Shabbat dinners in various people's homes and to encourage them to come to services afterward. Ms. Moskowitz provides the hosts with a Shabbat bag which includes a blessing card, two Shabbat candles, matches, and information from the *Shabbat Catalog* by Ruth Brin. She also provides suggestions for involving all the families in preparation of the Shabbat dinner. At the dinners, in addition to lighting candles, reciting *Kiddush*, and blessing *challah*, families are encouraged to share their experiences of the week, or to plan activities for discussion. Time is set aside for singing familiar songs, *niggunim* or *zemirot*, and concluding with *Birkat HaMazon*.

These programs were facilitated through synagogues. They may also be implemented through Community Centers, Family Service agencies, or other Jewish organizations. No matter who sponsors them, it is essential that the professional staff take an active role by hosting some of the dinners or acting as facilitators for any follow-up sessions.

It is possible to arrange to have all the Shabbat dinners hosted on a specific Shabbat during the month. As the program mushrooms, these may occur more frequently. Homes should be large enough to seat 3 or 4 families comfortably and to provide them with a warm Shabbat atmosphere.

Chapter

13

Another way to implement the program is to break into small groups of three or four families and host Shabbat dinners once a month, rotating from home to home. The groups change every three to four months. A preliminary workshop should precede the first set of family dinners. An intergenerational mix may be achieved through arbitrary assignment of families. Or, families with children of similar ages might prefer to be together. However the assignments are made, it is important to be sensitive to the needs and desires of congregants.

**Bibliography/Resources**    See the bibliography for Chapter 7, "The Joy Of Shabbat."

# Chapter 14

 **TITLE:**  Pre-Consecration Parent/Student Program

 **CONTRIBUTED BY:**: Esphira "Happy" Iscove

 **TOPIC:**  *Kodesh* — Holiness

 **TARGET AUDIENCE:**  Families with children in Grades K-1

 **TIME FRAME:**  2½ hour preliminary workshop; Consecration Service

 **STAFF:**  Coordinator, Rabbi, art specialist, song leader, classroom teacher

**Overview**   It is the custom in many congregations to have a Consecration Service for students who are just beginning their formal Jewish education. At Holy Blossom Temple in Toronto, parents and students come together prior to the actual service in order to prepare for this significant event in their children's lives. The program is structured to allow parents to engage in meaningful study on their level with the Rabbis and to be involved in interactional activities with their children. The focus of this program is on *Kedushah* (holiness) as a Jewish concept/value.

In addition to being applicable for families who have children beginning their religious education in a supplementary educational setting, the program is also applicable for day schools.

Chapter

14

**Purpose**   The specific goal of this program is to enhance the Consecration Service for the participating families. Ultimately, it is a way of enlisting parents as partners in their children's Jewish education by providing them with an opportunity to "learn" and "do" together.

**Preparation/Procedure**   It is necessary to prepare the groundwork for this program prior to publicizing it to the intended constituency. Gather written materials for reproduction, collect "mystery" objects, and arrange for arts and crafts materials. Outline the schedule for the day and recruit the staff.

This program generally consists of a 2 to 2½ hour session which takes place during religious school hours. Staff should include classroom teachers as facilitators, Rabbi, or Director of Education to lead a parent discussion, and a song leader. Give everyone a schedule for the day and an outline of his/her specific responsibilities. It is a good idea to have a brief orientation meeting one or two weeks prior to the program.

Letters should be sent to all eligible families, followed by personal phone calls. It is essential that each child have at least one parent present for this program; however, it is necessary to provide for the child who comes without a parent on the day of the program by having a teacher's aide or another congregant available.

**Program Description**   The following is the schedule for the day:

**Schedule**
Opening Session (45 minutes)
> Children: Meet in classrooms for administrative details, then rehearse for Consecration Service.

> Parents: Gather briefly for coffee, to put on nametags, and then to meet with leader for introduction to study on *Kodesh*.

*Kodesh* Activity (25 minutes)
> Children join parents for study together in small groups led by teachers.

Crafts Project (25 minutes)
> Children and parents create an *Aron HaKodesh* for the little Torah scroll. Parents write a special blessing to be inserted in the Holy Ark.

Worship Service (25 minutes)
> Children and parents worship together and listen to a relevant story.

*Oneg Shabbat* (30 minutes)
> *Kiddush, HaMotzi*, singing; fill in evaluation sheet.

*L'hitraot*

A brief description of each segment of the program follows.

Chapter

# 14

**Parent Discussion**   This discussion should be facilitated by someone who is familiar with the congregation and the Consecration ceremony. The leader must also have the skills and knowledge to lead a meaningful discussion on the value of a Jewish education and specifically on the idea of *Kedushah*. Begin by defining *kodesh* as special, unique, set aside. Then focus on an explanation of the Consecration ceremony, that people make things *kadosh*, what the idea of *kadosh* means to us, and why we say blessings.

**Kodesh Activity** The *Kodesh* activity includes a box of objects which may be found in the home and are *kadosh*: *mezzuzah*, *tzedakah* box, *chanukiah*, Jewish book (symbolic of a Jewish home library), *tallit*.

The purpose of the activity is to learn as much as possible about each object, specifically what makes it *kadosh*; how it helps our homes and lives to become uniquely *kadosh*, specially Jewish. The box is passed around and each person, one at a time, removes an object without looking into the box. That object is placed in the center of the table and identified. Some examples of questions to ask are:

What emotional significance does the object have for you? Does it conjure up any special feelings or memories? If you close your eyes, what do you imagine about the object?

Chapter

14

The facilitator then distributes a *Kodesh* Handout, an example of which follows:


KODESH HANDOUT

The Hebrew word *kodesh* means holy. There are many words derived from the same Hebrew root. Some of them are:

| | |
|---|---|
| *Kadosh* | Holy |
| *Kedushah* | Holiness |
| *Kidshanu* | Who has made us holy |
| *(Aron Ha) Kodesh* | Holy Ark |
| *Kaddish* | Mourner's prayer |
| *Kiddushin* | Marriage ceremony |
| *Kedushah LaTorah* | Consecration Service |

The English word HOLY means: to be separate, set apart, special . . . for religious purposes.

*"Kodesh"* Objects In Our Home
There are many objects which help to identify a Jewish home.

1. Identify the objects in this box. What emotional significance does each have for you? What memories does each conjure up for you?

2. Discuss the importance of each. Think about:
   *What* is each object used for?
   *Who* uses the object?
   *When* is it used?
   *Where* is the object used? (Is there a biblical injunction associated with it? Is it a custom?)
   *How* do we use the object?

3. Then think about the significance of the object, and/or recite the blessing associated with the object. (Can you find the word *kodesh* or its derivative in the blessing?)

The Blessings

*Mezzuzah*
*Baruch Atah Adonai, Eloheynu Melech Ha-olam, Asher Kidshanu B'mitzvotav V'tzivanu Likboa Mezzuzah.*
Blessed are You, O Eternal our God, Ruler of the Universe, who has sanctified us by Your commandments and commanded us to affix a *mezzuzah*.

Chapter

**14**

*Tzedakah* (box)
"We are not rewarded *for* our good deeds. We are rewarded *by* our good deeds. We are not punished *for* our misdeeds. We are punished *by* our misdeeds. The reward of a kind deed is that we become kinder. The punishment for a cruel deed is that we become more cruel. WE BECOME WHAT WE DO. The act itself weaves its consequences into the very fabric of our character and our conscience. There is nothing more certain in all the world than the certainty that every thought and act has its effect upon us, for good or ill, whether it is known to others or not."
(Rabbi Simon Greenberg)

*Chanukiah*
*Baruch Atah Adonai Eloheynu Melech Ha-olam Asher Kidshanu B'mitzvotav V'tzivanu L'hadlik Ner Shel Chanukah.*
Blessed are You, O Eternal our God, Ruler of the Universe, who has sanctified us with Your commandments and commanded us to kindle the lights of Chanukah.

*Baruch Atah Adonai Eloheynu Melech Ha-olam, She-asa Nisim La-avoteynu, Bayamim Haheym, Bazman Hazeh.*
Blessed are You, O Eternal our God, Ruler of the Universe, who performed miracles for our ancestors in those days, at this time.

Jewish Books/Torah
*Baruch Atah Adonai Eloheynu Melech Ha-olam Asher Kid-shanu B'mitzvotav V'tzivanu La-asok B'divrey Torah.*
Blessed are You, O Eternal our God, Ruler of the Universe, who has sanctified us with Your commandments and commanded us to study words of Torah.

*Tallit*
*Baruch Atah Adonai Eloheynu Melech Ha-olam Asher Kid-shanu B'mitzvotav V'tzivanu L'hitatayf Ba-tzitzit.*
Blessed are You, O Eternal our God, Ruler of the Universe, who has sanctified us with Your commandments, and commanded us to wrap ourselves in *tzitzit*.

**Discussion Questions On Ritual Objects**   At this point the facilitator begins a factual discussion about each of the above ritual objects. This discussion focuses on the who-what-when-where-why-how, as demonstrated by the following questions:

*Mezzuzah*
What is a *mezzuzah*?
Why do Jews put up a *mezzuzah*?
How do we go about placing a *mezzuzah* in our home?
Where should a *mezzuzah* be placed?
For this discussion it is important to have a Hebrew Bible available so that someone can look up the appropriate passages in the book of Deuteronomy. You may also want to talk about making your own *mezzuzot* holders and having a *Chanukat Habayit* (home dedication ceremony).

*Tzedakah* (box)
What is *tzedakah*?
Who is obligated to perform *tzedakah*?
When do we give to charity/perform acts of righteousness?
Where do we give charity or perform righteous acts?
How do we perform *tzedakah*?
Have samples of various kinds of *tzedakah* boxes available to show your audience. When leading this part of the discussion, you may wish to define the word *tzedakah*. Have a copy of Maimonides' *Eight Degrees Of Charity* available, as well as a list of places in your community where you can perform righteous acts or donate money for *tzedakah*.

*Chanukiah*
What is a *Chanukiah*?
How is it different from a *menorah*?
Why do we have a *chanukiah* in our homes?
How does one go about lighting the candles on a *chanukiah*?
Who may light the candles?
What does one say when lighting the candles?

Jewish Books
Questions about books in general:
Can you imagine life without books?
What would the world be like if we did not have books?

Questions about Jewish books:
How did the invention of the printing press change the form of
Jewish books?
What are the greatest Jewish books?
What makes a book Jewish?
What books belong in a Jewish home? Why?
You may wish to provide a basic bibliography for a Jewish home
library. Arrange to have a general display of several appropriate
books. It is a good idea to be prepared to assist families in pur-
chasing books by providing order forms or the name, address,
and phone number of a local store which carries the books on
your list.

Chapter

14

*Tallit*
What is a *tallit*?
Who wears a *tallit*?
When is a *tallit* worn?
Why is a *tallit* worn?
How does one go about putting on a *tallit*?
Once again it is important to have a Hebrew Bible available so
that participants can read the versus in Numbers and Deu-
teronomy which enjoin one to wear a *tallit*. You may also wish
to have several *tallitot* available in order to teach the appropri-
ate blessing. Allow people to wrap themselves and experience
the feeling of being sheltered and protected by a *tallit*.

**Crafts Project**   Parents and children together make a Holy Ark
for the miniature Torah scrolls children will receive at the Consecration Service. At Holy Blossom Temple, a congregant has

made up, at a reduced cost, boxes to fit the miniature Torah scrolls. If this is not possible to do in your school, include the dimensions for the box in the program publicity so that parents can bring the right sized box from home. Materials are provided to decorate the Holy Arks — cloth, glitter, tissue paper, pipe cleaners, markers, paint, scissors, and glue. Together parents and children decorate the Holy Ark. Parents are also requested to write a special blessing to insert into the Ark.

**Culminating Activities**   All gather for singing, services, and refreshments. Parents fill out an evaluation form, an example of which follows:

## GRADE ONE PARENT/STUDENT PROGRAM EVALUATION

Chapter

**14**

We hope that you enjoyed participating in today's Parent/Student Program. Please help us to plan similar programs for students and their parents by completing this form. Thank you.

I participated in _____ or _____ .
                    (morning program)     (afternoon program)

GENERALLY SPEAKING
(Parents answer, please)                                    YES     NO

1. Have you participated in a Grade 1
   program before?                                          ____    ____

2. Did you find today's program to be a posi-
   tive experience?                                         ____    ____

3. Did you find the program to be a
   "learning experience"?                                   ____    ____

4. Did you find the staff to be helpful?                    ____    ____

5. Did you experience the program as
   a special opportunity to work with your
   children in a way different from the usual
   daily meetings?                                          ____    ____

6. Do you think that these kinds of programs
   enhance the Religious School programs at
   our synagogue?                                           ____    ____

MORE SPECIFICALLY

1. ADULT STUDY
   We began our program with a discussion with the Rabbi.
   How did you perceive this activity?
   _____ excellent  _____ good  _____ fair  _____ poor

2. SMALLER GROUP ACTIVITY
   We looked at and discussed the contents of a "mystery box"
   containing several Shabbat objects. Discussion centered on
   what the items were and what made them *"kodesh."* How did
   you perceive this activity?
   _____ excellent  _____ good  _____ fair  _____ poor

3. CRAFTS PROJECT
   Children and parents created an *Aron HaKodesh* to house the
   Torah scroll children will receive at Consecration Service.
   How did you perceive this activity?
   _____ excellent  _____ good  _____ fair  _____ poor

Chapter

**14**

4. WORSHIP
   We moved to the Children's Chapel to worship together with
   our new Rabbi. How did you perceive this experience?
   _____ excellent  _____ good  _____ fair  _____ poor

5. ONEG SHABBAT
   Here we are, concluding our program with *Kiddush* and
   *HaMotzi* together. We hope that you have had a good morn-
   ing/afternoon.

Please add any additional comments here:

_____

_____

**Editor's Comments**  At Holy Blossom this program takes
place during the regular Religious School hours on Saturday
morning and/or afternoon. The Consecration Service follows
the next day, on Sunday morning, so that consecrants and their
families can conclude the weekend experience at home with a
celebratory lunch. However, this program would work as well
if held on a Sunday evening. Parents can spend Shabbat together
preparing for the service and the whole weekend will generate
a total experience.

Ms. Iscove has prepared several object boxes. One for Shabbat contains items pertaining to Shabbat and *Havdalah* — candles, candle sticks, *kiddush* cup, *challah* cover, spice box, braided candle, and a *Shabbat Manual*. A similar set of guided questions are prepared for the Shabbat box. This provides the program with a great deal of flexibility. It may also be adapted for family holiday experiences.

The *Kodesh* activity may also be revised to include personal family objects. Families may be asked to bring in Jewish artifacts from home and to share their histories and significance with other participants in the group. If the focus of the day is altered, the craft activity may then center around creating personal family heirlooms, family blessings, and prayers.

Chapter

# 14

## Bibliography/Resources

Donin, Rabbi Hayim Halevy. *To Be a Jew*. New York: Basic Books, Inc., 1972.

Fields, Harvey J. *Bechol Levavcha: With All Your Heart*. New York: Union of American Hebrew Congregations, 1976.

Gersh, Harry. *The Sacred Books Of the Jews*. New York: Stein and Day, 1972.

————. *When a Jew Celebrates*. New York: Behrman House, 1971.

Grishaver, Joel Lurie, and Huppin, Beth. *Tzedakah, Gemilut Chasadim and Ahavah: A Manual for World Repair*. Denver: Alternatives in Religious Education, Inc., 1983.

Hertz, J. H. *The Pentateuch and Haftorahs*. London: Soncino Press, 1972.

Kanof, Abram. *Jewish Ceremonial Art and Religious Observance*. New York: Harry N. Abrams, Inc., n.d.

Plaut, Gunther; Bamberger, Bernard J.; and Hallo, William W. *The Torah: A Modern Commentary*. New York: Union of American Hebrew Congregations, 1981.

Siegel, Richard; Strassfeld, Michael; and Strassfeld, Sharon, eds. *The First Jewish Catalog*. Philadelphia: Jewish Publication Society, 1973.

Strassfeld, Sharon, and Green, Kathy, eds. *The Jewish Family Book*. New York: Bantam Books, 1981.

Strassfeld, Sharon, and Strassfeld, Michael, eds. *The Second Jewish Catalog*. Philadelphia: Jewish Publication Society, 1980.

_____. *The Third Jewish Catalog*. Philadelphia: Jewish Publication Society, 1980.

Syme, Daniel. *The Jewish Home Series* 3. "Chanukah and Purim." New York: Union of American Hebrew Congregations, 1977.

_____. *The Jewish Home Series 1*. Book 1. New York: Union of American Hebrew Congregations, 1976.

Chapter

14

# Chapter 15

 **TITLE:** Leshev BaSukkah

 **CONTRIBUTED BY:** Frieda Hershman Huberman

 **TOPIC:** Sukkot in the synagogue and home

 **TARGET AUDIENCE:** Families with children of all ages

 **TIME FRAME:** One 2 hour preparatory workshop; 1½-2 hours for actual program

 **STAFF:** Coordinator, Rabbi, Cantor, and the Director of Education may also be involved.

**Overview**   Sharing Sukkot with the community enriches the celebration of the festival. This two session program acquaints synagogue members with the customs and traditions of the holiday and provides them with guidelines for building a *sukkah* at home. Because of the communal nature of the program, individuals who are building a *sukkah* for the first time have a ready-made support group. The synagogue staff plays a key role in the program.

**Purpose**   The main purpose of this program is to encourage families to build their own *sukkah*. In the process participants will become acquainted with the various *halachot* and *minhagim* associated with Sukkot.

Chapter

15

**Preparation/Procedure**   Publicize the program through flyers and the synagogue bulletin. There is no limit to the number of people who can participate in this program. However, if a meal is to be served in the *sukkah*, the program may need to be staggered to accommodate everyone.

The facilitators should be able to teach about the holiday. They should be knowledgeable about the customs, traditions, and laws of *Sukkot*. It is beneficial to have an art specialist and a song leader available for this program as well

Prior to the actual program, prepare all the materials needed for distribution, including guidelines for building a *sukkah*, decorating ideas, and song sheets. Prepare name tags for participants and a facilitator's check sheet of all necessary items.

**Program Description**   The following is a description of each of the two sessions:

Session I: Sukkah Designing and Decorating Workshop
At this session hold a discussion about the requirements for building a *sukkah*. Make available several models of different kinds of *sukkot* (free standing, two walls, three walls, etc.). Give participants an opportunity to design a *sukkah* for their homes.

Several stations are set up to make decorations for the *sukkah*, such as chains, stuffed fruit, New Year card collages, natural object pictures, etc. After families make various decorations, they may choose to take them home or to hang them in the synagogue *sukkah*.

Teach the blessing over the *lulav* and the *etrog*, and explain the *halachot* connected with them. If time permits include a values clarification exercise pertaining to the *lulav* and *etrog*.

Session II: Sukkah Family Meal and Program
This session begins with a family oriented *Kabbalat Shabbat* service followed by a dinner in the *sukkah*. If it is too cold to eat in the *sukkah*, set up a buffet in the *sukkah* and have people take their food into the synagogue building. Or, make *HaMotsi* and *Kiddush* in the *sukkah*, then go inside for the meal. If the *sukkah* can accommodate a small number of people only, have people eat in shifts and provide alternate activities for those who are waiting, such as singing, telling stories, or making decorations.

Each table is furnished with clues about a potential historical guest. (Sometime during the meal, the facilitator explains the concept of *Ushpizin*.) Participants need to figure out who their "guest" is, share what they know about the person, and discuss what question they would ask of that guest in their *sukkah*.

Each table is assigned a set of clues to the identity of one historical guest. The clues are written on a 3″ x 5″ card and placed in an envelope. Suggested clues follow:

Chapter

15

CLUES
Historical Guests

Abraham
My name was changed.
Terach was my father.
I've been called the father of the people.
I started something very important.
I don't believe in idols.

Miriam
I sang my songs of praise to God after the Exodus.
I liked to gossip.
I helped my now famous brother even when he was a baby.

Isaac
My father started it all.
I had a real close call.
The *shofar* is my favorite symbol.
My wife Rebekah had twins.

Joseph
I worked my way up to an important post.
In my youth I liked to brag.
My father gave me a special coat.
Pharaoh listened to my advice.

Moses
I took accurate dictation.
I sometimes got a little tongue-tied.
I never entered the Promised Land.
People refer to me as "our teacher" ("our Rabbi").
With God's help I split the sea.

David
My songs of praise are still recited today.
A city was named after me.
Bathsheva was my special love.
I was a poet and a soldier.
My son was a great builder.

Golda Meir
I spoke Hebrew with an American accent.
I moved to Israel to join a *kibbutz*, but soon became active
in politics.
I proved that a woman can be a great leader.
Labor was my party.

Esther
Winning contests was my thing.
At first I kept my Jewish identity a secret.
My husband was a king.
My charm helped save the Jews.

Deborah
My name means bee.
"Here comes the judge!"
I wasn't known just for my brains.
I also helped lead my people into battle.

Sarah
I was the first Jewish princess.
I was the mother of a people.
I almost lost my only son.
Thank God for rams!

Later on, representatives from each table come before the entire group. Using a "Twenty Questions" format, the entire assembly (except for each representative's own table) attempts to identify the guest. The program is rounded out by singing, dancing, and *Birkat HaMazon*.

Chapter

# 15

**Editor's Comments**   While each session stands on its own, both could be done at one meeting. The program might be augmented by a family home *sukkah* tour and/or progressive meal. The meal in the synagogue *sukkah* could be a Sunday brunch or lunch in conjunction with religious school, a *Seudah Shleesheet*, or a *Havdalah/Melaveh Malkah* repast.

Another way to make the synagogue *sukkah* available to the entire community is to invite a different group to use it each day. Families with young children and senior adults could come during the day for brunch or luncheon. Children in Grades 1-6 could attend an after school party in the *sukkah*. The *sukkah* could be reserved on one evening for the junior and senior high school students and another time for *havurot*. Each family could be asked to bring a meal for themselves and the synagogue could provide beverages and dessert.

During the day those who come to the *sukkah* can participate in the blessing of the *lulav* and *etrog*. Instead of the *Ushpizin* clues, there can be a discussion about the significance of the *lulav* and *etrog* and the nature of the festival of Sukkot. Each of the eight days of the festival has special signficance which is worthy of discussion. If there are many young children present, it would be appropriate to tell a story with puppets or a flannel board in the *sukkah*. On Hoshana Rabbah, march around the synagogue beating the willow branches, then gather together to read Psalms and other poetry.

For those who come for the evening, have people dressed as biblical heroes/heroines acting out parts. Or, play the "Who Am I?" game. Tape the name of a biblical hero/heroine on someone's back. In order to find out who the hero/heroine is, the person has to go around asking questions of others. This serves as an icebreaker and also as a way for participants to become acquainted with Bible personalities.

Chapter

**15**

### Bibliography/Resources

Drucker, Malka. *Sukkot: A Time to Rejoice.* New York: Holiday House, 1982.

Goodman, Philip. *The Sukkot and Simchat Torah Anthology.* Philadelphia: Jewish Publication Society, 1973.

Kelman, Victoria, ed. *Together: A Parent-Child Kit.* Issue 2. New York: Melton Research Center of The Jewish Theological Seminary of America, 1984.

Saypol, Judith, and Wikler, Madeline. *My Very Own Sukkot.* Silver Spring, MD, 1980.

Siegel, Richard; Strassfeld, Michael; and Strassfeld, Sharon, eds. *The First Jewish Catalog.* Philadelphia: Jewish Publication Society, 1973.

# Chapter 16

 **TITLE:** A Chanukah Program On Soviet Jewry

 **CONTRIBUTED BY:** Nachama Skolnik Moskowitz

 **DESIGN:** Adapted from a program at UAHC Camp Swig in the 1970s; designed in Tulsa with the help of Jay Weiner and Nurit Glick

 **TOPIC:** Involving families with the plight of Soviet Jews

 **TARGET AUDIENCE:** Families with children in Grades 2-8

 **TIME FRAME:** 2-2 ½ hours

 **STAFF:** Coordinator, classroom teachers and teaching assistants, Rabbi, Director of Eduation, liaison from local Soviet Jewry Committee

**Overview**   This program is a fact finding mission involving students and parents. It integrates information about Soviet Jews and the holiday of Chanukah. It was a one-time program, run jointly by two religious schools, for families with children in Grades 2 to 8. Participating families were divided into two groups, "Americans" and "Soviets." These roles were pre-assigned in a letter that went home to parents in advance. American and Soviet families interacted with each other, then everyone came together for a debriefing.

**Purpose**   The main purpose of the program was to acquaint American Jews with the plight of Soviet Jews, with particular emphasis on the lack of religious freedom and the lack of freedom to emigrate. It was also designed to help families learn what the American Jewish community is doing to help Soviet Jews and to show that there is a connection between Chanukah and the theme of religious freedom.

**Preparation/Procedure**   The staff for this program included the teachers of the classes involved, along with their high school age assistants. The Rabbi, Director of Education, and one outside speaker are also needed.

Prior to notifying families, it is necessary to preassign everyone to their roles. Half the families will be "American"; they will be given names that end in "stein" (Weinstein, Goldstein, etc.). The other half will be "Soviet Jewish families"; they will be given Russian sounding names. In the publicity, participants are encouraged to wear costumes and to bring objects which will enhance the day.

Meet with all facilitators one or two weeks in advance. Review the program and walk through it so that everyone is sure of his/her roles.

**Program Description**   The following is a suggested schedule for the event:

**Schedule**

| | |
|---|---|
| 9:45 | Registration |
| 10:00 | Separate preparation by "American" and "Soviet" families |
| 11:00 | "Americans" travel to the Soviet Union; "Soviet" families set up house. |
| 11:15 | Family visits |
| 11:35 | Debriefing |

**Preparation Of Families**

1. What the Americans do – The Americans are briefed by someone who has been to the Soviet Union. It is helpful if this person shows slides or pictures of the trip. The speaker is expected to describe how they were able to get in touch with Soviet Jews before the trip and once in the U.S.S.R. A major point to be emphasized is the need for Soviet Jews to have visitors.

Chapter
**16**

Once the Americans are briefed on the situation, they discuss what kinds of items need to be brought to the U.S.S.R. In preparation for their trip, they may select books from the library, find appropriate Jewish artifacts, or create artifacts that may be brought into the U.S.S.R. in several pieces (e.g., a disguised *chanukiah*). These materials should be available at the program site for people to select prior to leaving for the Soviet Union.

2. What the Soviet Jews will do – Those who are assigned the roles of Soviet Jewish families will use this time to learn about their own situations. The facilitator should set up role play situations which depict the difficulties Soviet Jews face when trying to emigrate. Have this group play the *Exodus* game and/or *Route To Freedom* so that the Soviets have specific things to discuss with the Americans.

**Travel and Setting Up House**   Once the preparations are completed, the Americans travel to the Soviet Union and the Soviet Jews set up a home in which to receive their visitors.

The Americans may take either a plane ride or go by boat. In either case provide a filmstrip or movie which depicts the situation. When the Americans arrive in the Soviet Union, customs officials are expected to confiscate about half the materials they are trying to bring in.

The Soviet Jews will utilize this time to set up an apartment to receive their guests. They may rearrange furniture, display artifacts brought from home, and, if possible, hang things on the walls. Refreshments should be arranged for the expected American visitors.

**Family Visits**    During the family visit time, it is necessary to have a minimum of two staff members with each family group. They help participants ask each other questions about life in the Soviet Union and in America. At this time, the Americans share their gifts with the Soviet Jews and refreshments are served. After the two groups part, everyone is brought to a central location where they are divided into small groups for debriefing.

Chapter

# 16

**Debriefing**    The following questions are suggested as guidelines for the debriefing session:

1. Ask participants to review the events of the day.

2. What is it like for a Jew living in the Soviet Union? Why does this situation exist?

3. How would you react as a Jew in the Soviet Union? Would you try to hide your Jewishness or announce it and try to leave the country? What about the consequences?

4. What are American Jews doing to help Jews in the Soviet Union?

5. What are some differences in Jewish practice between Jews living in America and Jews living in the Soviet Union?

6. If we think about the Maccabees and their fight for religious freedom, what might we say about the Soviet Jews and their desires? What can we as American Jews do to help our Soviet brothers and sisters?

7. What did you like best about the day? What did you like least?

**Editor's Comments**  In order for this program to be effective, it is necessary to have someone available who has first-hand knowledge of the Soviet Jewry situation. If you do not have such a person in your immediate community, your nearest Soviet Jewry Comittee may be able to provide you with someone with the appropriate background information.

This program represents a good opportunity to promote the Soviet Jewish Twinning Program for Bar or Bat Mitzvah. Obtain literature from the local Community Relations Commission or the nearest Soviet Jewry Committee. Have the literature available at the Chanukah program. Invite as a resource person someone who has participated in the twinning program.

This Chanukah program on Soviet Jewry can be expanded to include Jews who are oppressed in places other than the Soviet Union. The local Federation and/or Community Relations Commission can provide information about the situation of Jews in Arab lands and in other places where Jews are oppressed.

Chapter

**16**

## Bibliography/Resources

Blaser, Elissa. *Exodus*. New York: Behrman House.

*By Spirit Alone: Jewish Life In the Soviet Union Today*. A Four Lesson Unit based on the photo exhibit of Bill Aron. Los Angeles: Commission on Soviet Jewry of the Jewish Federation Council of Los Angeles, 1983. (6505 Wilshire Blvd., Los Angeles, CA 90048)

*Keeping Posted*. December 1978. New York: Union of American Hebrew Congregations.

*On the Move: A Game About Soviet Jewry*. Denver: Alternatives in Religious Education, Inc., 1974.

Orenstein, Sylvia. *Source Book On Soviet Jewry: An Annotated Bibliography*. New York: American Jewish Committee, 1981.

Ramm, Shoshana. *Route To Freedom: A Game Of Escape From the Soviet Union*. New York: Board of Jewish Education of Greater New York, 1976.

**Mediated Materials**
*By Spirit Alone: Jewish Life In the Soviet Union Today.* From a
photo exhibit by Bill Aron and Ahavia Scheindlin. Los
Angeles: Torah Aura Productions and the Commission on
Soviet Jewry of the Jewish Federation Council of Greater
L.A., 1985. (slide-tape presentation)

**Organizations**
National Conference on Soviet Jewry
10 East 40th Street, Suite 907
New York, NY 10016

Student Struggle for Soviet Jewry
210 West 91st Street
New York, NY 10024

Union of Councils for Soviet Jewry
1819 H Street N.W. Suite 410
Washington, DC 20006

Your local Jewish Community Relations Commission or Soviet
Jewry Committee

For a selected annotated bibliography on Soviet Jewry, write to:
Jewish Community Council of Greater Washington
1522 K Street N.W.
Washington, DC 20005

Chapter

16

# Chapter 17

 **TITLE:** Intergenerational Tu B'Shevat Seder

 **CONTRIBUTED BY:** Dayle Friedman

 **TOPIC:** Integrating school students with senior adults; education about Tu B'Shevat

 **TARGET AUDIENCE:** Families with children in Grades K-6; senior adults.

 **TIME FRAME:** 1-1½ hours, any size group

 **STAFF:** One facilitator, 2 or 3 assistants, songleader

**Overview**   The Tu B'Shevat *Seder,* originally a Sephardic tradition, has gained in popularity in recent years. As a family experience, it can be a helpful tool in educating about the holiday. At Central Synagogue in New York City, members of the Senior Adult Club joined with religious school students and their parents for a Tu B'Shevat *Seder.* There were two separate *Sedarim,* one for students in K-3 and one for students in 4-6.

**Purpose**   This program has a two-fold purpose: to educate families about Tu B'Shevat, and to foster intergenerational interaction and understanding.

**Preparation/Procedure**   In order for such a program to succeed, it is necessary to involve senior adults, teachers, and families. The senior adults should be individuals who are open to meeting and sharing memories with the children. Prior to the *Seder,* recruit the senior adults and inform them of the nature of the program. Explain that this is a school program and that their input will be welcomed and valued by the students, parents, and teachers. You may wish to explain the Tu B'Shevat *Haggadah* you will be using. If desired, ask the senior adults to bring some of the food for the *Seder.*

Teachers should spend at least one class lesson preparing the students for the *Seder.* Go over the Tu B'Shevat *Haggadah.* Learn the names of the seven species, the appropriate blessings, and some songs. In addition, spend some time preparing students for their interactions with the senior adults. Allow them to express feelings about old age, and help them understand that stereotypes often inaccurately characterize the aged as helpless, disengaged, or closed minded. Help students formulate questions they might wish to ask of the senior adults, such as their childhood memories of the Jewish holidays (Tu B'Shevat in particular) and their Jewish education. Make a list of things students might share about their religious school experience with the seniors. In addition, classes can prepare some of the foods to be eaten at the *Seder.*

In advance of the project, inform parents so that they will know what to expect when they arrive at school. Some of the ques-

Chapter

17

tions directed by students to the senior adults can also be asked of parents. You may wish to send home copies of the blessings for the different foods and the words to the songs so that parents and children can learn them together. Where appropriate, parents may also be asked to bring food or beverages to the *Seder*.

Be sure that everyone has an opportunity to participate as a reader during the *Seder*. If you have fewer parts than people, assign specific things for classes to do — e.g., recite *brachot*, sing songs, etc., and allow only the adults to read, or only the children to read.

For the *Seder* utilize any available Tu B'Shevat *Haggadah* (see Bibliography/Resources for suggestions).

Set up the physical facility with individual tables for 8 or 10 so that the generations can more easily interact with each other. Situate the leader in the middle of the room at a lectern with a microphone. Prepare enough *Haggadot* for everyone. Consider reproducing some of these in large print to accommodate younger children and senior adults. If you do not have a song leader, record the melodies on a tape and play them at the appropriate time. Assign seats in advance so that senior adults are interspersed among the participating families.

Chapter

17

**Program Description**   The basic program has two components — introductory/ice breaker activities and the actual *Seder*. You may begin by having everyone at each table introduce themselves to the others at the table and then name their favorite Jewish symbol/holiday/person, etc. Once you have gotten them started, suggest that the children ask some of the questions they have prepared and the adults share some of their Jewish experiences. If it is practical, ask everyone to introduce themselves to the rest of the group prior to beginning the *Seder*.

After the small group ice breaker, bring participants together at one large *Seder* table. If your facility cannot accommodate both small and large tables in one area, use individual classrooms for the small groups, then bring people together later on. For the actual *Seder*, have participants take turns reading the text of the *Haggadah* and have the song leader lead them in song.

At the end of the *Seder* allow each student an opportunity to put his or her own plant in a pot and take it home. In addition, the group may plant parsley or lettuce in wooden crates or in plastic swimming pools. The children can then care for the plants and use them for their religious school Passover *Seder.*

**Editor's Comments**    There are many ways to enhance an intergenerational Tu B'Shevat *Seder.* For instance, take two instant photos of the children and the senior adults interacting in their little groups. One copy can be used as a reminder to the children in follow-up classroom activities. Give the other copy to the senior adult. Consider tape recording some of the initial dialogues. As a follow-up write down some of the stories and prepare a booklet to be shared by the children, participating families, and senior adults.

Chapter

17

While the above program describes a Tu B'Shevat *Seder,* the model may be adapted to any activities involving families and senior adults, particularly those with holidays as a focus. You may wish to consider such a program for a class studying life cycle, history, or the Jewish community.

For an ongoing program that fosters intergeneration communication, see Chapter 5, "Bridging the Gap."

## Bibliography/Resources

Adler, Esther. *Forests and Personalities.* New York: Jewish National Fund, 1983.

_____. *Trees In the Bible.* New York: Jewish National Fund, 1982.

Ben-Zvi, Hava, comp. *New Year Of the Trees: Selected Resources.* Los Angeles: Bureau of Jewish Education, 1978.

Cone, Molly. *The House In the Tree: A Story Of Israel.* New York: Crowell, 1968.

Eckstein, Barry. *Tu Bi'Shevat Manual for Home-School-Community.* New York: Jewish National Fund, n.d.

Glatzer, Shoshana. *The New Year for Trees: A Challenge Kit for Tu Bi'Shevat*. New York: Board of Jewish Education of Greater New York, 1980.

Kelman, Victoria. *Together: A Child Parent Kit*. Issue 6, *Trees*. New York: Melton Research Center, 1985.

Ross, Betty Ann. *Dates As Sweet As Honey*. New York: Board of Jewish Education, 1982.

Simon, Norma. *Tu Bi-Shevat*. New York: United Synagogue Commission on Jewish Education, 1961.

Silverstein, Shel. *The Giving Tree*. New York: Harper, 1964.

**Tu B'Shevat Sedarim**

CAJE Curriculum Bank, Clejan Education Resource Center, University of Judaism, 15600 Mulholland Dr., Los Angeles, CA 90049.

*Chicken Soup*, January, 1984. (Clejan Education Resource Center, University of Judaism, 15600 Mulholland Dr., Los Angeles, CA 90049)

Eckstein, Barry. *Tu Bi'Shevat Manual for Home-School-Community*. New York: Jewish National Fund, n.d.

Hefter, Seymour. *Tu B'Shevat Haggadah*. Wilkes Barre, PA: Jewish Community Center of Wyoming Valley, 1977. (60 South River St., Wilkes Barre, PA 18702)

Kelman, Victoria. *Together: A Child Parent Kit*. Issue 6, *Trees*. New York: Melton Research Center, 1985.

Rappel, Yoel. *Seder Tu Bishvat*. New York: World Zionist Organization Department of Education and Culture, 1984.

Chapter

# 17

**Mediated Materials**

*My Tree In the Bar Kochba Forest*. Jewish National Fund, 42 East 69th St., New York, NY 10021. (filmstrip, 52 frames)

*A Seder for Tu B'Shvat*. Neot Kedumim, American Friends of Neot Kedumim, 270 W. 89th St., New York, NY 10024. (filmstrip, 44 frames)

# Chapter 18

 **TITLE:** Pesach Fair

 **CONTRIBUTED BY:** Sandy Dashefsky and Judy Press

 **DESIGNED BY:** Sandy Dashefsky and Judy Press

 **TOPIC:** Pesach

 **TARGET AUDIENCE:** Families with children in Kindergarten and above

 **TIME FRAME:** 1½-2 hours for actual program

 **STAFF::** Coordinator, classroom teachers, volunteers for "booths," "actors," guides

**Overview**   "Pesach Fair," modeled after science fairs in public schools, is an alternative to the traditional school *Seder*. The model has three components — exhibits, dramatic production, and booths. A school or agency may choose to do one part, combine two parts, or do all three parts. Preparation for the fair begins two to three months in advance of the actual event, thereby providing families with opportunities to study together and to delve deeply into a theme.

**Purpose**   The purpose of the "Pesach Fair" is to provide families with an opportunity to broaden their knowledge of Pesach and to participate in a Pesach celebration as a community of learners. Ultimately, it is designed to provide them with new insights about Pesach which they will bring to their own *Seder* tables.

**Preparation/Procedure**   This program requires 2-3 months of advance planning. Publicize the "Pesach Fair" to your constituency. Be sure to let everyone know that the culmination of their work will be on display at the fair and that creativity is the key. Send out a list of suggestions. Orient and involve the staff. Instruct them to prepare classroom lessons focusing on Pesach and have students make progress reports about their projects. Gather resource materials and let everyone know where these can be located. It is helpful to have a librarian or library volunteers to assist with research.

**Pesach Exhibits**   Two or three months before the actual fair, families prepare Pesach related projects which contain two parts — a written report based on research in texts, and a visual display. Families may create projects from a variety of media, such as: clay or wood sculptures, dioramas, video productions, filmstrips, slide shows, needlework, banners, posters, games, and poster displays, etc. Examples of these are: a mural of the Ten Plagues, a clay sculpture of Moses at the Red Sea, a video of "You Are There At the Exodus . . .").

Projects may be judged for content and creativity. Be sure that every entry receives some recognition. Special prizes may be awarded for exceptional exhibits. You may wish to set up a

variety of different categories and people may choose to participate in several different ones. Suggested categories are: class
projects, individual projects, small group projects, family
projects.

**Dramatic Presentation**   Plan a dramatic presentation which
involves both adults and children. A small group of individuals
might play the lead roles and the entire student body can be
involved in the chorus. The majority of the students can learn
the music as part of their music curriculum and then be
involved only in the final rehearsals.

**Booths**   Have each class develop a booth with a Pesach theme.
The class is responsible for planning and designing the booth
and for seeing to it that there will be personnel to staff the
booth. Possible Pesach booths might include:

Chapter

# 18

Craft Booth – Create Pesach buttons, *matzah* covers, or
pillowcases.

Pesach Game Room – Play games, such as *Passover Family Feud*
and *Pesach Bingo*.

A *Matzah* Factory – Bake *matzah*.

House Of Passover – Visitors have an opportunity to practice
*Seder* skills and taste *Seder* foods from around the world.

A Newsroom – Participants write articles to be published in the
"famous" *Pesach Inquirer.* Feature stories, editorial articles,
comics, weather reports, and advertisements are all included.

A "Sing-a-long" Room – Sing favorite Pesach songs and learn
some new ones.

Interview Room – "Meet" Moses, or maybe Pharaoh, and learn
more about them and their time.

Video-Land – Participants have an opportunity to view the video
*Operation Moses* about Ethiopian Jewry and to give a donation
to help settle Ethiopian Jews in Israel.

Decide in advance where all of the fair events will take place.
Plan a program and draw a map or floor plan if necessary.

**Program Description**   The actual day of the "Pesach Fair" will require 1½-2 hours of time. Allow a half hour for the dramatic presentation and 1-1½ hours for families to visit exhibits and booths. The day may begin or end with the dramatic presentation. It is not necessary to have a set schedule for visiting the exhibits and booths, except for scheduling times for the viewing of the video shows or films.

**Editor's Comments**   The model presented here may be adapted for other curricular areas. It has been used successfully for Shabbat and Torah. It is helpful to have the fair cosponsored by all the synagogue auxiliary organizations, such as the Sisterhood, Brotherhood, P.T.A., etc., in order to ensure a wide range of participation. This allows individuals who do not have children in school to participate in a variety of ways, particularly in the exhibits and the dramatic presentation.

## Bibliography/Resources

Cardozo, Arlene Rossen. *Jewish Family Celebrations*. New York: St. Martin's Press, 1982.

Cashman, Greer Fay. *Jewish Days and Holidays*. New York: SBS Publishing, Inc., 1979.

Chaikin, Miriam. *Ask Another Question: The Story and Meaning Of Passover*. New York: Clarion Books, 1985.

Drucker, Malka. *Passover: A Season Of Freedom*. New York: Holiday House, 1981.

Freedman, Jacob D. D. *Polychrome Historical Haggadah for Passover*. Massachusetts: Jacob Freedman Liturgy Research Foundation, 1974.

Goodman, Philip. *The Passover Anthology*. Philadelphia: Jewish Publication Society, 1961.

Goodman, Robert. *A Teachers Guide To Jewish Holidays*. Denver: Alternatives in Religious Education, Inc., 1983.

Greenberg, Dr. Irving. *Guide To Passover.* New York: CLAL, 1976.

Groner, Judyth R. *Where Is the Afikomen?* Rockville, MD: Kar-Ben Copies, 1985.

Halpern, Chaiky. *Mihu the Detective and the Mystery Of the Missing Chametz.* New York: Feldheim, 1979.

Klausner, Abraham. *The Bicentennial Haggadah.* New York: Emanual Press Publications, 1976.

Klein, Isaac. *A Guide To Jewish Religious Practice.* New York: The Jewish Theological Seminary of America, 1979.

Kustanowitz, Shulamit, and Front, Ronnie C. *A First Haggadah.* New York: Bonim Books, 1979.

Marcus, Audrey Friedman, and Zwerin, Raymond A. *But This Night Is Different: A Seder Experience.* New York: Union of American Hebrew Congregations, 1980.

Podwal, Mark. *Let My People Go: A Haggadah.* New York: Darien House, 1972.

Press, Chaim. *What Is the Reason? Pesach.* Missouri: Chain Press, 1977.

Rabinowicz, Rachel Anne, ed. *Passover Haggadah: The Feast Of Freedom.* New York: The Rabbinical Assembly, 1982.

Raphael, Chaim. *A Feast Of History: Passover Through the Ages As a Key To Jewish Experience.* New York: Simon and Schuster, 1972.

Raphael, Chaim, trans. *Passover Haggadah.* New York: Behrman House, 1972.

Rembrandt, Elaine. *Heroes, Heroines and Holidays.* Denver: Alternatives in Religious Education, Inc., 1981.

Rockland, Mae Shafter. *The Jewish Party Book: A Contemporary Guide To Customs, Crafts, and Foods.* New York: Schocken Books, 1978.

Chapter

# 18

Rosen, Anne. *A Family Passover.* Philadelphia: Jewish Publication Society, 1980.

Ross, Lillian. *Why Is This Season Different? A Pesach Manual.* Florida: Central Agency for Jewish Education, 1979.

Rosten, Norman. *The Wineglass: A Passover Story.* New York: Walker and Co., 1978.

Saypol, Judyth R., and Wikler, Madeline. *My Very Own Haggadah.* Silver Spring, MD: Kar-Ben Copies, 1974.

Schauss, Hayyim. *The Jewish Festivals: History and Observance.* New York: Schocken Books, 1978.

Schlein, Miriam. *Passover.* New York: Behrman House, 1983.

Shulevitz, Uri. *The Magician.* New York: Macmillan Publishing Co., 1973.

Siegel, Richard; Strassfeld, Sharon; and Strassfeld, Michael, eds. *The First Jewish Catalog.* Philadelphia, Jewish Publication Society, 1973.

Silberman, Shoshana. *A Family Haggadah.* Rockville, MD: Kar-Ben Copies, Inc., 1987.

Singer, Isaac Bashevis. *Elijah the Slave.* New York: Farrar, Straus and Giroux, 1970.

Strassfeld, Michael. *The Jewish Holidays: A Guide and Commentary.* New York: Harper and Row, 1985.

Waskow, Arthur. *Seasons Of Our Joy: A Handbook Of Jewish Festivals.* New York: Bantam Books, 1982.

**Mediated Materials**

*My Exodus.* Torah Aura Productions, 4423 Fruitland Ave., Los Angeles, CA 90058, 1984. (videotape, 22 min.)

*Operation Moses.* United Jewish Appeal, 99 Park Ave., New York, NY 10016, 1985. (film, 27 min.)

Chapter

**18**

# Chapter 19

 **TITLE:** Shabbat Can Be

 **CONTRIBUTED BY:** Robin Eisenberg

 **TOPIC:** Enhancing Shabbat in the home

 **TARGET AUDIENCE:** Families with children in Grades K and 1

 **TIME FRAME:** 2 ½ to 3 hours

 **STAFF:** Overall coordinator, classroom teacher, one facilitator per station

**Overview**   The book *Shabbat Can Be* by Raymond A. Zwerin and Audrey Friedman Marcus is the focal point of this program. Families go to stations where they engage in activities which will enhance Shabbat in their lives. A parallel track is set up for parents to study about Shabbat and learn Shabbat skills.

**Purpose**   The purpose of the program is to help parents of younger children to integrate Shabbat into their lives on an ongoing basis by introducing them to appropriate activities that can be done at home. It is also designed to help parents learn the skills of making Shabbat at home.

Chapter

19

**Preparation/Procedure**   Secure a large room or several rooms where you can set up work stations. Arrange for at least one facilitator per station. Have someone available to study with parents while children have a parallel session with the classroom teacher. Engage a music specialist and a crafts specialist.

**Program Description**   The following is the overall schedule of the program:

**Schedule**
> Parallel Activities (45 min.)
>> Introduction and Orientation
>> Parent Study
>> Classroom Lesson Pertaining To Shabbat

> Parents and Children Together
>> Read *Shabbat Can Be* (15 min.)
>> Stations – each family can do as many as they wish (60 min.)
>> Shabbat Skills (15 min.)

> Culminating Activity
>> Shabbat Contracts (15 min.)

**Parent Study**   The Director of Education or the Rabbi studies a text about Shabbat with the parents. Material may be taken from a variety of sources, such as the Talmud, the writings of

Abraham Joshua Heschel, *The Sabbath: Time & Existence* by David Zisenwine and Karen Abramovitz, or directly from the Torah. It is important to introduce the parents to text study as an aspect of Shabbat celebration. Provide each person with a copy of the text and write down sample questions. If they so desire, families can take the material home and study it further.

**The Stations**   The following is a description of each of the stations:

1. Shabbat Can Be . . . A Time for Special Words
   a. Make copies of popular Shabbat prayers and songs.
   b. Each family selects prayers and songs they would like to include in their Shabbat at home.
   c. Provide folders and blank paper so that people can collect their selections and add extra pages for pictures or personal Shabbat words.

2. Shabbat Can Be . . . A Time for Stories
   a. Each family takes one of the story starters and writes their own ending. Save the story to share with the group later and to use at home on Shabbat. Some examples of story starters are:
   In our family we prepare for Shabbat by . . . .
   I'm glad that Shabbat comes every week because . . .
   In our family Shabbat is special because . . . .
   "*Shabbat Shalom*" in my family means . . . .
   When I see the Shabbat candles, I . . . .
   When I hear the *Kiddush*, I . . . .

3. Shabbat Can Be . . . A Time for Sharing
   a. Read information about *tzedakah*. Decide on how you can share with others who are less fortunate. Put your ideas on a *tzedakah* wall chart. Then make a family *tzedakah* box.

4. Shabbat Can Be . . . A Time for Special Food
   a. As a family, go into the synagogue kitchen and, following the directions you will find there, bake *challah*.

5. Shabbat Can Be . . . A Time for Celebration
   a. Read the information about *Kiddush*. Discuss the meaning of *Kiddush* in your lives. Make wine cups using the materials provided.

Chapter

19

   b. As an alternate activity, read the information about Shabbat candles. Make a pair of Shabbat candlesticks out of clay. The clay will dry overnight and can then be painted.

6. Shabbat Can Be . . . A Time for Special Thoughts
   a. Tell the story about the two neighboring shopkeepers, one who sold cooking oil and the other who sold spices. The oil seller, after seeing the spice merchant counting out one hundred gold coins, ran out into the street shouting that his coins were missing. When asked who took them, he blamed the spice merchant. Shortly afterward, the police found the one hundred gold coins at the spice merchant's. He, of course, insisted that they were his, and that he had earned them. The policeman brought the two feuding merchants to a judge. The judge asked for a pitcher of warm water and dropped the coins into it. No drops of oil floated to the top, suggesting that the oil seller had never handled the coins. The judge ruled that the coins belonged to the spice merchant.

   What is the moral of the story? What does this say about fairness?

   b. Still another activity involves the reading of Exodus 20:9-10. Make up a prayer for people in other lands who are not allowed to come and go as they please, or to worship as they want, or to work at the job they enjoy.

   Ask the question: How can you feel rich without a penny in your pocket? Make a mural to which each family adds its interpretation of this line from *Shabbat Can Be*.

**Shabbat Skills**   Gather everyone together and teach them the blessings for candles, wine, and *challah*. If these skills are already known to the group, teach the *Birkat HaMazon* and *Eyshet Chayil*. Provide the words for "*Shalom Aleichem*" and teach them to everyone. Be sure that you have made copies of all the blessings in Hebrew, in transliteration, and in translation.

**Culminating Activity**   Provide each family with a Shabbat Contract Form. Tell them to review what "Shabbat Can Be" for them and then to write a family contract agreeing to do certain things on Shabbat at home. Be sure everyone signs the contract. Go around the room and ask each family to share what "Shabbat Can Be" for them.

**Editor's Comments**  This program lasts 2½ to 3 hours. It can be lengthened by including a lunch or brunch, or by allowing an extra ½ hour for the stations and for a more intensive skill session, or by adding a music session. Or, if you want to keep the program under 3 hours and add other kinds of sessions, eliminate the parallel study and classroom lesson. You can also conclude the program with an actual Shabbat meal or *Kabalat Shabbat* worship service.

*Challah* covers and *challah* boards, for instance, can be made at the food station while waiting for the *challah* to rise or bake. The story station can contain stories which parents can read to their children at home. These are but a few of the endless varieties of stations that are possible. For more ideas for stations, see *The Learning Center Book Of Holidays and Symbols* by Deborah Levy and Audrey Friedman Marcus.

Chapter

19

Arrange for a display of appropriate children's books from the congregational library and allow parents to check them out. You can also provide a form so that parents can order the books for their home library. In addition to providing background information about *tzedakah*, show one or two episodes of *Profiles In Chesed* (Torah Aura Productions) to provide a visual demonstration of *tzedakah* in action.

This program helps families to initiate Shabbat observances in their homes on an ongoing basis. Encourage participants to get together to celebrate Shabbat in small groups, two or three families together. If possible, help them get started by giving or selling each family a copy of the *Shabbat Manual* or *The Art Of Jewish Living: The Shabbat Seder* by Ron Wolfson. Provide a list of places where *challah* can be bought, as well as a tape of the songs and blessings. Give everyone a class list complete with parents' names, addresses, and telephone numbers.

**Bibliography/Resources** See the bibliography for Chapter 7, "The Joy Of Shabbat."

# Chapter 20

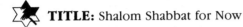 **TITLE:** Shalom Shabbat for Now

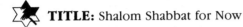 **CONTRIBUTED BY::** Janice Alper

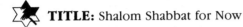 **TOPIC:** Shabbat afternoon and *Havdalah*

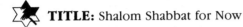 **TARGET AUDIENCE:** Families with children of all ages

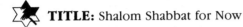 **TIME FRAME:** 2-3 hours on Shabbat afternoon

 **STAFF:** One facilitator for every 20-25 people

**Overview** This program takes place on a Shabbat afternoon and extends through *Havdalah*. Family members engage in Torah study, learn *Havdalah* skills, participate in a *Seudah Shleesheet*, and worship together. This program may be implemented for any number of people of varying ages, provided the activities are carefully planned.

**Purpose** The purpose of the program is to increase each family's awareness of Shabbat as families come together as a community to bid good-bye to Shabbat.

**Preparation/Procedure** This program works best in a large room with enough seating to accommodate all the people who attend. Set aside separate areas for study skill centers. These may be on the perimeter of the large room, or they may be set up in adjoining areas or classrooms. Designate a place where people can sit down to eat. Have a telephone committee ascertain who is coming so as to have an idea of the number of people and the ages of the children. If desired, assign people to tell Shabbat stories or lead singing. You will need one facilitator for every 20-25 people.

In class sessions prior to the program, have students prepare spice boxes which will be used at *Havdalah*. Review the *Minchah* and *Ma'ariv* services for Shabbat, as well as the blessings for the *Havdalah* service.

If time permits, students may prepare personal booklets containing the *Minchah* and *Ma'ariv* services and *Havdalah*. They may also learn songs and *niggunim* and prepare Shabbat stories which will be presented at the *Seudah Shleesheet*.

**Program Description** The program includes four parts: 1) Introductory Activities; 2) Concurrent Learning Sessions; 3) *Seudah Shleesheet*; and 4) Services: *Minchah/Ma'ariv* and *Havdalah*. An overview of each part follows:

**Introductory Activities** Begin the day by singing familiar Shabbat songs. Have everyone sit in a circle. Ask everyone to

**Chapter**

**20**

introduce themselves to the rest of the group, then begin a continuous story. The facilitator begins the story with a Shabbat theme, tells a few lines, and the next person adds to the story, and so on. The story is made up as people go along. It works best if there are about 20 people in a group. If that number is exceeded, break into two or more groups. It is helpful to go around the group twice for the story. The facilitator should make an effort to tie the story together and remind people to stick to the Shabbat theme. Examples of some story starters are:

One Shabbat afternoon as I was getting everything ready for *Havdalah* . . .

Once upon a time, a long time ago, I saw the Shabbat Queen. She came into my room and said . . .

One Shabbat when I was praying in synagogue, this thought crossed my mind . . .

Chapter

# 20

**Concurrent Learning Sessions**   The following two sessions occur simultaneously. Each family goes to both. The simplest way to do this is to divide families according to the ages of their children — i.e., those with children third grade and below start with study, then go to skills, and vice versa. Families with children in both age groups have to decide on their own which order works best for them.

1. Shabbat Study – Since it is traditional to study the Torah portion for the coming week on Shabbat afternoon, the Shabbat study session should center around this. Be prepared to divide families into groups according to the ages of the children. For families with younger children, focus the study around storytelling, a puppet show, or a dramatization. For families with intermediate aged children and above, use the slide-tape presentation *Torah Toons*, the book *Sedra Scenes* by Stan J. Beiner, or actual primary text materials from the *Chumash* and *Midrash*.

2. *Havdalah* Skills – At this session, families review the *brachot* for *Havdalah*, learn about the symbols of *Havdalah*, and the melodies for the service. Allow families time to reflect about Shabbat in their lives and why it is necessary to make a separation between Shabbat and the rest of the week. Give

each family a handout with the *Havdalah* service and background material about *Havdalah*.

**Seudah Shleesheet**    While enjoying the *Seudah Shleesheet* meal, engage families in singing *niggunim* and ask different people to read or tell Shabbat stories.

**Services: Minchah/Ma'ariv and Havdalah**    Bring everyone together for *Minchah/Ma'ariv* services. Conduct these services in the sanctuary or, weather permitting, outside on a patio or in an open area. At the *Havdalah* service which follows, families have an opportunity to practice the skills learned in the *Havdalah* skills session. It may be advisable to have an alternate activity for younger children while older children and parents are davening.

Chapter

## 20

**Editor's Comments**    This program lends itself to many alternate activities. For instance, study does not have to be limited to the portion of the week. Parents may examine the *halachot* of Shabbat and discuss them. Other texts about Shabbat may be used, such as writings from the medieval commentators, or more modern writings by such authors as Kaplan, Heschel, Wiesel, Singer, etc. An article worthy of discussion in a Jewish periodical can be the stimulus for study.

Robin Eisenberg of Temple Beth El, Boca Raton, Florida, suggests family skits. In advance, write on 3 ″ x 5 ″ cards simple situations which families can act out together. Some examples are:

Pretend:
You are preparing a Shabbat meal.
You are a *challah*, first the dough, then rising into a soft, golden loaf.
You are calling the Shabbat Bride on the phone. What is her response?

Say something:
I am _____. Every week we say "Shabbat Shalom," which means Sabbath peace. To me, Sabbath peace means _____.

My name is _____. On Shabbat I feel good because
_____.

Another way to do this is through paper bag dramatics. Into grocery bags place eight to ten items. Be sure to combine Jewish artifacts, along with articles of clothing, household things, tools. Anything goes. Tell families to create a skit about Shabbat, during which the whole family participates and each item in the bag is used.

Another activity suggested by Ms. Eisenberg is "Shabbat has kept Israel." Provide families with quotes about Shabbat, such as:

"More than Israel has kept the Sabbath, the Sabbath has kept Israel" (Ahad Ha'am).

"Remember the Sabbath day to keep it holy" (Exodus 20:8).

Chapter
20

Ask families to consider what the quotes mean to them and comment on them, then have them create a quote that is meaningful for their own family. Families should share their comments and quotes with the rest of the group.

The program may be varied in other ways as well. It may be held at a time other than Shabbat afternoon. Families can come together to make *Havdalah* sets, to learn the skills of *Havdalah*, and to engage in study.

## Bibliography/Resources
See the bibliography for Chapter 7, "The Joy Of Shabbat."

# Chapter 21

 **TITLE:** Family Education Day In Mitzvahland

 **CONTRIBUTED BY:** Sharon Katz, Robert E. Tornberg, and Annette Fish

 **DESIGNED BY:** Annette Fish

 **TOPIC:** Personalizing *mitzvot*

 **TARGET AUDIENCE:** Families with children in Grades K-6

 **TIME FRAME:** One 2-4 hour session

 **STAFF:** One coordinator and assistants for each station

**Overview**  This school-wide program utilizes several stations to focus on *mitzvot*. Families have the opportunity to learn or relearn about *mitzvot* in Jewish tradition and to choose to do particular *mitzvot* with their families. The program provides interactional and hands-on activities.

**Purpose**  The purpose of the program is to help parents and children understand and identify the concept of *mitzvah* and to help them choose to do certain *mitzvot*.

**Preparation/Procedure**  The program is designed for families with children in Kindergarten through Grade 6. It can be adapted for smaller groups or for specific grade levels. It is set up in such a way that families stay together throughout the day.

Several classrooms are set up as "*mitzvah* stations." A large room or outside area may be used instead. In each station is some printed background material and information about a particular *mitzvah*. Be sure to provide a folder for each family in which to collect this printed matter. Families will enjoy decorating the folder and personalizing it.

It is important to have a knowledgeable person at each station. Utilize the teaching staff or community volunteers. Be sure to orient these individuals both as to the overall program and as to their individual stations.

**Program Description**  This program may take from two to four hours, depending on whether or not a meal is included. The meal or snack serves to help families focus on *mitzvot* as they recite the appropriate blessings before and after eating. The number of stations will depend on the length of time available for the program and the number of participants.

It is advisable to have an opening and closing activity for the day. The opening segment should orient everyone to the program by providing an overview of the activities and procedures. The closure should bring people together again and allow them to share their experiences.

**Stations**   Here are some suggestions for *mitzvah* stations:
1. Kiddush – Create a family *Kiddush* cup (4 stops within the station). Give each family a large glass goblet. Have families move with it from one stop to another. The three stops are the three themes of the *Kiddush* – creation, redemption, and revelation. At the creation stop, review the story of creation. At the redemption stop, retell the story of the Exodus from Egypt. Then move on to the revelation stop and discuss how the Torah was given to the Jewish People. At each of these three stops, provide the families with the appropriate section of the *Kiddush*. After visiting each stop, participants add a design to their cup which reflects that section of the *Kiddush*. Use non-toxic permanent marking pens. At a fourth stop, practice singing the *Kiddush*.

2. Candles and Challah (2 stops within the station) – At the first stop, provide background material about candle lighting. Discuss why we light a minimum of two candles and why it is traditional to cover our eyes. Teach the blessing for lighting the candles.

Chapter

# 21

At the second stop, provide background material about *challah*. Discuss the reason we cover the *challah*, why there are two *challot* on the Shabbat table, and why they are braided. Recite the blessing over *challah*. Compare the formula for this blessing with the blessing over candles. Point out that a *mitzvah* blessing requires an action. At this station you may also include some of the following activities at additional stops: Making Shabbat candlesticks, braiding or baking *challah*, making a *challah* cover or *challah* board.

3. Tzedakah (one required stop, several optional stops) – At the first stop, families should receive background materials about *gemilut chasadim* and *tzedakah*. Have a general discussion about the two concepts. Include in your discussion the concept of *tzedakah* as justice.

Give each family a copy of Maimonides' eight levels of *tzedakah*. Ask them to discuss how their *tzedakah* activities correspond to the various levels. This station provides information on various *mitzvot* — rescuing captives, feeding the hungry, respecting elders, lending money to the needy, caring for orphans, strangers, etc. At each stop denote the particular *mitzvah* or *mitzvot* to be studied. Once the preliminary discussion is completed, families may select those other stops which interest them. Some suggestions are:

a. Have a display of various *tzedakah* boxes. Provide materials to make a family *tzedakah* box. Have families decide when (on a regular basis) they will put money in the *tzedakah* box.

b. Compile a list of people in your community who would benefit from personal contact with the families. Some examples are: Individuals in nursing homes, single people (young and old) who would welcome a Shabbat or holiday dinner invitation, a person needing tutoring in a particular subject, individuals for whom a phone call on a regular basis (once a week or once a month) would be meaningful, someone who has no transportation to get to synagogue or to an important appointment, a family that is bereaved. Ask families to review the list and make a family contract to act on one or more of the opportunities presented.

c. Have information available about various causes or agencies which require communal support, such as: American Association for Ethiopian Jews, local Soviet Jewry Committee, Jewish Family Service, Mazon. Ask families to develop a campaign demonstrating how they will go about publicizing the cause they adopt and methods of raising funds for it.

d. Talmud Torah (Ongoing Study) – At this station have a facilitator available to lead the family in some type of study. The content may range from the portion of the week to other primary source texts — Talmud, *Midrash*, *Responsa*, simple stories, newspaper articles, etc. Conduct a guided discussion during which families can glean a lesson from the material. When the study is completed, the facilitator discusses the *mitzvah* of *Talmud Torah* with the families. Focus on how families now have Jewish study in their lives and how they can increase it. Provide a packet of materials for families to take home and study. This can include a short text piece, along with questions for discussion.

Chapter

21

**Editor's Comments**    In a school-wide program, it is necessary to have a variety of activities at each station so that families can participate in those which are new to them. Directing the program to specific age levels automatically limits the kinds of activities and the content levels. Ms. Fish originally set up 12 stations for her program.

A values clarification exercise or similar whole group activity enables families to process what they have learned and to decide how to implement *mitzvot* in their own lives. This also ends the day on a positive note.

If desired, *mitzvot* can be put into categories — e.g., Shabbat, interpersonal relations, holidays, etc. Provide a page or a packet of pre-printed coupons, each of which list specific *mitzvot*, such as lighting Shabbat candles, visiting a sick friend, inviting someone for Shabbat dinner, building a *sukkah*, hearing the *Megillah* read on Purim. Leave some coupons blank so that families can fill them in for themselves — be kind to my brother/sister, read and discuss a Shabbat story together, have a family *chametz* hunt, etc. — when they go home. Families and children can be very creative in response to such instructions. Collect the coupons in school. When you have collected the desired number (25 or 50 for a class), hold a special event — a group visit to a home for the aged for a party; a special program in class, such as a movie day or a party; cooking as a group and donating the food to a children's shelter, etc.

Chapter

21

## Bibliography/Resources

Chill, Abraham. *The Mitzvot: The Commandments and Their Rationale.* Jerusalem: Keter Publishing House, 1974.

Grishaver, Joel, and Huppin, Beth. *Tzedakah, Gemilut Chasadim and Ahavah: A Manual for World Repair.* Denver: Alternatives in Religious Education, Inc., 1983.

Millgram, Abraham. *Sabbath: Day Of Delight.* Philadelphia: Jewish Publication Society, 1965.

Neusner, Jacob. *Mitzvah.* Chappaqua, NY: Rossel Books, 1981.

Siegel, Richard; Strassfeld, Michael; and Strassfeld, Sharon, eds. *The First Jewish Catalog*. Philadelphia: Jewish Publication Society, 1973.

Strassfeld, Sharon, and Strassfeld, Michael, eds. *The Third Jewish Catalog*. Philadelphia, The Jewish Publication Society, 1980.

**Mediated Materials**
Grishaver, Joel. *Profiles In Chesed*. Los Angeles: Torah Aura Productions, 1983. (slide-tape presentation, 20 min.)

Chapter
# 21

# Chapter 22

 **TITLE:** Come Let Us Bless

 **CONTRIBUTED BY:** Janice Alper

 **TOPIC:** *Birkot Hanehenin* (blessings of the senses), *Birkot HaMitzvah* (blessings that are a *mitzvah*), and *Birkot Hoda'ah* (thanks-creating blessings)

 **TARGET AUDIENCE:** Families with children in Grade 4

 **TIME FRAME:** 1-1½ hours

 **STAFF:** One facilitator (classroom teacher), 2 assistants

**Overview**   This is a program to introduce various kinds of blessing to families. It is designed to show parents and children that, in the Jewish tradition, we praise God for providing us with wonderful things, some unusual, some commonplace. Using stations, individual families move at their own pace. During the course of the program, a blessing book is compiled so that the learning experiences can be transferred to the home.

**Purpose**   The goal of the program is to acquaint participants with various kinds of Jewish blessings.

**Preparation/Procedure**   First, it is necessary to collect the appropriate materials for the stations. Have enough copies available for the anticipated number of people. Provide staff with an overview of the program and define their specific responsibilities. Remember that people learn through a variety of modalities. For this reason, you may wish to record on tape the blessings which they will recite in the stations, as well as have them available in print. It is also a good idea to have the blessings written in Hebrew and transliteration, and to supply the appropriate translations.

Chapter

# 22

The physical setting should consist of an area large enough to accommodate three stations at which people may gather in groups and also a separate working area for each family. The facilitator should be prepared to move people along smoothly and to answer any questions that arise.

**Program Description**   Before participants engage in the activities of the stations, bring them together in one place for an overview of the day. Begin by having a service at the start of the day. Invite everyone to share in this experience. Follow with a discussion about why Jews have worship services, and the Jewish tradition of blessing as a way of thanking God for the goodness we receive. Then proceed to the stations as follows:

### The Stations
Station I: *Birkot Hanehenin* (Blessings Of the Senses)
Teacher prepares items for this station which appeal to the

senses: Different kinds of foods; things with aromas, such as flowers, a spice box, or perfume; mounted pictures of a rainbow, a king or queen, rain; a teacher-made cassette tape of something newsworthy, either good or bad news. For each set of items, provide the appropriate blessings. These may be excerpted from *The First Jewish Catalog* edited by Richard Siegel, Michael Strassfeld, and Sharon Strassfeld or *Higher and Higher* by Steven M. Brown. Place the following instructions and handout in the station for each family to read:

### STATION I – BIRKOT HANEHENIN
### Instructions

At this station you will see many different things. Look them over together. You may handle them if you wish. Next, as a family, decide what all of these have in common. Then complete the activities on the handout about *Birkot Hanehenin*. To help you, there is a sheet containing the appropriate blessings.

### HANDOUT (FOR STATION I)
### Birkot Hanehenin

Taste
Each family takes an apple, a piece of bread, and a carrot. There is enough for each family member. Refer to the blessings provided in the blessings sheet and find the appropriate blessing for each of these items. Why do you suppose there is a different blessing for different foods?

Smell
Smell the spice box, the flowers, and the perfume. What is the blessing said for each one? (Refer to the blessings sheet.)

Sight
Look at all the pictures that are in this station. Each one represents something different. Look them all over and recite the appropriate blessing for each one. (Refer to the blessings sheet.)

Hearing
Listen to the tape of the news. Recite the appropriate blessing

for each thing you heard about. (Refer to the blessings sheet.) Now that you have responded to all the items at Station I, please find a quiet place to discuss the significance of all these *brachot*. You may want to consider why we have blessings or benedictions for specific things and how all of these blessings represent our response to God's world. You may summarize your discussion below.

Now you are ready to go on to Station II, *Birkot HaMitzvah*.

Station II: *Birkot HaMitzvah* (Blessings That Are a Mitzvah) Teacher prepares a display of things which require a *mitzvah* blessing. Some items you may collect are Shabbat candles, *tallit*, *shofar, chanukiah, matzah, lulav* and *etrog*, etc. It is a good idea to limit the number of items to four. Once again, provide in the station a handout containing the appropriate blessings for each item. Place the following instruction sheet in the station:

**Chapter 22**

STATION II – BIRKOT HAMITZVAH
Instructions

There are four symbols on this table. Each requires an action that is a *mitzvah* to perform. For each action there is a specific blessing. First, list the action required for each symbol. Then recite the blessing associated with each action.

| SYMBOL | ACTION |
|---|---|
| Shabbat Candles | _____ |
| *Tallit* | _____ |
| *Shofar* | _____ |
| *Lulav* and *etrog* | _____ |

What is the difference between blessings that are a *mitzvah* and *Birkot Hanehenin*? Write your answer below:

Now you may proceed to Station III, *Birkot Hoda'ah*.

Station III: Birkot Hoda'ah (Blessings Of Thanksgiving)
At this station participants will focus on things for which they

are thankful. Prior to introducing the blessings, give out the following worksheet and handout:

WORKSHEET – STATION III
Birkot Hoda'ah

Please list ten things for which your family is thankful.

1.

2.

3.

4.

5.

6.

7.

8.

9.

10.

Now you may proceed to the next station.

STATION III — BIRKOT HODA'AH
Instructions

*Birkot Hoda'ah* are blessings which are intended to praise, petition, and express gratitude to God. Examples of such blessings — *Birkot HaShachar* (Morning Benedictions), *Birkat HaMazon*, (the blessings after the meal), *Shehecheyanu*, and the Torah blessings — may be found on the blessings sheet.

1. What formula is used in these blessings?

Chapter

# 22

2. Look over the Torah Blessings.
   What words are used in the blessings to praise?
   For what are we expressing thanks?

Now you may proceed to Station IV, Creating Personal Blessings.


Station IV: Creating Personal Blessings
This station provides an opportunity for families to create personal blessings. Provide the following instructions, along with material about how we create prayer. (A good reference is *Bechol Levavcha* by Harvey Fields.)

STATION IV – CREATING PERSONAL BLESSINGS
Instructions

**Chapter**

# 22

By now you probably realize that, as Jews, we express appreciation through *brachot*.

We have examined three types of blessings today — *Birkot Hanehenin*, *Birkot HaMitzvah*, and *Birkot Hoda'ah*. Each of these blessings represent our response to God's world. Now it is time for your family to compose a blessing or a prayer which reflects your personal response to God's world. It may be a blessing of thanks, praise, petition, or action, or it may even contain all of these elements. If you choose to write a blessing, make up your own new formula for the blessing. Once you have completed this exercise, try to determine when you might use your blessing or prayer in your family life.

When all participants have completed all of the stations, gather the whole group together to conclude the program. Invite families to share reactions and to share the blessings they wrote if they so desire. You may also wish to end with a story or some music.

**Editor's Comments**   This program was designed to tie in with a fourth grade curriculum that focuses on personal choices, values, identity, and prayer. It can be altered in a variety of ways. For younger children there are books and songs which can help families focus on blessings. (Examples of such books are *Prayer*

•

*Is Reaching* by Howard Bogot and Daniel B. Syme and *Prayers and Blessings* by Miriam Schlein. An appropriate song is "We Say *Shehecheyanu.*")

One way to carry out this program is to separate parents and children after the initial orientation and have each group focus on a discussion about God. When they come together again, they can discuss their views of God and talk about why we bless God for the things we have.

The program may also be restructured to introduce the concept of prayer, why we pray, and how we pray. Various *tefillot* from the Shabbat service may be substituted for the individual blessings. Structuring it in this manner also allows for a discussion of God. A consideration of Shabbat as a day of rest and prayer may also be included.

A variation of this program planned in conjunction with a Shabbat morning service will introduce the structure of the service to those unfamiliar with it and reinforce the conceptual elements of the service for those with a basic familiarity. The service can be divided into three core elements: The *Shema* and its blessings represent the oneness of Israel, Creation, and reverence for God. The *Tefillah* reinforces the concept of *Kedushah* (holiness), what it means to be holy, how we can strive to be holy. The Torah service links us to our history by recreating the Exodus from Egypt and the giving of the Torah. Participants can walk through stations representing parts of the service (similar to the Blessing stations). At each station they learn the concepts of the core elements of the service. As a culmination, participants come together for a service which includes an opportunity to reflect on discoveries made in the activity centers.

Chapter

## 22

## Bibliography/Resources

Birnbaum, Philip. *Daily Prayer Book.* New York: Hebrew Publishing Co., 1949.

Bogot, Howard. *I Learn About God.* New York: Union of American Hebrew Congregations, 1982.

Bogot, Howard, and Syme, Daniel B. *Prayer Is Reaching.* New York: Union of American Hebrew Congregations, 1981.

Brichto, Mira. *The God Around Us*. New York: Union of American Hebrew Congregations, 1958.

Brown, Steven M. *Higher and Higher: Making Jewish Prayer Part Of Us*. New York: United Synagogue of America, Department of Youth Activities, 1979.

Cone, Molly. *Hear O Israel*. Book 4, *About God*. New York: Union of American Hebrew Congregations, *1973*.

————. *Hear O Israel*. Book 1, *First I Say the Shema*. New York: Union of American Hebrew Congregations, 1971.

Fields, Harvey J. *Bechol Levavcha: With All Your Heart*. New York: Union of American Hebrew Congregations, 1976.

Garfiel, Evelyn. *The Service Of the Heart*. New York: The Burning Bush Press, 1958.

*Gates Of Prayer: The New Union Prayerbook*. New York: Central Conference of American Rabbis, 1975.

Klein, Isaac. *A Guide To Jewish Religious Practice*. New York: The Jewish Theological Seminary of America, 1979.

Kushner, Harold. *When Children Ask About God*. New York: Reconstructionist Press, 1971.

Millgram, Abraham. *Jewish Worship*. Philadelphia: Jewish Publication Society, 1971.

Rossel, Seymour. *When a Jew Prays*. New York: Behrman House, 1973.

Schlein, Miriam. *Prayers and Blessings*. New York: Behrman House, 1983.

Siegel, Richard; Strassfeld, Michael; and Strassfeld, Sharon, eds. *The First Jewish Catalog*. Philadelphia: Jewish Publication Society, 1973.

Chapter

22

Soncino, Rifat, and Syme, Daniel B. *Finding God: Ten Jewish Responses*. New York: Union of American Hebrew Congregations, 1986.

**Mediated Materials**
*Byron Bee Looks for God*. Polansky Association, P.O. Box 6369, Silver Spring, MD 20906. (videocassette or slides, 16 min.)

Chapter

# 22

# Chapter 23

 **TITLE:** Create Your Own Jewish Heirlooms

 **CONTRIBUTED BY:** Carol K. Ingall

 **DESIGNED BY:** Minna Ellison, Ruth Ross, and Carol K. Ingall

 **TOPIC:** The value of creating personal heirlooms which enhance family holiday celebrations

 **TARGET AUDIENCE:** Families with children in Grades 3-6; any size group

 **TIME FRAME:** One 1½-2 hour session

 **STAFF:** 2 facilitators, 2 assistants

**Overview**   The Bureau of Jewish Education of Rhode Island facilitates a series of holiday workshops for the community. These take place on an ongoing basis. Each has a specific focus. "Create Your Own Jewish Heirlooms" is one such workshop. It is aimed at families who have children 8-11 years old. Through the creation by each family of a Jewish "heirloom," the celebration of the holiday or festival is enhanced.

**Purpose**   The primary function of this holiday workshop is to promote more involvement with the holiday and to provide direction for further study.

Chapter

23

**Preparation/Procedure**   The workshops are held in various congregations throughout the community. The agency staff is trained to teach others how to create a family heirloom for a specific holiday. Staff members are briefed by the host congregation about the nature of their group, their level of observance, and their level of participation. With this information, the staff can prepare an appropriate presentation for the participants.

A host congregation is expected to publicize the program to its constituency. The congregation provides the physical setting, refreshments, and pays a set fee per family to the Bureau of Jewish Education. The Bureau provides a professional educator, supplies, and handouts containing information about the holiday selected.

**Program Description**   Families come together for a brief activity during which they introduce themselves to each other. Since the focus of the day is on creating family heirlooms, it works well to have each person introduce himself/herself and then describe a favorite Jewish object. Another way to do this is to have each participant say one thing he/she likes about the specific holiday under discussion. A third suggestion is for each group member to talk about a personal memory of the specific holiday.

After the introductory activity, the facilitator provides background information about the holiday. This may be done by reviewing the contents of a specific booklet or of handouts which will be sent home, by reading a story, or by viewing a videotape, filmstrip, or movie.

The facilitator goes on to discuss heirlooms. Points to consider in the discussion are: What is an heirloom? What kinds of heirlooms do you have in your home? Why create an heirloom? This discussion will be enhanced by bringing in heirlooms from people's homes, or from museums, or even pictures of heirlooms.

Provide an opportunity for families to sit together to plan their creations. Once this is done, help them select the medium they will use. For example, to make *chanukiot*, provide clay, tin, or plaster of paris; for calendars provide canvas and paint, wood, or cloth; for *challah* boards provide stones for a mosaic, sheets of plexiglass and permanent markers, or china dishes and non-toxic paints. Allow families enough time to complete their heirlooms, but be sure to have an alternate activity or project for families who finish before the others.

Chapter

23

When all the heirlooms are finished, bring the group together. Have each family share its creation. Ask them to tell what they expect for the holiday and what they hope will happen to the "heirloom" as time goes on.

**Editor's Comments**    This program, while an excellent project for a Central Agency to initiate, can also be sponsored by a particular religious school or congregation. Such a program could take place throughout a one or two year period, so that all the holidays are covered and everyone has an heirloom created specifically for each holiday. The program may also be adapted for life cycle events.

It is important that families actually use the heirlooms they have created. Provide opportunities for them to do so at Shabbat dinners, school or community *Sedarim*, Purim feasts, or meals in the *sukkah*. When inviting families to these events, remind them to bring the heirlooms they have made.

A good additional project is to create a history of the heirlooms. As part of the creative process, families can make booklets containing background information about the holiday and the special traditions, customs, blessings, etc., associated with it. They should take an instant photograph of their heirloom and paste it into their booklets with a description that includes when it was made, by whom, the materials used, and its physical features. Add several blank pages in the booklets for families to record the occasions when they use the heirloom and any special feelings or thoughts they have when they do so.

This program can be enhanced still further through the creation of a "museum." Ask congregants to bring in real family heirlooms and talk about them to the group or put them in a display area for a limited period of time with appropriate explanations. Representatives of a local Jewish museum may also be asked to come and facilitate a discussion about heirlooms and Jewish artifacts.

For a related program, see Chapter 24, "Exploring Jewish Roots Via Wimpel Making."

## Bibliography/Resources

Resources for this program will depend on which holiday is chosen. The following are recommended for general use:

Becker, Joyce. *Jewish Holiday Crafts*. New York: Bonim Books, 1978.

_____. *Hanukkah Crafts*. New York, Bonim Books, 1977.

Kanof, Abram. *Jewish Ceremonial Art and Religious Observance*. New York: Harry N. Abrams, Inc., n.d.

Kelman, Victoria, ed. *Together: A Parent-Child Kit* . New York: Melton Research Center, 1984.

Rockland, Mae Shafter. *The Work Of Our Hands*. New York: Schocken, 1973.

Sharon, Ruth. *Arts and Crafts the Year Round*. Vols. I & II. New York: United Synagogue Commission on Jewish Education, 1965.

Chapter

23

Springer, Selma and Friends. *Designs Of Judaica: A Needle Art Handbook*. Santa Monica, CA: SIMCHA, 1986.

Ungerleider-Mayerson, Joy. *Jewish Folk Art: From Biblical Days To Modern Times*. New York: Summit Books, 1986.

Chapter

23

# Chapter 24

 **TITLE:** Exploring Our Jewish Roots Via Wimpel Making

 **CONTRIBUTED BY:** Debra Cohn-Levine

 **DESIGN:** Based on a program originally designed by Linda Thal, Leo Baeck Temple, Los Angeles

 **TOPIC:** Consecration and *Brit Toledot* - tracing family traditions

 **TARGET AUDIENCE:** Families with children entering a new phase of Jewish education (Kindergarten or Grades 3 and 4)

 **TIME FRAME:** 2-3 hours plus ceremony

 **STAFF:** Facilitator

**Overview**   The family wimpel project takes place prior to Consecration for children in Kindergarten, or before the *Brit Toledot* ceremony, a Hebrew naming celebration for students who are beginning formal Hebrew studies in Grades 3 and 4. It is designed to enable the exploration of the concepts of *kedushah* and the importance of naming to Jewish identity, as well as to facilitate the development of personal relationships with Torah. In a session just for parents, the significance of Consecration and *Brit Toledot* is discussed. Parents and students then come together to make a wimpel which will be on display in the synagogue at the time of the Consecration or *Brit Toledot* ceremony. Participating families are encouraged to make the wimpel into a family heirloom which will be used to wrap the Torah at the child's Bar or Bat Mitzvah ceremony and at other significant religious occasions in the child's life.

Chapter

# 24

**Purpose**   The purpose of the program is to help parents focus on their links with Jewish tradition through names given to their children, as well as to connect with the Jewish future of their families. It is also designed to help parents make a stronger commitment to the Jewish education of their children.

**Preparation/Procedure**   Determine the appropriate grade level for this project. If the focus is on Consecration, it will most likely be geared to Kindergarten and Grade 1. If the focus is on *Brit Toledot*, it will probably be geared to Grades 3 or 4. Once this decision is made, send out a letter describing the program, along with a naming form which is to be returned to the synagogue. A sample of this form follows.

NAMING FORM

Child's name: _____    _____
                    English                        Hebrew

Named after whom (or for what reason was this name chosen):
_____
_____

Child's date of birth: _____    _____
                          Month/Day/Year              Time of Birth

Child's Mother's name: _____     _____
                              English            Hebrew
Named after whom (or for what reason was this name chosen):
_____
_____

Child's Father's name: _____     _____
                              English            Hebrew
Named after whom (or for what reason was this name chosen):
_____
_____

If you or your child(ren) have not been given Hebrew names, we
can help you select one if you fill in as much of the above information as possible. Indicate below your preference in selecting
a Hebrew name:

_____ That it has the same first initial as my English name.

_____ That it has a comparable meaning to my English name.

Chapter

# 24

(For example: Someone with the name Leonard might have been
given the Hebrew name Levi because of the sound similarity, or
the Hebrew name Aryeh, because Aryeh and Leonard both
mean "lion.")

We will _____ will not _____ be able to attend the family
naming program on (insert date). Bear in mind that your child
will be unable to work on the project without at least one
parent present.

_____
             Parent(s) Signature

In order to make the wimpel, collect the following materials:

   Strips of muslin

   Glad Rags Fabric Markers or fabric paint

   Metallic markers (gold and silver)

   Hebrew and English cut-out letters (3″ for tracing) or
   Hebrew and English stencils

   Pictures of Jewish symbols and objects

*The Name Dictionary* by Alfred J. Kolatch

*A Dictionary Of Jewish Names and Their History* by Ben Zion Kaganoff

*The Standard Guide To the Jewish and Civil Calendars*

Compile a list of participants and write down their Hebrew names and birthdates. Stencil or write these on to the wimpels in advance. This may be done with a soft lead pencil. Be aware that some children may not have Hebrew names. If this is the case, help the families to choose a name, or simply spell out their child's English name in Hebrew characters.

Prepare Consecration or *Brit Toledot* certificates to be presented to the children at the appropriate ceremony. Discuss with the Rabbi when the ceremony will take place and what the parents and children will do at the service.

Chapter

24

If at all possible, obtain a sample of a wimpel for display purposes. Prepare the necessary materials for each station. For Station I you will need a tape of the *Shehecheyanu* for parents to listen to, an instruction sheet, pens and pencils. For Station II you will need copies of the Kolatch and Kaganoff name dictionaries, an instruction sheet, pens and pencils. For Station III you will need copies of *The Fabric Of Jewish Life* by Barbara Kirshenblatt-Gimblett and Cissy Grossman and *Designs Of Judaica* by Selma Springer and friends, an instruction sheet, pens and pencils. Prepare the instruction sheets for each station. Examples of these sheets follow:

STATION I
Instruction Sheet

Listen to the tape and practice saying the *Shehecheyanu*. (Remember to rewind the tape for the next group.)

*Shehecheyanu*
*Baruch Atah Adonai Eloheynu Melech Haolam Shehecheyanu V'kiyemanu V'higiyanu Lazman Hazeh.*
Blessed are You, O Eternal our God, Ruler of the universe, for

giving us life, for sustaining us, and for enabling us to reach this season.

List three occasions on which you have used or would like to use the *Shehecheyanu* with your family:

1.

2.

3.

STATION II
Instruction Sheet

In the name dictionaries, look up your child's name, your name, that of your spouse, and your family name. Jot these definitions down, then when your child arrives, explain the history and meaning of his/her Hebrew name. Practice saying the name with him/her.

Chapter

**24**

My child's name means _____
_____

My name means _____
_____

My spouse's name means _____
_____

Our family name(s) mean(s) _____
_____

STATION III
Instruction Sheet

1. Look at the wimpels in the books *The Fabric Of Jewish Life* (pp. 19 and 97) and *Designs Of Judaica* (pp. 15 and 16).

2. Jot down three wishes you would like to add to your child's wimpel. The three traditional wishes are: May this child grow up to a life of Torah, *chupah* (wedding canopy), and *ma'asim tovim* (good deeds). Use these and/or make up your own wishes. Be creative!

a.

b.

c.

3. Use the list of suggestions below to aid you in designing your wimpel.

a.   Illustrate the meanings of the names.

b.   Illustrate the three wishes.

c.   Add the astrological sign.

d.   Add a symbol or symbols of the 12 tribes of Israel.

e.   Add Jewish ritual objects.

f.   Add symbols of hobbies, family traditions, occupations.

g.   Add anything that describes the life and personality of the child and family.

h.   Add the English name and birthdate and illustrate these.

Chapter

24

i.   Add a border-trim.

j.   Add the symbols of the holiday falling in the month of birth.

k.   Look up the Torah portion and *Haftarah* of the week your child was born. Draw symbols which describe their contents or use quotes from them.

l.   Look up the day of the week on which your child was born. Then look at Chapter 1 of Genesis and illustrate what was created on that day.

m. Make drawings based on the "Psalm of the day" for the day of the week on which your child was born (see the traditional *Siddur*).

n. Make an acrostic out of your child's name by finding verses which begin with each letter of his/her name.

o. Find and use a verse in the Bible which contains your child's name.

**Program Description**   The program has three parts: a parents meeting, wimpel making, and a Consecration or *Brit Toledot* ceremony. Each of these parts is discussed below.

**Parents' Meeting** (one hour, while children are in class)

1. Discussion of Consecration or *Brit Toledot* with reference to:

a. *Kedushah/Shehecheyanu*

b. Naming

c. Relationship with Torah

   d. *Wimpels* as a concrete expression of *Kedushah* and
      naming.

2. Stations – each station contains a worksheet, examples of
   which appear previously in the Preparation/Procedure section. The stations are:
   a. Station I: Review or learn *Shehecheyanu.*
   b. Station II: Look up names of family members.
   c. Station III: Look at wimpels and write three wishes for
      your child's wimpel.

**Wimpel Making** (one hour)
1. Parents and children do this together. Set up tables with
   materials which one or two families can share.

2. If names and birthdates have not been stenciled onto the
   wimpels, they are put on now.

3. Parents and children draw pictures which reflect the meanings
   of their names.

4. Parents write the three wishes for their children on the
   wimpels.

5. Everyone colors in the letters and names stenciled or drawn
   on the wimpels.

Chapter

24

**Consecration or Brit Toledot Ceremony**   Consecration or
the *Brit Toledot* may be held as part of a Shabbat morning or Friday evening service. Parents bring the wimpels and display them
in the sanctuary. At some time during the service, families are
called on to explain to the congregation the wimpel they have
made. Parents may also recite a special blessing, say the *Shehecheyanu,* or write personal notes to their children for this
ceremony.

**Editor's Comments** Making wimpels is a pleasant and
meaningful way for a family to link itself with its Jewish roots.
In this program the wimpels are prepared for a particular
ceremony. It may be valuable to include a way to present the
wimpels to the children at some time during the ceremony,
either by draping them around the children or by handing them

their wimpel wrapped as a gift. Some families may wish to show and explain their wimpels to the congregation.

If desired, provide a time for families to complete their wimpels at a follow-up session, since families may not have the appropriate materials at home. If everything is stenciled or drawn onto the muslin in advance, the children can color or paint the wimpels in class.

Provide for children whose parents do not attend the program. Set a time and date by which to have the naming forms returned. At this point it is necessary to call those who have not responded and obtain the information on the phone. If parents indicate they will not be present for the program, suggest that they send an older sibling or grandparent. Have aides available to assist those children who do not have family members with them.

Chapter

24

Set up a fourth station for parents and children together as an activity that looks to the future. Families can imagine future occasions when the wimpel might be used for the child. They can also talk about where they will keep or display the wimpel between celebrations. As an additional follow-up activity, make a decorative box in which to store the wimpel safely.

The Hebrew Union College Skirball Museum of Los Angeles has a large collection of wimpels. The collection is available as slides for a nominal fee. (See Bibliography/Resources for the address.)

The wimpels that are created in the program outlined here can be used as a means for tracing family roots. Parents and children can create a wimpel for every member of the family to show the chain of tradition. They can keep records of each time the wimpel is used in a life cycle ceremony, thus enabling the family to focus on the chain of tradition.

For a related program, see Chapter 23, "Create Your Own Jewish Heirlooms."

## Bibliography/Resources

Kaganoff, Benzion C. *A Dictionary Of Jewish Names and Their History.* New York: Schocken Books, 1977.

Kirshenblatt-Gimblett, Barbara, and Grossman, Cissy. *The Fabric Of Jewish Life: Textiles From the Jewish Museum Collection*. Vol. 1. New York: The Jewish Museum, 1977.

Kolatch, Alfred J. *The Name Dictionary*. New York: Jonathan David, 1967.

Springer, Selma, and Friends. *Designs Of Judaica: A Needleart Handbook*. Santa Monica, CA: Simcha, 1986. (P.O. Box 5680, Santa Monica, CA 90405)

Strassfeld, Sharon, and Green, Kathy, eds. *The Jewish Family Book*. New York: Bantam Books, 1981.

Strassfeld, Sharon, and Strassfeld, Michael, eds. *The Second Jewish Catalog*. Philadelphia: Jewish Publication Society, 1976.

Ungerleider-Mayerson, Joy. *Jewish Folk Art: From Biblical Days To Modern Times*. New York: Summit Books, 1986.

"What's In a Name." *Keeping Posted* 18, no. 1 (October, 1972).

Chapter

# 24

**Mediated Materials**
Slides Of Wimpels:
Media Resource Department
Hebrew Union College-Skirball Museum
3077 University Avenue
Los Angeles, CA 90007

# Chapter 25

 **TITLE:** And Let Them Make Me a Sanctuary

 **CONTRIBUTED BY:** Janice Alper

 **TOPIC:** The synagogue as a place of worship and as a communal institution

 **TARGET AUDIENCE:** Families with children in Grade 1

 **TIME FRAME:** 1½-2 hours

 **STAFF:** Classroom teacher, teacher's aide, Rabbi, Cantor, Director of Education, song leader, other individuals who help to make the synagogue function

**Overview**   This program was developed as a culmination to a unit of study on the synagogue. After intensive study and preparation, students "teach" their parents all that they have learned.

**Purpose**   The purpose of the program is to have parents become acquainted with the synagogue as if through the eyes of their children.

**Preparation/Procedure**   In anticipation of the forthcoming family day, students select the parts of their synagogue they wish to talk about and rehearse several times what they will say. A list of questions for parents is prepared and handed out by the teacher in order to elicit response from the children. Background materials are also prepared for the parents about the history of the synagogue.

**Program Description**   During the course of the year, the students study the synagogue by participating in services and by interviewing the Rabbi, Cantor, and Director of Education about their jobs and roles in synagogue and communal life. The students see first-hand how holidays are celebrated in the synagogue. Early in the year, they make a tour of the synagogue. At that time various people from the congregation tell them how the synagogue functions. They visit the sanctuary with the Rabbi and Cantor, the social hall and kitchen with a member of the Sisterhood as guide, the synagogue office, the preschool, the library, another class, etc.

Following the tour, several sessions are devoted to the various parts of the sanctuary. The Rabbi shows the students the *Sifrei Torah* and discusses them. The Rabbi explains the symbolism of the Holy Ark and calls all other significant aspects of the sanctuary to the attention of the students. Also, throughout the year, as each holiday occurs, there is a discussion in class about how it is celebrated both in the synagogue and at home. The students also visit another synagogue, so as to compare that building and its function with their own.

On the family day, parents are invited to come to school with their children. They first attend the school worship service with them. After services families introduce themselves to each other. The teacher then describes the program. He/she gives background about what the students have been studying and urges the parents to ask questions of the students during the program.

A tour of the synagogue follows with students acting as docents. The following areas of the synagogue are visited:

Sanctuary

Offices of the Rabbi, Cantor, Director of Education, and Administrator

Library

Youth Lounge

Preschool

Social Hall

Kitchen

Chapter

# 25

At each stop the student docent describes the events and activities that take place in that particular area and how these events and activities help to foster a synagogue community. Parents are encouraged to ask questions, either original or from the prepared list.

After the tour families come together to review what they have seen. If time permits, they build model synagogues or Holy Arks out of corrugated cartons or shoe boxes.

**Editor's Comments**    Originally designed to be integrated into a first grade curriculum, this program may also be adapted and used as an all-school program for families. This format may also be used to focus on synagogue functions, holidays, or life cycle events. It could also serve as an orientation program to the synagogue for potential members, new families, and non-Jewish visitors. In the latter instance, there should be special activities in each area for children and adults as they proceed through the building – e.g., learning a song in the the Cantor's office, hearing a story in the library, having a snack in the kitchen, looking at a *Sefer Torah* in the sanctuary, etc.

As an adjunct to the program, an educational element may be added which focuses on the history of the synagogue in Jewish life. This can be tied in with the history of a particular congregation with the help of the congregation's historian or a knowledgeable "old timer." Try to find pictures of synagogues from various periods of time to enhance the cognitive historical material. This material would make an idea exhibit with legends for each display item.

If the synagogue is involved in an Interfaith Council, the format described may serve as a means of educating the community about Judaism. In addition to the synagogue tour, one area of the building can be designated for activities and information on a specific Jewish holiday, Shabbat, or life cycle event.

Chapter

25

## Bibliography/Resources

Bogot, Howard I. *Yoni*. New York: Union of American Hebrew Congregations, 1982.

*Encyclopaedia Judaica*. "Synagogue." Vol. 15. Jerusalem: Keter Publishing House, 1971.

Freeman, Grace R. *Inside the Synagogue*. New York: Union of American Hebrew Congregations, 1963.

Friedman, Audrey, and Zwerin, Raymond A. *Our Synagogue*. Series A. New York: Behrman House, 1974.

Greenberg, Simon. *The Conservative Movement In Judaism*. New York: United Synagogue of America, n.d.

Jick, Leon. *The Americanization Of the Synagogue, 1820-1870*. Waltham, MA: Brandeis University Press, 1976.

Kaplan, Uri. *The Synagogue*. Jerusalem: Keter Publishing House, 1973.

Krinsky, Carol Herselle. *Synagogues Of Europe: Architecture, History, Meaning*. Cambridge, MA: The MIT Press, 1985.

*NATA/UAHC Temple Management Manual*. New York: Union of
   American Hebrew Congregations, 1984.

Weisser, Cantor Michael. *My Synagogue*, New York: Behrman
   House, 1984.

Chapter

25

# Chapter 26

 **TITLE:** Israel: Back To the Future

 **CONTRIBUTED BY:** Sandy Dashefsky and Judy Press

 **TOPIC:** A historical and cultural view of Israel

 **TARGET AUDIENCE:** Families with children of preschool age and up

 **TIME FRAME:** One session of 3 hours

 **STAFF:** Coordinator, facilitators for each station, music specialist, dance specialist, back up personnel

**Overview** "Israel: Back To the Future" is a one-day family education unit that culminates with a Yom HaAtzma'ut *Seder*. It involves an historical and a cultural approach to the study of Israel. The program consists of four stations — Back In Time, Heroes/Heroines Of Israel, Israel Today, and Next Year In Jerusalem. At each station families create something together which will be utilized in the *Seder*. Activities at each station are suitable for all family members from preschool and up.

**Purpose** The purpose of this program is to acquaint participants with various aspects of Israel, both historical and cultural. It allows families to learn about Israel from a variety of perspectives and to realize that Israel has a place in their lives.

Chapter

26

**Preparation/Procedure** Each station involves a variety of activities from which participants may choose. The preparation for each of the four stations and for the *Seder* is materials specified below:

Station I: Back In Time – Cut up a complete puzzle for each family.

Station II: Heroes/Heroines Of Modern Israel – Gather information about the various personalities.

Station III: Israel Today – Gather a variety of media, such as books, activity kits, filmstrips, slides, or videotapes. Other needs include: recipes and ingredients for food preparation and items for table and room decoration, such as scissors, glue, construction paper, poster board, markers, paint, glitter, fabric scraps, etc.

Station IV: Next Year In Jerusalem – Have available pencils, paper, styrofoam, cardboard boxes, glue, etc.

The *Seder* – Reproduce the outline of the *Seder* so that everyone will have a copy of it. Include the words to songs that will be sung. Also needed are: paper plates, cups, flatware, napkins, and wine or grape juice.

Orient the staff to the program. Place staff members at the different stations. At some stations two or three people may be needed. Instruct them to help participants. When there are choices of activities, remind staff members to guide participants toward choosing several different ones. The staff should include a music and a dance specialist.

Two areas are needed for this program, a large room for the *Seder* and another area for the stations. Each station can take place in individual classrooms if a second large area is not suitable.

Allow three hours for the program – 20-25 minutes in each station and one hour for the *Seder*. It is suggested that families team up to create groups of 4-6 people.

**Program Description**   The following are the handouts for each of the four stations:

Chapter

26

STATION I: BACK IN TIME
Handout

The Land of Israel has a long and diverse history. In biblical times it was called Canaan and Israel and Judah. Then it was called Palestine. Today, once again, it is called Israel. It is here in the Middle East that Jewish history began 4,000 years ago. Throughout these four millenia, Jews have maintained a presence in the Land. Even when we were dispersed and in exile, Israel was in our hearts and prayers. Although the land was repeatedly conquered, no other people ever attained independence there or saw it as the center of their peoplehood.

Use the puzzle pieces (see below) to learn about the long and complicated history of the Land of Israel. The puzzle comes in three layers. The top layer gives the dates of each of the major events in the history of Israel. The middle layer tells what these major events were. The bottom layer, with stars on each puzzle piece, tells about famous people, places, or things that are associated with each event. Put the three layers of the puzzle together and you will begin to appreciate the long path the Jews have traveled from the time that our ancestors lived in Canaan until the rebirth of the State of Israel in 1948. An example of such a puzzle follows, reduced in size.

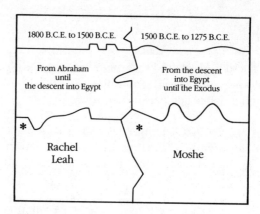

STATION II: HEROES/HEROINES OF MODERN ISRAEL
Handout

Many people played an important role in the founding of the State of Israel. Four of the most famous include: Theodor Herzl, Ahad Ha-Am, David Ben-Gurion, and Golda Meir. Each family should become a specialist on one of these heroes/heroines. Use the information provided at the station. Once your family knows all about its hero, choose *one* of the following activities to do as a family:

1. As the hero/heroine, prepare a one paragraph statement that tells who you are, and why you have accepted the invitation to be at our *Seder*.

2. As the hero/heroine, write a poem or song about yourself.

3. As the hero/heroine, write a riddle or quiz about yourself. *Seder* guests will try to guess who you are or what the answers to your quiz are.

4. Create a Coat of Arms for your hero/heroine which will be displayed at the *Seder*.

5. Publish a Chronicles-style newspaper for an important day in the life of your hero/heroine.

6. Each member of the family write an entry into a diary/journal as if you were:
   a. The hero/heroine
   b. The spouse or girlfriend/boyfriend of the hero/heroine
   c. The child or grandchild of the hero/heroine
   Note: Younger children can draw a scene from the life of the hero/heroine.

7. Get together with a family who is studying a different hero/heroine. Talk about the differences and similarities between your personalities.

8. While the heroes/heroines of Israel were helping to secure the soil of Israel, millions of their sisters and brothers were being murdered by the Nazis. Write a memorial tribute from your hero/heroine to these murdered Jews. Tell them about the work you have been doing for the new State of Israel which they never lived to see. (Perhaps if there had been a State of Israel when they were being persecuted, many lives might have been saved.)

## STATION III: ISRAEL TODAY
### Handout

Chapter

# 26

Today Israel is a modern nation that plays a key role in international affairs. Many excellent books, articles, filmstrips, videotapes, and films have been produced telling about life in Israel. In addition, many people visit Israel and take slides that give a good picture of life in Israel today. Select one media presentation from those provided to learn about life in Israel, then do one of the following activities for the *Seder*:

1. Prepare a dish to be eaten at the Yom HaAtzma'ut *Seder*. Some suggestions: falafel (frozen or from mix), humous, tehina, fruit soup, any unfrosted sheet cake (or cupcakes) to be decorated as a birthday cake for celebrating Yom HaAtzma'ut.

2. Make a travel poster to help turn the dining room into an Israeli-style *chadar ohel*.

3. Make a table centerpiece that depicts an aspect of life in Israel today.

4. Use magic markers to transform the paper tablecloths into a mural with an Israeli motif.

5. Make placemats depicting life in Israel today.

6. Make namecards with an Israeli theme on them.

STATION IV: NEXT YEAR IN JERUSALEM
Handout

Since the destruction of the Temple in 70 C.E., Jews have
dreamed of returning to Jerusalem. Jews did not give up the
dream of rebuilding Jerusalem. In 1967, after the Six Day War,
the old city of Jerusalem was returned to the Jewish people.
With the return of the old city, the ancient Western Wall of the
Temple was once again in Jewish hands. Today, even though the
city of Jerusalem is in Israeli territory, we still dream of the day
when all residents of Jerusalem, Jew, Arab, and Christian alike,
can live in peace. This is the meaning of the blessing with
which we conclude our Pesach *Seder*: "Next Year In Jerusalem."
This is a prayer for peace for the people of Jerusalem, Israel, and
the world.

**Chapter**

**26**

1. Create a peace banner. Devise a new symbol of peace for your
   banner. Display your banner at the *Seder.*

2. The traditional *Haggadah* ends with the words "Next Year In
   Jerusalem." Write a prayer or poem to be recited at the end of
   the *Seder* that tells of your wishes for peace in Jerusalem.

3. Write a prayer for the *Seder* for the release of the Soviet Jews.

4. Write an acrostic prayer for peace in Israel. You can use the
   following words:

   | P | S | J | I | Y |
   |---|---|---|---|---|
   | E | H | E | S | O |
   | A | A | R | R | U |
   | C | L | U | A | R |
   | E | O | S | E | |
   | | M | A | L | N |
   | | | L | | A |
   | | | E | | M |
   | | | M | | E |

5. Create a model of the Western Wall (*HaKotel HaMa'aravi*)
   from cardboard boxes or sheets of styrofoam. Write prayers
   for peace and place them in your *kotel.*

6. Write a poem about Natan Shcharansky's arrival in Israel.

7. Write a letter/proclamation to the Prime Minister of Israel.
   Share some of your suggestions for peace in the Middle East.

8. Legend tells us that the prophet Elijah never died. Instead, he was carried to heaven, and he reappears from time to time dressed as a beggar to test whether or not the Jewish people are doing *mitzvot*. According to the legend, when Elijah returns undisguised, there will be peace in the world. As a family prepare a dramatization about the appearance of Elijah dressed as a beggar at the door of a poor or wealthy family. Present it at the *Seder.*

**The Seder**    The parts of the *Seder* correspond to the four stations.

Back In Time
The holiday of Yom HaAtzma'ut, Israel Independence Day, celebrates the fulfillment of God's promise to Abraham: "I will give this land to your offspring."

Chapter

26

We raise the first cup of wine at our Yom HaAtzma'ut *Seder* to remember all of our ancestors who lived, loved, and yearned for the Land of Israel. We say the traditional blessing for wine, followed by the blessing of thankfulness for reaching this special day in the life of the Land of Israel. (Say the *brachah* and drink the wine or grape juice.)

We now join in singing a familiar song about King David, who helped to build ancient Israel into a strong nation. (All join in singing "*David Melech Yisrael.*")

Continuing our tribute to King David, we will now learn the dance, "*V'David*" (Optional).

Heroes/Heroines Of Israel
Four famous builders of Israel have been invited to our *Seder.* We will ask each of them to say a few words. (Each builder of Israel now reads his/her prepared speech, poem, or riddle. Those families who prepared Coats of Arms can display them now.)

On this day we remember the heroism of all of the builders of Israel who brought about the birth of the modern nation of Israel. We especially celebrate the vision of Theodor Herzl who proclaimed: "If you will it, it is no dream." These famous words of Herzl have been set to music and have become a popular song. (All join in singing: "*Im Tirtzu.*")

As the heroes/heroines of Israel worked the soil by day, they sang and danced by night. Their most popular dance of course, was the *hora*. In tribute to the heroes and heroines of modern Israel, let us all rise and dance a hora.

At this joyous time, we also remember the brutal days of the Holocaust and the memory of those who gave their lives *al kidushat HaShem*. As a memorial to our brothers and sisters destroyed by the Nazis, we have written these poems. (Families who wrote tributes to Holocaust victims read them now.)

Chapter
**26**

Let us rise and join in singing "*Ani Ma'amin*" in memory of the victims of the Holocaust.

Israel Today
It is now time to sample some traditional foods from Israel. Before eating, say the appropriate *brachah* and eat foods from Israel.

One of the most popular songs in Israel today tells of the bitter-sweet nature of life in Israel. Let us learn the words and music for the beautiful song, "*Al Kol Ayleh.*"

One of the most popular dances in Israel today is "*Od lo Ahavti Dye.*" Let us learn this delightful dance (optional).

Next Year in Jerusalem
We raise this final cup of wine at our *Seder* as a cup of hope – a vision of peace for the future. At this time, we recite a special prayer on behalf of our sisters and brothers in the Soviet Union who are yearning to be free to live Israel.

We also pray for peace in the land of Israel. Using the letters of some very special words, we offer these hopes for peace, *shalom*. (Families who wrote acrostics, made peace banners, or prepared Elijah skits, display or perform them now.)

The last prayer in our *Seder* is the traditional *Seder* blessing, "Next Year In Jerusalem." Here are some of our wishes for the next year. (Families who wrote "Next Year In Jerusalem" wishes read them now.) Let's join in singing "Next Year In Jerusalem" — "*L'Shanah HaBa'ah Be'rushalayim.*" A popular Israeli dance that looks ahead to better days is "*Machar,*" which means tomorrow. Let us learn this dance now.

We conclude our *Seder* with a giant birthday cake celebrating Israel's independence. As we light the birthday candles, we all join in singing "*Yom Huledet Sameach.*" (Each person gets a piece of the cake, or the cake can be donated to a local soup kitchen.)

**Editor's Comments**   This is an ambitious program which may be tailored to one's own needs. It is suggested that all of the activities be maintained. However, the number of choices might need to be limited once participants move beyond the "Back In Time" station. This program may also be integrated with the school curriculum by having different classes prepare materials for each station in advance. In addition, follow-up activities should take place in classes where students share their family's experience.

Chapter

26

## Bibliography/Resources

Adler, David A. *A Picture Book Of Israel*. New York: Behrman House, 1979.

_____. *Our Golda: The Story Of Golda Meir*. New York: Viking, 1984.

Bahat, Dan. "Twenty Centuries Of Jewish Life In the Holy Land: The Forgotten Generations." *The Israel Economist* (1975).

Bar-Zohar, Michael. *Ben-Gurion: The Armed Prophet*. New York: Prentice Hall, 1967.

Ben-Gurion, David. *Israel: A Personal History*. New York: Funk & Wagnalls, 1972.

Borovetz, Frances. *Israel Ditto Pak K-3*. Denver: Alternatives in Religious Education, 1982.

_____. *Israel Ditto/Copy Pak*™ *4-6*. Denver: Alternatives in Religious Education, 1982.

Burstein, Chaya. *What's An Israel?*. Rockville, MD: Kar-Ben Copies, 1983.

Comay, Joan. *Israel: An Uncommon Guide*. New York: Random House, 1969.

Davidson, Margaret. *The Golda Meir Story*. New York: Scribner, 1982

Eban, Abba S. *My Country: The Story Of Modern Israel*. New York: Random House, 1972

Edelman, Lily. *Israel: New People In An Old Land*. New York: Nelson, 1958.

Elon, Amos. *Herzl*. New York: Holt, 1975.

_____. *The Israelis: Founders and Sons*. New York: Holt, 1971.

Essrig, Harry. *Israel Today*. New York: Union of American Hebrew Congregations, 1977.

Fine, Helen. *Behold the Land*. New York: Union of American Hebrew Congregations, 1968.

Frankel, Max, and Hoffman, Judy. *I Live In Israel*. New York: Behrman House, 1979.

Ganz, Yaffa. *Our Jerusalem*. New York: Behrman, 1978.

Gidal, Sonia. *My Village In Israel*. New York: Pantheon, 1959.

Grand, Samuel. *The Children Of Israel*. New York: Union of American Hebrew Congregations, 1972.

Hill, Jeri. *Let's Explore Israel*. New York: KTAV, 1978.

Chapter

**26**

Jaffe, Bernette. *Builders Of Israel*. Denver: Alternatives in Religious Education, 1984.

Kubie, Nora B. *The Jews Of Israel: History and Sources*. New York: Behrman House, 1975.

Learsi, Rufus. *Israel a History Of the Jewish People*. Cleveland: World, 1949.

Lehman, Emil. *Israel: Idea and Reality*. New York: United Synagogue, 1962.

Meir, Mira. *Alina: A Russian Girl Comes To Israel*. Philadelphia: Jewish Publication Society, 1982.

St. John, Robert. *They Came From Everywhere*. New York: Coward, 1962.

Shamir, Maxim. *The Story Of Israel In Stamps*. North Hollywood, CA: Wilshire Book Co., 1969.

Slater, Robert. *Golda: The Uncrowned Queen Of Israel*. New York: Jonathan David, 1981.

Zion, Jacob, ed. *My Shalom, My Peace*. Israel: American Publishing Co., 1974.

Chapter

# 26

**Mediated Materials**
Filmstrips
*The Beauty Of Nature In Israel Stamps*. World Zionist Organization, Publications Dept., 515 Park Ave., New York, NY 10022. (61 frames)

*Beneath These Stones*. World Zionist Organization, 1977. (filmstrip, 80 frames)

*David's City*. Board of Jewish Education of Greater New York, 426 West 58th St., New York, NY 10019, 1977. (65 frames)

*Ilana Goes To Israel*. The Learning Plant, P.O. Box 17233, West Palm Beach, FL 33416. (28 frames)

*Moki and the Life Giving Water.* The Learning Plant. (29 frames)

*My Israel.* Board of Jewish Education of Greater New York, 1978. (128 frames)

*A Stamp Tour Of Israel.* World Zionist Organization, 1970. (filmstrip, 51 frames)

*Study Tour Of Israel.* World Zionist Organization, 1964-72. (set of 7 filmstrips, 51-65 frames each)

*Uzi and Zuzu.* The Learning Plant. (26 frames)

*Yediat Ha'aretz.* The Learning Plant. (set of 16 filmstrips, 45-56 frames each)

Chapter
# 26

# Chapter 27

 **TITLE:** Jews Around the World Festival

 **CONTRIBUTED BY:** Frieda Hershman Huberman

 **TOPIC:** Jewish heritage; commonality of Jewish experiences

 **TARGET AUDIENCE:** Families with children in Grades 4-8

 **TIME FRAME:** One session of 2-3 hours

 **STAFF:** One overall facilitator; many volunteers to staff the stations, guide role play, coordinate activities, and provide information

**Overview**   This is a one time program which may stand on its own or be integrated into a camp weekend or *Shabbaton*. It utilizes a round robin approach to teach participants about Jews who originated from different countries. It includes cultural activities and, of course, food. While it is designed for students and families in Grades 4-8, it may be adapted for junior high and high school students as well.

**Purpose**   The purposes of the program are as follows:

1. To demonstrate the diversity of our Jewish ethnic heritage.

2. To instill a sense of pride in participants' ethnicity, especially for non-Ashkenazim.

3. To involve parents in the educational process as teachers and participants.

4. To promote in the school a sense of community and of *K'lal Yisrael*.

**Preparation/Procedure**   This program requires extensive use of community volunteers. The volunteers are oriented and trained by the professional staff. It is also the role of the professional staff to recruit the volunteers, coordinate publicity, secure necessary supplies, and arrange the facility for the program.

**Program Description**   A round robin format is used with parent representatives acting as facilitators. The countries are selected to reflect the students' ethnic backgrounds, and also to include those of Eastern European or non-Ashkenazic origin. The activities are chosen based on the volunteers' backgrounds, interests, and strengths.

At each station the parents give a brief lecture on some facet of their country's unique history and customs, how the Jewish community functions there, and the status of that Jewish community today. They then lead a participatory activity with the families at their station. The countries and activities may include:

| Israel | Map making |
| Iran | Learning Farsi words |
| Egypt | Drawing pictures/writing poems of peace |
| Morocco | Calligraphy |
| Mexico | Storytelling |
| Yemen | Dance |
| Ethiopia | Writing letters to the U.S. government on behalf of Ethiopian Jews |
| Hungary | Learning a Yiddish song |
| Chile | Paper cutting |
| U.S.S.R. | Writing letters to Refuseniks |

Chapter

27

When the round robin is completed, everyone joins together in sampling various foods.

**Editor's Comments**  The program as presented here requires ten stations. It may be coordinated to group people together into such categories as Eastern European, Arabic, Mediterranean, South America, and Asian Jews.

The program may be expanded by including a segment during which people trace their family roots. In advance, a question-naire may be sent to participants, enabling them to investigate their family members' places of origin. Then plot these on a world map. In this way everyone present gets a sense of the background of the people in the community.

The program will be greatly enriched if some people come in costume. Most communities have ethnic arts councils or museums with ethnic arts experts who will help authenticate a costume. Consult the book *The History Of the Jewish Costume* by Alfred Rubens to find the appropriate clothing.

Another enhancement to this program is to have artifacts avail-able which represent the different cultures. Set up a museum-type display with various items, such as *kipot*, Torah covers, *chanukiot, Seder* plates, prayerbooks, *Kiddush* cups, and the like. Assign one person to be in charge of this and to provide explanations for the items. The person in charge may also have a crew of docents to describe the items and compare them.

## Bibliography/Resources

Angel, Marc D. *La America: Sephardic Experience In the United States*. Philadelphia: Jewish Publication Society, 1982.

Ausubel, Nathan. *Pictorial History Of the Jewish People*. New York: Crown Publishers, Inc., 1961.

Birmingham, Stephen. *The Grandees*. New York: Harper, 1971.

Cowan, Ida. *Jews In Remote Corners Of the World*. New Jersey: Prentice-Hall, n.d.

Grand, Samuel. *Jews In Distant Lands*. New York: Union of American Hebrew Congregations, 1977.

Patai, Raphael. *Tents Of Jacob: The Diaspora Yesterday and Today*. New York: Prentice-Hall, 1971.

Pollak, Michael. *Mandarins, Jews and Missionaries: The Jewish Experience In the Chinese Empire*. Philadelphia: Jewish Publication Society, 1980.

Rubens, Alfred. *The History Of the Jewish Costume*. London: Peter Owen, 1981.

Shulman, Abraham. *The Old Country: The Lost World Of East European Jewry*. New York: Charles Scribners Sons, 1974.

Vishniac, Roman. *Polish Jews: A Pictorial Record*. New York: Schocken, 1973.

**Chapter 27**

### Mediated Materials

*Falashas Of Ethiopia*. Union of American Hebrew Congregations, 838 Fifth Ave., New York, NY 10021, 1962. (filmstrip, Part 1 – 45 frames; Part 2 – 48 frames)

*Glimpses Of Jewish Life In France.* Union of American Hebrew Congregations, 1976. (filmstrip, Part 1 – 92 frames; Part 2 – 85 frames)

*Jews In Italy.* Union of American Hebrew Congregations, 1964. (filmstrip, 59 frames)

*The Jews In Russia.* Board of Jewish Education of Greater New York, 468 West 58th Street, New York, NY 10019, 1973. (filmstrip set, Part 1 – 36 frames; Part 2 – 44 frames; two cassettes)

*Jews Of Prague.* Union of American Hebrew Congregations, 1968. (filmstrip, 59 frames)

*Rebirth After 500 Years: Jewish Communities In Spain.* Union of American Hebrew Congregations, 1977. (filmstrip, 87 frames)

*Scenes From Canadian Jewish History.* Union of American Hebrew Congregations, 1967. (filmstrip, 44 frames)

*Scenes Of Jewish Life In England.* Union of American Hebrew Congregations, 1977. (filmstrip, 85 frames)

Chapter

27

# Chapter 28

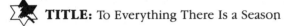 **TITLE:** To Everything There Is a Season

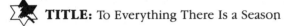 **CONTRIBUTED BY:** Janice P. Alper

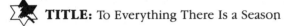 **TOPIC:** Life Cycle

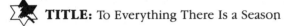 **TARGET AUDIENCE:** Grade 5 students and their parents

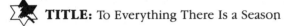 **TIME FRAME:** One session of 2-3 hours

 **STAFF:** One facilitator and two assistants

**Overview**   This program was developed several years ago for a Conservative synagogue. Since then it has been replicated in a camp setting and in a Reform congregation. During the program families move to various stations where they become acquainted with the Jewish life cycle.

**Purpose**   The purpose of the program is to provide cognitive information about Jewish life cycle events and to help families gain heightened awareness of these events. The goal is to stress how these events have helped to preserve Jewish tradition within a cohesive Jewish community.

**Preparation/Procedure**   The program is designed to last from 2 to 3 hours and ideally there are six stations. In preparing for the program, it is necessary to have appropriate background materials at each station (see below under Program Description), along with materials necessary to produce finished products. The optimal environment is a large room with six long tables (one for each station) and several tables at which families can work together. The stations are:

Station I: A Time to Be Born (Birth/Naming)

Station II: A Time to Speak (Bar and Bat Mitzvah/Confirmation)

Station III: A Time to Embrace (Jewish Wedding)

Station IV: A Time to Gather Stones (Jewish Home)

Station V: A Time to Mourn (Death)

Station VI: Putting Materials Together (Making a Life Cycle Book)

**Program Description**   When families have gathered together, have them introduce themselves to each other. Provide an orientation to the program. Tell families to proceed at their own pace. Some may finish all stations, others may not. The purpose of the program is to enable families to work together and to share ideas. The following are sample instructions to be placed in each station:

STATION I: A TIME TO BE BORN
(Birth/Naming)

"To everything there is a season, and a time to every purpose under the heavens. A time to be born . . . ." (Ecclesiastes 3:1-2)

There are many wonderful customs, traditions, laws, and ceremonies associated with the birth of a Jewish child. At this station you will receive information regarding the above. You may choose to review some of it now with your family or just retain it for your booklet and read it at a future time.

Family Activities
1. Naming Certificates – Complete a certificate for everyone in the family. Names may be written in Hebrew and/or English. Lists of Hebrew names are available for reference, as well as a 100 year calendar to locate your Hebrew date of birth. Then answer these questions:
   a. Who will have the honor of carrying the baby up to the *bimah*?
   b. Who will hold the baby on the *bimah*?
   c. Who else will participate in the service? How will they participate?

Chapter

28

2. Acrostics – As part of a naming ceremony, it is sometimes customary to find biblical verses which spell out the name of the child. Bibles have been provided to help you find a name verse, or, you may create an acrostic using the first letters of your name.

3. Preparing for the Celebration Of the Birth Of a Child, for the *Brit Milah*, or *Brit HaBat*
   a. Who will you ask to be the *K'vatterine* (godmother) and *K'vatter* (godfather)?
   b. At a *Brit Milah* who will bring in the baby and hand him to the *Sandak*?
   c. Who will you ask to be the *Sandak*?
   d. Who will you ask to take the baby from the *Sandak* and return him to his mother?
   e. Who else would you like to honor at a *Brit Milah* or *Brit HaBat*?

### STATION II: A TIME TO SPEAK
#### (Bar and Bat Mitzvah/Confirmation)

"To everything there is a season and a time to every purpose under the heaven . . . a time to build up . . . a time to laugh . . . a time to speak . . . ." (Ecclesiastes 3:1, 3, 4, 7)

You may find the attached information about Bar/Bat Mitzvah (from *The Second Jewish Catalog*) very interesting. For many young people, this ceremony is the culmination of their Jewish education; for others, it is truly a beginning. While the ceremony of Bar Mitzvah has been practiced for several hundred years, the ceremony of Bat Mitzvah was introduced less than 100 years ago.

**Chapter**

# 28

There is also a section from the same book on Confirmation which you may include in your family life cycle book.

Family Activities
1. Read the section on origins of Bar and Bat Mitzvah, then complete the activity sheets.

2. Find your Torah portion, read about it, and summarize it.

How to Find Your Torah Portion

1. Locate your Hebrew date of birth, as suggested in Station I; add 13 and find the date – for example, if you were born on Wednesday, September 18, 1940, corresponding to the 15th of Elul, 5700, you would locate the date of Bar/Bat Mitzvah on the 15th of Elul 5713, which is August 26, 1953.

2. Find the column that says "Sabbath," and you will find the appropriate Torah portion for the week. In the case of our example, it is *Ki Tavo*. If you look at the list of Torah portions, you will see that *Ki Tavo* is in the Book of Deuteronomy.

### GENESIS

| | | |
|---|---|---|
| *Beresheet* | *Chayay Sarah* | *Vayeshev* |
| *Noah* | *Toledot* | *Miketz* |
| *Lech Lecha* | *Vayeytze* | *Vayigash* |
| *Vayera* | *Vayishlah* | *Vayechi* |

## EXODUS

| | | |
|---|---|---|
| *Sh'mot* | *Yitro* | *Ki Tisa* |
| *Vaera* | *Mishpatim* | *Vayakhel* |
| *Bo* | *Terumah* | *Pikude* |
| *Beshalach* | *Tetzaveh* | |

## LEVITICUS

| | | |
|---|---|---|
| *Vayikra* | *Metzora* | *Emor* |
| *Tzav* | *Acharay* | *Behar* |
| *Shemini* | *Kedoshim* | *Bechukotai* |
| *Tazriya* | | |

## NUMBERS

| | | |
|---|---|---|
| *Bemidbar* | *Korach* | *Pinchas* |
| *Naso* | *Chukat* | *Matot* |
| *Beha'alotecha* | *Balak* | *Mas'ay* |
| *Shelach Lecha* | | |

Chapter

# 28

## DEUTERONOMY

| | | |
|---|---|---|
| *Devarim* | *Shofetim* | *Vayelech* |
| *Va'etchanan* | *Ki Tetze* | *Ha'azinu* |
| *Ekev* | *Ki Tavo* | *V'zot HaBerachah* |
| *Re'eh* | *Nitzavim* | |

Station II: Activity 1
For those who have become Bar/Bat Mitzvah:

1. One thing I learned when I became Bar/Bat Mitzvah was

   _____ .

2. As an adult in the Jewish community, I became responsible for

   _____ .

3. I felt _____ after my Bar/Bat Mitzvah ceremony was
   over  because  _____ .

4. Some things I remember about my Bar/Bat Mitzvah ceremony
   are: _____
   _____
   _____

5. Now discuss this with your child.

Station II: Activity 2
For students who have not yet had a Bar/Bat Mitzvah ceremony:

1. At my Bar/Bat Mitzvah service, I want to honor _____ .

2. A Jewish practice I especially look forward to continuing is _____ because _____ .

3. When I become Bar/Bat Mitzvah, I hope my family will _____ .

4. As an adult in the Jewish community, I will _____ _____ .

5. Now discuss these questions and your answers with your parents.

Chapter

**28**

### STATION III: A TIME TO EMBRACE
### (Jewish Wedding)

"To everything there is a season, and a time to every purpose under the heaven; A time to plan . . . a time to build up . . . A time to embrace . . . A time to love." (Eclesiastes 3:1, 2, 3, 5, 6)

A Jewish wedding is a beautiful ceremony. It is rich in history and symbolism. It is a time when family, extended family, and the community rejoice in the founding of a new Jewish home.

At this station you will find some background on marriage from the book *When a Jew Celebrates* by Harry Gersh, pp. 44-55, as well as the words of an actual Jewish wedding ceremony.

Family Activities
1. Parents – write a *Ketubah*, marriage contract.

2. Children – make bride and groom paper bag puppets.

3. Entire family – plan a wedding.

Planning a Wedding
1. Decide where the wedding will take place, who will perform

the ceremony, what color dresses, flowers, tablecloths, and accessories.

2. Decide on the music, attendants, ushers, bridesmaids, Maid of Honor, Best Man, flower girl. Design an invitation, plan a menu.

When you are through with all of your notes, save them for your family book.

### STATION IV: A TIME TO GATHER STONES TOGETHER
### (A Jewish Home)

"To everything there is a season, and a time to every purpose under the heavens; A time to cast away stones, and a time to gather stones together . . . A time to seek, and a time to lose . . . a time to keep silence, and a time to speak." (Ecclesiastes 3:1, 5, 6, 7)

Chapter

# 28

In our tradition a Jewish home is regarded as a *Mikdash Me'at*, a small sanctuary. The home is the place where values are taught and *mitzvot* become a way of life. There are many symbols inside a home that identify it as Jewish. The *mezzuzah* identifies a Jewish home from the outside.

At this station you will collect some information about a Jewish home and have an opportunity to identify objects which make your home Jewish.

Family Activities
1. Take an inventory of Jewish items in your home.

2. Make a *mezzuzah* and have a *Chanukat Habayit* ceremony (dedication of the home).

3. Design a family Coat of Arms.


Station IV: Activity 1
Inventory Jewish items from home:
    *Siddur*
    *Seder* plate

*Kiddush* cup
Candle holders
*Challah* cover
*Matzah* cover
*Mizrach* plaque
*Mezzuzah*
Pictures with Jewish content
Items with Hebrew writing on them
*Challah* board
*Tallit*
*Tefillin*
*Havdalah* candle
Other items

Ceremonies Practiced At Home:
Lighting candles
Saying *Kiddush*
Blessing *Challah*
Blessing children
Reciting *Birkat HaMazon*
Making *Havdalah*
*Seder*
Lighting Chanukah candles
Other ceremonies

*Mitzvot* Practiced At Home:
Welcoming guests
Studying together
Visiting the sick
Building a *sukkah*
Giving money to charity
Honoring parents
Other *mitzvot*

Chapter

# 28

Station IV: Activity 2

Make a *mezzuzah* holder for your home.

1. Fashion a *mezzuzah* holder out of clay. Be sure to leave a place in which you insert the *klaf* (parchment scroll) and a hole at the top and bottom so you can nail it to your doorpost. Once the holders are finished, we will fire them for you and they will be returned to your children at school.

Station IV: Activity 3
Design a family Coat of Arms
1. Decide on all the things you like to do as a family and list
   them below.

2. Come up with a design that represents your family in a Jewish way. Be sure to include your name and some or all of the
   things you like to do as a family.

3. Put the design on 8½" x 11" paper for your book.


### STATION V: A TIME TO MOURN
### (Death)

"To everything there is a season, and a time to every purpose
under the heaven. A time to weep, and a time to laugh . . .
A time to mourn . . . A time to rend, and a time to sew . . . ."
(Ecclesiastes 3:1, 4, 7)

Chapter
28

Birth and death are part of the same process. At a time of birth
we rejoice and celebrate; when someone dies it is a time of sadness. A part of the mourning ritual involves reciting *Kaddish*, a
prayer which sanctifies the name of God. The special ceremonies and customs associated with death help mourners to accept
their loss and make the transition back to daily life.

Family Activities
1. List some Jewish mourning customs and discuss how they
   help us in working through a loss.

2. Together write a condolence note to "someone" who has
   experienced a loss.

3. Talk about ways to reach out to someone in mourning.

4. Everyone writes about "How I want people to remember me."


### STATION VI: PUTTING MATERIALS TOGETHER
### (Making a Life Cycle Book)

At this station you will have an opportunity to compile all the
materials you gathered today. Heavy paper has been provided

for you to make a cover for your family life cycle book. As a family design a cover, punch holes in all the pages, and put the book together with brads. This book can now be made a part of your family's Jewish library.

**Editor's Comments**   This program may be used in its entirety or in part. If time is limited, the first two stations (Birth/Naming and Bar/Bat Mitzvah) are the most relevant for 5th Grade students. It may be desirable or necessary to keep everyone together for this program. If this is the case, have backup activities available for those people who finish quickly. Still another way to run this program is to have one or two stations in several rooms.

If desired, mount pictures which show the transition from one phase of life to another – i.e., from birth to Bar/Bat Mitzvah, learning to ride a bike, entering school, birthday cakes, etc. Another activity is to involve participants in finding their Jewish birthdays. For this have several copies of the 100 year calendar available and an instruction sheet which shows people how to find their Jewish birthdays.

This program may be extended over the course of a full school year. Buzz Hellman, teacher at Baltimore Hebrew Congregation (7401 Park Heights Avenue, Baltimore, MD 21208) implements such a program in the second grade. The children make two stuffed dolls who get married, move into a home, and have a child. Parents are invited to participate throughout the school year. They decorate a *ketubah*, prepare for celebrations, and join in class discussions. The children write invitations to parents for various events. Background information about the life cycle events is sent home to be shared by both parents and children.

Rabbi Shira Milgram and Dr. David Elcott developed a program several years ago at Valley Beth Shalom in Encino, California which linked the birth of Isaac with the birth of the students. Parents and children together listened to a recounting of the biblical story of the birth of Isaac. Each parent then told his/her child what he/she experienced when the child was born. The stories were compiled into a class book which was distributed to all participants.

Another strategy for this program is to develop a special family prayer or blessing for each event. Provide the traditional sources so that participants know what is expected. Then suggest that they write their own blessings which will be used on the various life cycle occasions. Collect these into a booklet and distribute it to everyone in the class.

This program can serve as a culmination to year-long study of the life cycle. Have students work in groups to prepare displays and explanations of each of the events studied. One way to do this is to set up a large room as a life cycle museum. Parents move from one life cycle event to another as students explain what is taking place at each station. Help the students develop interactive activities at each station so that parents are not just spectators — e.g., writing contracts at the Jewish wedding station, creating life maps or family coats of arms at the station on death and mourning, making *tzitzit* for a *tallit* at the Bar/Bat Mitzvah station. A mock marriage provides a joyous way to end the day.

Chapter

28

## Bibliography/Resources

Cardozo, Arlene Rossen. *Jewish Family Celebration: The Sabbath, Festivals and Ceremonies*. New York: St. Martin's Press, 1982.

Davidovitch, David. *The Ketuba: Jewish Marriage Contracts Through the Ages*. Tel Aviv: Lewin-Epstein Publishers, 1968.

Gersh, Harry. *When a Jew Celebrates*. New York: Behrman House, 1971.

Grollman, Earl A., ed. *Concerning Death: A Practical Guide for the Living*. Boston: Beacon Press, 1974.

Klein, Isaac. *A Guide To Jewish Religious Practice*. New York: Jewish Theological Seminary of America, 1979.

Kolatch, Alfred J. *The Complete Dictionary Of English and Hebrew First Names*. Middle Village, NY: Jonathan David, 1984.

Strassfeld, Sharon, and Green, Kathy, eds. *The Jewish Family Book*. New York: Bantam Books, 1981.

Strassfeld, Sharon, and Strassfeld, Michael, eds. *The Second Jewish Catalog*. Philadelphia: Jewish Publication Society, 1974.

**Mediated Materials**

*The Jewish Home*. Board of Jewish Education of Greater New York, 426 West 58th St., New York, NY 10019. (filmstrip, 43 frames)

*A Seal Upon Thy Heart*. Board of Jewish Education of Greater New York. (videocassette, 30 min.)

**Game**

Moskowitz, Nachama. *The Jewish Life Cycle Game*. Denver: Alternatives in Religious Education, Inc., 1984.

Chapter

28

# Chapter 29

**TITLE:** Pyramid Of Life

**CONTRIBUTED BY:** Shirley Barish

**TOPIC:** Jewish view of death

**TARGET AUDIENCE:** Students in Grade 6 and their families

**TIME FRAME:** One 2 hour session

**STAFF:** One facilitator

**Overview**   "Pyramid Of Life" is a sixth grade family enrichment program with two parts: understanding death as a part of the natural process of life, and building a pyramid of life. Participants learn that Jewish values teach us to affirm life even in the face of the reality of death. Participants work in family units and share feelings and reactions within the structure of the family.

**Purpose**   The purpose of the program is three-fold: to help participants become aware of death as a natural part of the life cycle, to answer questions about death, and to deal with their own feelings and those of others. The program is also designed to help parents communicate with their children about death.

Chapter
29

**Preparation/Procedure**   Inform parents of the date of the program and try to ensure that each child in the class is accompanied by an adult. Prepare a booklet containing brief readings and questions to which participants will respond (have one copy of the booklet for each family). Order the film *The Day Grandpa Died*, and arrange for the Rabbi to come and talk about the *Kaddish*. Review the program with the facilitator. Arrange for a movie projector or VCR and supplies (markers, gummed paper, Instruction Sheets, pyramid sheets).

**Program Description**   An outline of the 2 hour session follows:

**Session Outline**
  I. Introduction
    A. Talk about:
      1. The difficulty in discussing death, in saying "dead"; euphemisms for death – "passed on," "went away," "gone forever."
      2. The seeming mystery which surrounds death – what happens when one dies?
      3. The fear of death is part of being human, yet we try to protect children from the idea of death. If possible, have facilitator talk about his/her own reaction to/concern about/fear of death.

II. Movie: *The Day Grandpa Died*
  A. Give a brief resume of the film *The Day Grandpa Died*.
  B. Show the film. Then, in family groups, immediately following the film, encourage reactions.
  C. Distribute the booklets, one per family, and one pencil per person. The booklet is based on *Explaining Death To Children* by Earl A. Grollman. The following are two examples of exercises from the first part of the booklet:

### EXERCISE

Remember then thy Creator in
   The days of thy youth . . .
Before the silver cord is
   snapped asunder,
And the golden bowl is
   shattered . . .
And the dust returneth to
   the earth as it was,
And the spirit returneth
   unto God who gave it.
   (Ecclesiastes 12:1,6)

Chapter

# 29

(Talk with each other for a few minutes about how the family in the film *The Day Grandpa Died* helped the boy and each other to accept and understand what had happened.)

### EXERCISE

When you die, you're dead.
Try saying that word: DEAD.
How do you feel
when you say the word DEAD?
What's the first thing you think of when you say the word DEAD?

(Talk with each other, for a few minutes, about HOW YOU FEEL and WHAT YOU THINK ABOUT when you say the word DEAD.)

The following is the last exercise in the booklet:

EXERCISE

A bell is not a bell
until you ring it.
A song is not a song
until you sing it.
Love isn't love until
you give it away —
The act of giving —
of giving away —
Is in return – on our part —
for God's gift of life.
If life is sensed as a surprise,
as a gift – a preparation —
an opportunity – as a task —
a moment of achievement —
Then death ceases to be a radical,
absolute denial of what life
stands for.
Life isn't life
until you live it.

**Chapter**

**29**

(Talk with each other for a few minutes about what you
do to show appreciation for your life.

Judaism is said to be a way of life. What are some of the
things we do as we try to live the best life we can — i.e.
be kind, be respectful? Make your list below.)

D. Personal Reaction To Death
1. Ask the participants to read the booklet and respond in
   writing to the instructions on each page. Explain that
   their responses are personal and for their eyes only.
2. Sharing upon completion of the booklets (about 25-30
   minutes). Members of each group share what they
   wish from the books such as: How do you show
   anger? How do you show your sadness? What is
   wrong, if anything, with crying? How does crying give
   you relief? How do you show your hurt? If time permits, continue the discussion, possibly ending with
   the sharing of the final page of the booklet.

E. *Kaddish* – The Rabbi gives a talk about the *Kaddish* — its development, traditions associated with it, and its meaning for Jews. Other points to consider are the *Kaddish* as a core theme in the *Siddur*; the *Kaddish* as recited on the *Yahrzeit*, during *Yizkor*; and *Kaddish* as it relates to our hope of redemption, our Messianic hopes, etc.

III. Pyramid Of Life – This part of the program was adapted from *More Values Clarification* by Sidney Simon and Jay Clark and takes 45 minutes.

A. Introduction — Explain:

A pyramid is most solid when large stones are at its foundation, and smaller and smaller stones are toward the top. While each stone is important to the structure, those on top could be removed without the entire pyramid collapsing. Each of us, in the years granted, builds a "Pyramid Of Life." Our Jewish tradition encourages us to affirm life even though we know our life will end. If we are to face death in a healthy manner, we have to build a strong "Pyramid Of Life."

Chapter

29

During this part of the program, participants will become aware of those things in their lives which are important to them in terms of building a good life for themselves and for those with whom they live.

B. Preparing to Build a Pyramid (Note: For this activity there are 9 different Instruction Sheets; each family gets a different one.)

1. Pass out Instruction Sheets to each person in the group. Have all supplies for the activity readily available.

2. Have someone in each group read the instruction sheet out loud to the participants in that group.

a. Within the group, talk about the meaning of the text.

b. Some discussion will be necessary before anyone in the group can write their own "life" words. Encourage parents to help children understand the full meaning of any words they use.

c. Once everyone understands the text, distribute several pieces of colored gummed paper to each person. Ask each person to write their own "life" words (words representing values which are most important to them), one word per strip of paper.

d. Once these "life" words are written, pass out a pyramid sheet (simply a triangle shape which fills an 8½" x 11" sheet of paper) to each *family*. Remind the group that the base of the pyramid as its foundation must contain those values deemed the most important by the family group.

Samples of two Instruction Sheets follow. The opening paragraph is the same on all the sheets.

INSTRUCTION SHEET I
Pyramid Of Life

The Jewish concepts and traditions concerning death are unique, just as the Jewish way of life is unique. In a realistic manner we are taught that death is a part of life. To undertand this and come to grips with it is a motif that can be traced all the way through Jewish tradition. How does one come to grips with the reality of death? By building a "Pyramid Of Life."

Read the following story:
A traveler once saw an old man planting a carob tree. "When will the tree bear fruit?" asked the traveler. "Oh, perhaps in seventy years," the old man answered.

"Do you expect to live to eat the fruit of that tree?"

"No," said the old man, "but I didn't find the world desolate when I entered it, and as my fathers planted for me before I was born, so do I plant for those who come after me." (Talmud)

What "life" words come to mind after reading the above? What value words are needed to build a "Pyramid Of Life"?
What attitudes toward life do you need to survive happily and effectively?

Individually, write down all the "life" words which have come to mind, such as: *remembering, ecology, children.*

Use the colored strips of paper and write your *one* word
on each strip.

As a group, build your "Pyramid Of Life." Put those words
from each person which the family group thinks are the
most important at the base and work your way up.


INSTRUCTION SHEET II
Pyramid Of Life


The Jewish concepts and traditions concerning death are
unique, just as the Jewish way of life is unique. In a realistic manner we are taught that death is a part of life. To
undertand this and come to grips with it is a motif that
can be traced all the way through Jewish tradition. How
does one come to grips with the reality of death? By
building a "Pyramid Of Life."

Chapter

29

Read the following:
A good name is better than precious oil; and the day of
death than the day of one's birth. (Ecclesiastes 7:1)


Two ships were once seen near land. One of them was
leaving the harbor, and the other was coming into it.
Everyone was cheering the outgoing ship, giving it a
hearty send-off. But the incoming ship was scarcely
noticed.

A wise man standing nearby exclaimed: "Rejoice not over
the ship that is setting out to sea, for you know not what
destiny awaits it, what storms it may encounter, what
dangers lurk before it. Rejoice rather over the ship that
has reached port safely and brought back all its passengers in peace" (*Midrash*).

What "life" words come to mind after reading the above?
What value words are needed to build a "Pyramid of Life"?
What attitudes toward life do you need to survive hap-
pily and effectively?

Individually, write down all the "life" words which come to mind, such as: *family, peace, safety.*

Use the colored strips of paper and write your *one* word on each paper.

As a family group, build your "Pyramid Of Life." Put those words from each person that the family group thinks are the most important at the base and work your way up.

C. Building a Pyramid
   1. Each family builds its own pyramid.
      a. Encourage families to talk out the values which they as individuals have thought most important. What makes a value so important to that person?
      b. When the family has reached consensus as to where on the pyramid the different "life" words belong, they should begin building the pyramid. Allow enough time for each family to arrange the words inside the pyramid, going from the bottom to the top. When the groups finish, ask each to share their pyramids, describing the reasons for the order of their "life" words.

D. Closure
   1. Rank Order exercise on the verse "Teach us to number our days that we may attain a heart of wisdom" (Psalm 90:12).
   2. Pass out the Rank Order sheets, a sample of which follows:

      Which of the following is most important? Rank each from "A" (most important to you) to "E" (least important to you).

      _____ To number our days means to stay healthy and live a long life.
      _____ To number our days means using each day to help each other.
      _____ To number our days means cherishing life more than money or material things.
      _____ To number our days means filling our days with meaning regardless of how long we live.
      _____ To number our days means trying to learn something new each day of our lives.

**Editor's Comments**   The film *The Day Grandpa Died* is a fine trigger for discussion of a Jewish view of death. Also excellent as discussion triggers are books such as *Bubby, Me, and Memories* by Barbara Pomerantz or *The Fall Of Freddie the Leaf* by Leo Buscaglia. While these materials are geared primarily to younger children, they are provocative enough for discussion with older children as well.

An alternate activity to building a "Pyramid Of Life" is for families to create a "life map." Each family receives a piece of mural paper and draws on it a long horizontal line. Using markers they show their family's journey from the marriage of the parents to the present, and also their hoped for future projections. The values and ideas which are most important to the family can be written at the beginning of the line and can be traced all along it. This exercise can also be useful in illustrating the continuity of life.

Chapter

29

Follow-up activities can include a visit to a Jewish mortuary or cemetery. Such a visit can help take the mystery out of a funeral and may serve to clear up many misconceptions the children may have about death. Coupled with this, the Rabbi can talk about the customs and traditions connected with a Jewish burial – i.e., tearing a garment, burial within 24 hours in a plain pine box, shoveling the earth, etc. The Rabbi can also address the issue of mourning, particularly in relation to one's personal needs.

## Bibliography/Resources

Buscaglia, Leo. *The Fall Of Freddie the Leaf*. Thorofare, NJ: Charles B. Slack, 1982.

Fassler, Joan. *My Grandpa Died Today*. New York: Human Sciences Press, 1971.

Grollman, Earl A., ed. *Explaining Death To Children*. New York: Beacon Press, 1967.

Kübler-Ross, Elisabeth. *On Death and Dying*. New York: Macmillan Co., 1969.

————. *Questions and Answers On Death and Dying*. New York: Collier Books, 1974.

Lamm, Maurice. *The Jewish Way In Death and Mourning*. New York: Jonathan David Publishers, 1972.

Marcus, Audrey Friedman; Bissell, Sherry; and Lipschutz, Karen. *Death, Burial and Mourning In the Jewish Tradition*. Denver: Alternatives in Religious Education, Inc., 1976.

Pomerantz, Barbara. *Bubby, Me, and Memories*. New York: Union of American Hebrew Congregations, 1982.

Riemer, Jack. *Jewish Reflections On Death*. New York: Schocken Books, 1974.

Simon, Sidney, and Clark, Jay. *More Values Clarification*. San Diego, California: Pennant Press, 1975.

Spiro, Jack. *A Time to Mourn*. New York: Bloch Publishing, 1967.

Chapter

29

**Mediated Materials**
*The Day Grandpa Died*. Jewish Community Library, Jewish Community Building, 6505 Wilshire Blvd., Los Angeles, CA 90048. (film, 11 min.)

# Chapter 30

 **TITLE:** Tzedakah Encounter

 **CONTRIBUTED BY:** Cherie Koller-Fox

 **DESIGNED BY:** Cherie Koller-Fox and Matia Angelou

 **TOPIC:** *Tzedakah* education integrated into family life

 **TARGET AUDIENCE:** Families with children in Grade 4 and above (may be adapted for families with younger children); any size group

 **TIME FRAME:** Several months preparation; 2-3 hours for actual program

 **STAFF:** Overall coordinator; one facilitator per group; back up staff well acquainted with the content material

**Overview**   At the Harvard Hillel Children's School, *tzedakah* is an integral part of the curriculum from preschool onward. At each grade level, there are educational materials and projects which involve the students and their families in *tzedakah* and *chesed*. ("*Tzedakah*" here refers to the notion of giving money, while "*chesed*" is used to connote giving of oneself.) The "Tzedakah Encounter" is one piece of the total curriculum. It enables families to learn about a variety of agencies, projects, and funds which are of benefit to the community and which rely on the support of interested people. The program began as a Chanukah event, but for the past seven years has taken place at the end of the school year.

In various groups, families learn about each potential charity and especially about the "Tzedakah Hero" who is associated with it. A "Tzedakah Hero" is a person who is actively involved with the inner workings of an agency or project. Such a person might be the founder of the organization or someone who was closely involved with its establishment and, therefore, serves as a role model for both parents and children. After presentations by the hero (or staff representing him or her), families vote on how much of the money collected in their groups to give to each agency or project. They then make a donation to the Tzedakah Fund. This program was the model for "The Great Tzedakah Encounter" which took place at the CAJE Conference at the University of Maryland in 1986.

The program may be adapted for large and small groups and can also be used as a community project.

**Purpose**   The purpose of the program is to provide families with a way to incorporate *tzedakah* into their lives in a meaningful, ongoing way. It is also designed to demonstrate that each individual can make a difference. The ballot and advocacy process can help people clarify their priorities in terms of *tzedakah*.

### Preparation/Procedure
I. Tzedakah Committee
  Set up a Tzedakah Committee early in the school year.

A. Structure

If the Tzedakah Committee is recognized as a standing committee of the congregation, then the Rabbi and congregational leadership might wish to determine its membership. There should be a liaison between the Tzedakah Committee and the teaching staff to facilitate the integration of the curriculum with the plan of the committee.

B. Tasks

The following are the tasks of the Tzedakah Committee:

1. Each committee member studies the subject of *tzedakah* and *chesed* on his/her own.
2. As a group, investigate a variety of *tzedakah* groups (i.e., charities). The term "tzedakah group" is used instead of charity, because the word charity does not express the Jewish concept of *tzedakah*. Set criteria to determine which agencies, projects, or charities are worthy of support. Secure brochures, background information and annual financial reports for each project under consideration.
3. Decide whether to give to Jewish or non-Jewish *tzedakah* groups or to both.
4. Decide, together with the educator(s), which aspects of *tzedakah* to emphasize during the program.
5. Open and administer a separate *tzedakah* account from which to distribute funds.

Chapter

30

II. Teaching Staff Functions

The following are the functions of the teaching staff:

A. Interacts with committee and serves as a resource to them about *tzedakah* and *chesed*.
B. Determines the program for the "Tzedakah Encounter"
   1. Decides how the study material should be presented — i.e., primary source material, audiovisual presentation, participatory theater
   2. Prepares a time schedule for the day (see section entitled "Schedule")
   3. Each member of the Tzedakah Committee or teaching staff is asked to study one group in detail. They should read the brochures, letters and financial reports submitted to the committee by each group. The ideal situation is to have a Tzedakah Hero from each group appear in person. Since this is rarely feasible, video

tapes or slides will help to explain the function and merit of each agency or project. If the use of such audiovisual aids is not possible, the staff person or committee member must be prepared to represent the interests of that group.

4. Prepare support materials for the program, including a map or floor plan of the rooms where the program will take place to facilitate group movement. Prepare brochures and/or a page of background information about each group, including names and addresses. Design a ballot for each family containing instructions for the voting process. Each family needs to be a assigned to a learning group, a hero, and a team. This is done by designing a ticket with the information on it, which is randomly handed out to families as they arrive.

5. Send letters to all potential participants explaining the value of *tzedakah* and the rationale for the "Tzedakah Encounter." Include a list of the agencies, projects, and charities which are being considered as recipients of the funds raised.

Note: When doing this program for the first time, suggest in advance that each family make a token contribution to the Tzedakah Fund ($5-$10). Explain that this donation enables everyone to participate equally and to have a say in how the money is distributed. This reduces the anxiety that people have about being solicited for contributions. When the program is organized for the second time, and people are more familiar with it, you can ask them to make voluntary contributions without setting limits. When this program is introduced for the first time, it may be combined with a holiday such as Chanukah which has the theme of giving.

**Program Description**    When participants come in, they are handed materials which include a "ticket" with schedule and room assignments, a ballot, a summary sheet listing all the charities and detailed information about each one. An overall schedule for the day can be found below. Explanations of the various components of the program follow this schedule.

**Schedule**

Orientation and Study (1 hour)
  Hand out "tickets" and materials.

  Learn about some aspect of *tzedakah*.

Learn About Your Tzedakah Group (30 min.)
  Presentations about the different organizations to small groups of families

  Families write letters or draw pictures to be sent to the organization they are studying.

Team Meetings and Balloting (75 min.)
  Families advocate for their *tzedakah* group.

  Balloting — each family decides how to divide the money.

  Collect ballots and checks.

Culminating Activity (15 min.)
  Action Project (this could be done at any time before, during or after the program)

  Refreshments

  Tabulate results and, if possible, announce.

Chapter

30

**Components Of the Program**    A description of the various components of the program follows:

1. Study – The first part of the program introduces participating families to the concepts of *tzedakah* and *chesed* through text study, slide or videotape presentations, participatory theater, stories, etc. For example, the slide-tape presentation *Profiles In Chesed* could be shown. Text study could include both classical and modern texts. Be sure to include texts that are appropriate for all ages or set up parallel age appropriate program with the same subject matter. Participatory theater (as developed by Sally Fox) uses characters which have a dilemma and share their problem with the whole group. Then the group has a chance to offer advice to the character. A dialogue ensues until the dilemma is resolved. For example, the character might be a child who decides not to help any

body because he or she is frustrated by how many people need help and aware that he/she can't help everyone. The audience helps the "child" understand that if *each* person does something to help, the world will be a better place. Possible subjects for discussion are: Maimonides' Eight Degrees Of Charity, *halachot* pertaining to *tzedakah*, why the donor benefits as much as the recipient, modern views of charity versus the Jewish view of *tzedakah* and *gemilut chasadim*.

2. Learn About Your Tzedakah Group – One to three families from each team go to an assigned place where they hear a presentation about their *tzedakah* group by the hero or the staff person or Tzedakah Committee member who is standing in. A letter from the charity may be read, or the hero may offer a visual presentation or poster display. Each person talks about the group he or she represents, describes how it works, who benefits from it, and why it is needed. Literature should be available and time set aside for questions. Once the presentation is over, allow time for families to write letters or draw pictures that will go to the group being presented.

Note: If the number of families is very small, it is still desirable to separate them as described above. The number of *tzedakah* groups can be limited to accommodate the size of the group. But the advocacy process described below helps involve people and cannot work if everyone has heard about all the groups together.

3. Team Meetings and Balloting – This part of the program consists of advocacy and the balloting.
   a. Advocacy – Regroup families into teams so that there is at least one family representing each *tzedakah* group on each team. Each family advocates for the *tzedakah* group they learned about. The presentations include a brief description of the organization, the work it does, and why the family believes it is worthy of support. Limit presentations to 3 minutes, with 2 minutes for questions. The facilitator keeps time. If there are fewer groups to represent or more time, it is possible to allow more time for the presentations and discussions.

b. Balloting – The facilitator assigns a treasurer for the team. Once the presentations are completed, each family meets together and writes a check to the Tzedakah Fund. They give it to the treasurer, and receive a ballot. No matter how large or small a contribution, each family receives one ballot. The ballot contains a list of all the recipients of money from the Tzedakah Fund. Families take time to discuss their priorities with each other. When their family discussion is finished, each family completes the ballot, designating what percentage of the total funds raised should go to each *tzedakah* group. (If this becomes an annual event, the committee may discuss alternative methods of allocating the money.)

The instructions on the ballot should explain the procedure and be followed by the list of causes next to a line for the percentage figure. Sample instructions to families follow:

Chapter

30

1. Each family is entitled to one ballot.

2. Review together the list of groups and individuals that are in this packet and which you have heard discussed for the past hour.

3. On the line next to the name of the cause below, write the percentage of the total monies that we have collected that you would like to see allocated to each one. *Make sure that your total does not exceed 100%, or your ballot can't be counted.*

   For example: You can pick out four *tzedakah* groups from the list and give each one 25% of the total. Or, you might weigh one organization more heavily, giving it 40%, then giving 20% to a second group, 10% to a third, and 5% to the six remaining groups. If you feel strongly about only two groups, divide the money evenly between the two. *You can vote any way you choose, as long as the total is 100%.*

4. The percentages on each ballot will be averaged and the money awarded accordingly.

5. We hope to be able to give you the totals today and, of course, the final allocation sheet will be sent in the mail with the report cards. If you want to make an additional

gift to a particular group, the addresses have been included on the information sheet.

6. A sheet of school stationery has been included so that you and your children can write a note to your favorite group or individual to be included with the check. These notes often mean as much in terms of encouragement as the money itself.

Special ballot question:
Please check: Yes _____ No _____

A percentage (10%) of the money raised should remain in a discretionary fund at the school to deal with emergency needs among our own families, for local emergencies in the course of the year, and to provide incentive money to match contributions that our students make during the school year. At the end of the year, money left over would return to the general Tzedakah Fund.

**Chapter**

# 30

|  | Percentage They Should Get |
|---|---|
| List of Charities | |
| 1. Ma'on Latinok – Home for Retarded Children in Israel | _____ |
| 2. The Shalom Center – Anti-nuclear advocacy | _____ |
| 3. Rabbanit Bracha Kapach – for Jerusalem poor | _____ |
| 4. Partnership – friendship between Arabs & Jews | _____ |
| 5. New Israel Fund – supports Israeli social change | _____ |
| 6. New England Chapter of P'Tach (Special Needs) | _____ |
| 7. Yad LaKashish – Lifeline for the Old in Israel | _____ |
| 8. Transition House Battered Women's Shelter | _____ |
| 9. American Association for Ethiopian Jews | _____ |
| 10. Action for Soviet Jewry – Natalya Katz Project | _____ |
| Total | 100% |

**Culmination**   As a conclusion to the program, bring everyone together and provide refreshments. Tabulate the ballots and announce the results. This is also one possible time to do an action project, such as pack boxes of food or clothing for the needy or write letters on behalf of Soviet Jewry.

**After the Program**  After the "Tzedakah Encounter," the Tzedakah Committee Chairperson or the Director of Education sends the contributions to the various charities. Accompanying each contribution is a letter from the school or congregations which identifies the donor and explains the *tzedakah* process in which families were involved, along with all the letters written and pictures drawn by participants. These letters are usually answered and the answers should be circulated among the students and their parents.

**Parallel Program for Primary Grades**  If there are several families with children in Grades K-2, Ms. Koller-Fox and Ms. Angelou suggest a parallel program for them. Parents and children are together during the study portion of the program, then parents go to hear about the charities and participate in the team meetings. Children rejoin their parents for the balloting. During their separate session, children listen to three presentations about charities that are appropriate for them. Look for groups that help people who are in trouble, or are sick or handicapped. The participatory theater idea (modified) is quite effective. A teacher can "play" either the person in need or the hero helping people in need. The *Keren Ami* money that has been collected in school is converted into 50 cent pieces and each child receives four of them. After the children have listened to the presentations, the three representatives join the children. Each has a jar and the chilren decide where to donate their money by putting their 50 cent pieces into the jars. Because they have one more coin than groups, they can be "fair," but still have to decide which group is most important to them.

Chapter

30

**Some Suggestions for Follow-up:**
Institute *chesed* (doing) projects for each holiday.

Teach mini-courses on *tzedakah.*

Involve teen-agers in planning the program and then in actually teaching younger children about *tzedakah.*

Encourage every Bar/Bat Mitzvah to contribute to the cause of his/her choice and every family to give three percent of the cost of the affair to Mazon, or a charity of its choice.

Organize summer *tzedakah* projects. (CAJE Curriculum Bank has examples.)

Have *tzedakah* assemblies every six weeks or so to recognize the accomplishments of each student.

**Editor's Comments**   An alternate way to handle the charities is to organize them by category. For example, at one "Tzedakah Encounter," the focus might be on agencies in Israel; at another such program, the focus might be on local groups. Charities can also be categorized by the nature of the services they provide, such as education, medical, shelter, etc.

When this program becomes ongoing in your community, there are additional issues which one must face. Often people will give their money, but they begin to question why they are doing so. One way to respond to this phenomenon is to invite a speaker to remind participants that they are being provided with an opportunity to perform a *mitzvah*. Be aware, too, that each new group needs to be educated about the value of community, why it is necessary to hold a vote, and why it is necessary to give funds communally. The process of educating your constituency about these issues creates a connection between your own synagogue and/or agency and the larger community.

You also need to provide people with an opportunity to perform acts of *chesed*. Since such acts are easier to perform in groups than on an individual basis, select one or two sites during the year where families can become involved. At the Harvard Hillel Children's School, families spent one day before Pesach at Project Mazon, a community-wide program, providing food. They also picked up *chametz* and distributed it to food pantries for the needy and delivered Passover packages to the elderly. At another time they spent an entire day at a nursing home working in the stead of Christian employees on Christmas day.

It is most important that the educator(s) and the Tzedakah Committee feel comfortable asking others for money. Prior to initiating the program, it is important to reinforce the *mitzvah* of *tzedakah* with those who will be facilitators by reminding them that they, too, are benefiting by having the opportunity to ask for funds. Once the leadership is aware of this, they can then inspire others.

## Bibliography/Resources

Epstein, Jerome M. *Tzedakah: A Matter Of Priorities*. New York: United Synagogue Youth, n.d.

Koller-Fox, Cherie, and Angelou, Matia. "A Family Tzedakah Project for the Summer Months." *Bikurim* 3, no. 2 (March 1986): 17-20. (CAJE, 468 Park Ave. S., New York, NY 10016)

Grishaver, Joel Lurie, and Huppin, Beth. *Tzedakah, Gemilut Chasadim and Ahavah*. Denver: Alternatives in Religious Education, Inc., 1983.

Grishaver, Joel Lurie, ed. *Tzedakah Programs That Work*. New York: Coalition for Alternatives in Jewish Education, 1987.

Olitzky, Kerry M. *My Jewish Community*. Denver: Alternatives in Religious Education, Inc., 1986.

Raz, Simcha. *A Tzaddik for Our Time*. New York: Feldheim, 1976.

Siegel, Danny. *Angels*. Spring Valley, New York: Town House Press, 1977.

_____. *Between Dust and Dance*. New York: United Synagogue of America, Department of Youth Activities, 1978.

_____. *Gadol Kevod HaBriot: Jewish Perspectives On Beauty and Ugliness*. New York: Leaders Training Fellowship of Jewish Theological Seminary, 1973.

_____. *The Giants of Jerusalem*. New York: United Synagogue Youth, n.d.

_____. *Gym Shoes and Irises*. Spring Valley, New York: Town House Press, 1982.

_____. *Tzedakah, Jewish Giving, a Privilege*. New York: United Synagogue Youth, n.d.

Chapter

# 30

Siegel, Danny; Huppin, Beth; and Novick, Bernard. *Tzedakah: Righteous Action A Teachers Guide*. New York: Coalition on Alternatives in Jewish Education, 1987.

Strassfeld, Sharon, and Strassfeld, Michael, eds. *The Second Jewish Catalog*. Philadelphia: Jewish Publication Society, 1976.

Summer, Barbara Fortgang. *Tzorchi Tzibbur: Community and Responsibility In the Jewish Tradition*. New York: United Synagogue Youth, 1976.

*Tzedakah: Not Charity, But Justice*. Part I and II. Miami: Central Agency for Jewish Education, 1977.

Zwerin, Raymond A. *For One Another*. New York: Union of American Hebrew Congregations, 1975.

Chapter

# 30

**Mediated Materials**

*Best Boy*. International Films, 159 W. 53rd St., New York, NY 10019, 1981. (film, 104 min.)

*Profiles In Chesed*. Torah Aura Productions, 4423 Fruitland Ave., Los Angeles, CA 90058, 1983. (slide/tape presentation, 40 min.)

**Source for Tzedakah Materials**

"The Great CAJE Tzedakah Encounter" – program materials and names and addresses of the recipients are available from CAJE.

CAJE Curriculum Bank, Clejan Educational Research Center, University of Judaism, 15600 Mulholland Drive, Los Angeles, CA 90077.

# Chapter 31

 **TITLE:** Tzedakah Fair

 **CONTRIBUTED BY:** Nachama Skolnik Moskowitz

 **DESIGN:** Adapted from a program designed by Linda Thal

 **TOPIC:** Providing information about *tzedakah* to the community and encouraging active involvement in *tzedakah*

 **TARGET AUDIENCE:** Entire community

 **TIME FRAME:** 2½-3 hours for the actual program; 4-6 months advance preparation

 **STAFF:** The ideal staff: an overall coordinator, representatives from various agencies, classroom teachers, Rabbi, Cantor, Director of Education, song leader, dance and art specialists. (The program can also be run without all these staff specialists.)

**Overview**   This program requires the participation and support of all auxiliary groups in the synagogue community, as well as the participation of personnel from various communal agencies. It is designed to encourage immediate involvement in *tzedakah* giving and focus on Jewish agencies as prime recipients. It involves an actual "fair" during which various individuals tell about their agencies and projects. Additionally, there are alternative activities pertaining to *tzedakah* in which people participate throughout the day.

**Purpose**   There are several goals for this program:
1. To inform congregants of the activities, goals, and needs of a variety of worthy organizations to which money raised as *tzedakah* could be sent.

2. To increase awareness of participants of the Jewish attitudes and values related to giving *tzedakah*.

3. To help parents broaden their awareness of the value of *tzedakah*, and to have them teach their children to make *tzedakah* a priority in their lives.

4. To provide an opportunity for students to participate with adults in *tzedakah* giving.

**Preparation/Procedure**   The following are the steps necessary when preparing for a Tzedakah Fair.
1. Contact all synagogue affiliated groups — women's and men's auxiliaries, caring community, youth group, senior adults, etc., and enlist their assistance with the fair. The groups may be involved in any of the following ways:
   a. Contacting outside agencies
   b. Actual setup of the fair
   c. Running booths
   d. Telephone committee
   e. Logistics

2. Contact communal agencies, both Jewish and non-Jewish to enlist their participation as booth presenters. In the letter let people know the date, the length of time of the fair, the anticipated number of people, and any space restrictions. Include an application form (see sample below) for them to return to

you, telling you who to contact, who will be present, and a diagram of how the booth should be set up.

### APPLICATION
### Tzedakah Fair

ORGANIZATION:

CONTACT PERSON/BOOTH WORKERS:

What will people learn about your organization from visiting your booth?

What will your booth look like? What graphics, pictures, films, hands-on activities will you display?

Where would you like your booth to be — in the auditorium or a classroom?

What will you need for the setup?
_____ long tables (how many? _____)
_____ round tables (how many? _____)
_____ a back wall
_____ access to electricity
_____ projection screen.
_____ other: _____ .

Thank you for helping make our Tzedakah Fair a success!

Committee contact _____

3. Recruit and orient staff.

4. Prepare a schedule of the day and reproduce in-house materials.

5. Contact families by letter and phone to let them know about the program.

6. Prepare a floor plan of the fair booths and reproduce it.

7. Obtain shopping bags or large envelopes so that people can collect materials. Pre-stuff the bags with an overview of the day, a map, and appropriate readings on *tzedakah*.

Chapter

# 31

Chapter

# 31

**Program Description**  The following schedule is suggested:

**Schedule**

9:00     Registration (collect an "admission fee" of canned goods or used clothing)
Refreshments

9:30     Worship service

10:15    The Fair
1. Booths representing the communal organizations and agencies

2. Scheduled activities to supplement the booths:
Storytelling
Mediated materials
Parents' discussion
Maimonides' Ladder Of Tzedakah Bingo

3. Ongoing activities to supplement booths:
Making *tzedakah* boxes
Banner design based on quotes from *Pirke Avot*
A visit to a hospital (*Bikur Cholim*); set up a mock bed and provide a tape of one person talking to another in the hospital.
Thematic song teaching

11:30    *Tzedakah* decisions in classes

12:00    *L'hitraot*

The program as described here allows families to learn about a variety of charitable organizations and agencies, and to move through the fair at their own pace. In classes students are asked to decide on two places to send their *tzedakah* money. One should be Jewish and the other may be of their choice. Having parents present in the decision making helps the families focus on *tzedakah* as an ongoing process.

**Supplemental Activities** (brief descriptions)
Storytelling – have someone in the library to read or tell stories on the theme of *tzedakah*.

Parents' discussion – the Rabbi helps parents clarify how they handle *tzedakah* giving with their children.

Making *tzedakah* boxes – display several *tzedakah* boxes. Participants may choose to make a *tzedakah* box in one of four different ways, depending on the level of difficulty and how much time they wish to put into it.

Banner designs – provide families with a set of quotations about *tzedakah*. Participants develop a representation of the quote of their choice on cloth.

Sign language demonstration – teach a *brachah*.

Mediated materials – schedule films and slide shows throughout the morning.

*Tzedakah* card project – make cards to send to people in the hospital for Rosh Hashanah.

Roving theater – students prepare 3-5 minute scenarios they can put on at various locations during the fair.

Chapter

# 31

**Editor's Comments** It is likely that 45 minutes is the maximum time one can concentrate on the fair itself. Having a variety of scheduled activities provides more mobility and enables people to stay involved. This necessitates integrating the supplemental activities into the entire schedule by allowing anywhere from 5 to 30 minutes for each of the activities — visiting booths, viewing films, storytelling or discussion.

Several of the supplemental activities can be integrated into the overall program. After the parents' discussion with the Rabbi, plan a family values clarification exercise on *tzedakah* during which families come up with a contract that spells out how they will become actively involved with specific *tzedakah* projects.

Every family should be given an opportunity to make *tzedakah* boxes. As part of the process, have each family discuss when they will put money into their box and to which organization they will be giving the money. Make a list of all the organizations families pick and post it on a bulletin board. Set a time to collect the money and post the overall total that is collected.

An alternate way to handle this program is to present the agencies and organizations thematically. For example, general presentations could be made about groups of agencies, such as those dealing with medical care, child welfare, education, etc. Then participants could visit individual booths.

As an additional activity, a discussion with the Rabbi is appropriate for students in Grades 6-8 or for all participants.

For another *tzedakah* program, see Chapter 30, "Tzedakah Encounter."

## Bibliography/Resources

Grishaver, Joel, and Huppin, Beth. *Tzedakah, Gemilut Chasadim and Ahavah: A Manual for World Repair.* Denver: Alternatives in Religious Education, Inc., 1983.

Strassfeld, Sharon, and Strassfeld, Michael, eds. *The Third Jewish Catalog.* Philadelphia: Jewish Publication Society, 1980.

Thal, Linda. "Spectrum Of Tsedakah." *Compass Magazine* (Fall 1983).

Chapter

**31**

### Mediated Materials

*Commitment To Life.* Alden Films, 7820 20th Ave., Brooklyn, NY 11214, 1980. (film, 18 min.)

*A Gift Of Life.* Alden Films, 1972. (film, 15 min.)

*If I Forget Thee.* Hadassah, 50 West 58th St., New York, NY 10019, 1975. (film, 28 min.)

*Kirk Douglas Reports From the Technion.* Alden Films. (film, 11 min.)

*Miracle At Intervale.* Board of Jewish Education of Greater New York, 426 West 58th St., New York, NY 10019, 1981. (filmstrip, 100 frames)

*Profiles In Chesed.* Torah Aura Productions, 4423 Fruitvale Ave., Los Angeles, CA 90058, 1983. (8 five min. slide-tape presentations)

*Project Renewal.* United Jewish Appeal, 1290 Avenue of the Americas, 1979. (film, 18 min.)

*Shield Of Life.* Alden Films, 1972. (film, 15 min.)

*Strangers — A Visit With the Falashas.* New York: Board of Jewish Education of Greater New York. (filmstrip)

*The Team.* Alden Films, 1972. (film, 28½ min.)

*Time for Survival.* Alden Films, 1976. (film, 21 min.)

*Wisdom Hath Builded Its House.* Alden Films, 1969. (film, 22 min.)

Chapter

# 31

For additional resources, see the bibliography for Chapter 30, "Tzedakah Encounter."

# Chapter 32

 **TITLE:** Beresheet: A Retreat Weekend for Families With Young Children

 **CONTRIBUTED BY:** Judy Aronson

 **TOPIC:** Integrating Torah study into family life; planning for the future of the congregation

 **TARGET AUDIENCE:** Families with young children; individuals and families who desire to strengthen their ties with the congregation

 **TIME FRAME:** One weekend

 **STAFF:** Coordinator, teachers and teaching assistants, song-leader, dance instructor, arts and crafts teacher, babysitters

**Overview** This retreat weekend was sponsored by Shir Chadash — New Reform Congregation, Woodland Hills, California, during the congregation's first year of existence. The theme of Beresheet was chosen because the congregation was at a beginning stage and because such a weekend presented an opportunity for people to come together to discuss the future of the congregation. The retreat setting allowed participants to observe Shabbat, reflect about creation, and spend quality time together without interruption.

**Purpose** This retreat program served to reinforce for participants the ongoing process of Jewish study. It was designed to bring parents and children together for reflection, study, and *chevrah*. In this particular congregation, the retreat was intended to help set some future directions for the congregation.

Chapter

32

**Preparation/Procedure** It is important that the setting enable people to be physically comfortable. A camp setting is acceptable if there are cabins for couples with private or semi-private baths, adequate space for children, meeting rooms, and play areas. Be sure to visit the site in advance to see where your group will be housed and where activities will take place.

The staff should include Rabbi, Director of Education, Cantor, teacher aides, song leader, dance instructor, art specialist. Babysitters should be hired, even if children are going to be sleeping with their parents. Assign someone to be the photographer. Enlist the teacher aides to serve as facilitators for the Family Feud game, and have them make up questions on Jewish subjects.

Plan a schedule which allows for in-depth discussions, recreation, and ancillary activities, such as crafts, dance, and drama. Send participants the schedule in advance along with a "What To Bring List." If you are in a place where those in attendance have to set tables, serve food, or even cook your own food, draw up a schedule and a brief set of instructions.

As with any retreat, you will need *shironim*, *Siddurim*, a *Sefer Torah*. Have a supply of extra items such as storybooks, board games, projector and films, or VCR and videotapes, sports equipment, etc. By all means remember to pack an adequate first aid kit.

**Program Description**    The following is an outline of the retreat schedule.

**Schedule**
Friday

|       |                                                                 |
|-------|-----------------------------------------------------------------|
| 4:00  | Arrival – settle into cabins, guided tour of camp site          |
| 6:00  | *Kabbalat Shabbat* and dinner                                   |
| 8:30  | Discussion: *Beresheet* — what does it mean to begin something new? |
|       | Assign *pesukim* to each family for Shabbat morning worship service (see below). |
| 10:00 | Friendship circle                                               |

**Chapter**

# 32

Saturday

|       |                                                                 |
|-------|-----------------------------------------------------------------|
| 9:00  | Wakeup and breakfast                                            |
|       | Free time                                                       |
| 10:00 | Services – listen for your family's *pasuk*.                    |
| 11:00 | *Tiyul*/nature walk – observe and display beautiful things that God has created. |
| 12:00 | Lunch                                                           |
|       | Free time                                                       |
| 1:30  | *Chugim* – Drama, dance, storytelling, music                   |
| 3:00  | Activities for the family                                       |
| 4:30  | Parallel parent child activities                                |
|       | Parents: Discussion — How do you feel about creating a congregation? Future directions |
|       | Children: Lesson on creation                                    |
| 5:30  | Dinner                                                          |
| 6:30  | Craft: Everyone makes *Havdalah* spice boxes to take home.     |
| 7:30  | Gather for *Havdalah* Service.                                 |
| 8:00  | Evening Activity – *Family Feud*                               |
| 9:30  | Children go to bed.                                            |
|       | Parent Discussion: How do you see yourself as part of the congregation? |

|        | What role will you take?                                                |
|--------|-------------------------------------------------------------------------|
| 10:30  | Parent friendship circle                                                |

Sunday

| 8:00  | Wake up and breakfast |
|-------|-----------------------|
| 9:00  | Clean cabins and pack |
| 10:00 | Parallel parent-child activities |
|       | Parents: Discussion – concrete programs; suggestions for the congregation |
|       | Children: God in my life |
| 11:00 | Parent-child activity: Describe the creation of the world as if . . . (see below). |
| 12:00 | Lunch |
| 1:00  | Friendship circle; *L'hitraot.* |

## Chapter 32

The Friday evening activity related to the assignment of *pesukim* and the Sunday morning activity during which families describe the creation of the world from different perspectives are described below.

**Pasuk Activity**    Read through the story of creation in English. Discuss the main ideas. Reread it in Hebrew, translating as you go along. Assign each family a particular *pasuk* or part of a *pasuk* to listen for during the Torah reading at services on Shabbat morning. In advance, prepare each *pasuk* on a piece of paper with pointed Hebrew, Torah script, or transliteration and translation. Once the *pesukim* have been assigned, open the *Sefer Torah* and show the families where their particular *pesukim* occur.

**Describe the Creation Of the World As If . . .**    Reread the story of creation. Assign each family to rethink the story of creation based on the different perspectives of:

1. A baseball player (soccer player, football player, etc.)

2. An artist

3. A computer expert

4. A musician

5. A physician

6. An actor/actress

7. An architect

8. A gardener

9. An astronaut

10. A policeman/policewoman

Once this assignment is completed, have each family share their descriptions of creation.

**Editor's Comments**   The retreat model outlined here may be adapted to any subject. The Torah study applies to any portion of the Torah and may be enhanced with guided reading and *midrashim*.

In order for a retreat such as this to be successful, it is necessary that the number of participants be no less than ten families and no more than 25 families. Pre-registration helps to clarify the programming in terms of children's ages and family needs. Young families often have to bring infants and toddlers. It may be necessary to provide for them as well. If you have a large number of teen-agers, you may want to set up some activities for them together with their parents which do not necessarily involve younger children.

Chapter

32

## Bibliography/Resources

Beiner, Stan. *Sedra Scenes*. Denver: Alternatives in Religious Education, Inc., 1982.

Chill, Arthur A. *A Guide To Sidraot and Haftarot*, New York: KTAV, 1971.

Grishaver, Joel Lurie. "Family Kallah: A Program Guide." *Alternatives Magazine* 4 (Spring 1974):26-29.

Hertz, J.H. *The Pentateuch and Haftorahs*. London: Soncino Press, 1972.

Lipis, Philip L., and Katzoff, Louis. *Torah for the Family.* Jerusalem: World Jewish Bible Society, 1977.

Loeb, Sorel Goldberg, and Kadden, Barbara Binder. *Teaching Torah: A Treasury Of Insights and Activities.* Denver: Alternatives in Religious Education, Inc., 1984.

Plaut, W. Gunther; Bamberger, Bernard J.; and Hallo, William W. *The Torah: A Modern Commentary.* New York: Union of American Hebrew Congregations, 1981.

Reisman, Bernard, and Abraham, Harriet. *Jewish Families Together: A Model Weekend Retreat for Family Life Enhancement.* New York: William Petschek National Family Center, American Jewish Committee.

Zielenziger, Ruth. *Teaching Genesis.* Teacher's Guide. New York: Melton Research Center, 1981.

Chapter

32

**Mediated Materials**

Grishaver, Joel Lurie. *Torah Toons* I and II. Torah Aura Publications, 4423 Fruitdale Ave., Los Angeles, CA 90058, 1983-84. (slide-tape presentations, 5-7 min. each)

# Chapter 33

 **TITLE:** Bar/Bat Mitzvah Family Retreat

 **CONTRIBUTED BY:** Sherry Bissell Blumberg

 **TOPIC:** Bar/Bat Mitzvah preparation, Shabbat, *mitzvot*

 **TARGET AUDIENCE:** Students in Grade 7 and their families

 **TIME FRAME:** One weekend or one overnight

 **STAFF:** Coordinator, Rabbi, Cantor, music specialist, craft specialist, counselors for children

**Overview** This program is a retreat for families whose children will become Bar or Bat Mitzvah within the coming year. It is part of an ongoing series of family programs connected with the Bar/Bat Mitzvah class at Temple Israel in Long Beach, California. There are three family programs which precede the retreat and one following the retreat.

The first program which precedes the retreat deals with expectations of Bar/Bat Mitzvah. At this program parents and children make a plan for the service. At the second program, families talk about continuing the chain of tradition by having a Jewish home. The third program focuses on the concept of *mitzvah* as families design and/or make a *tallit* for the Bar/Bat Mitzvah and discuss *tzedakah* and *gemilut chasadim*. At the session following the retreat, those families whose child has already become Bar or Bat Mitzvah, talk about the experience. Others talk about special moments in their family's lives. The chain of tradition is symbolically continued by passing the Torah from one family to another.

The retreat is designed to help families spend quality time together in a Jewish setting with a primary focus on Bar or Bat Mitzvah. Several activities center around Shabbat, others around Jewish history and, if the retreat is scheduled near a holiday, such as Purim or Pesach, there is a learning segment pertaining to that holiday. Since this is part of an ongoing series of family programs, families are often responsible for some aspects of the programming.

**Purpose** The purpose of the retreat is to provide families with an opportunity to study and learn about Judaism in a comfortable atmosphere with no outside distractions. The program is also intended to bring families in the community closer together by providing them with common Jewish experiences.

**Preparation/Procedure** The family retreat should be scheduled early in the year so that the thematic elements can be determined and people can plan for it in advance. Once the date has been set, the appropriate site found, and the theme decided upon, publicize the retreat to the constituency and place it on the synagogue and community calendars. Be sure that the support staff — the Rabbi, specialists, teachers — all have the date cleared.

When planning a retreat, there are several administrative decisions that need to be made in advance:

1. Fee – is it included in school registration or is there a separate fee for the retreat?

2. How many nights – one or two?

3. Transportation – buses or carpools or both?

4. Food – will there be someone at the campsite to cook or will it be necessary to bring your own food?

5. Sleeping arrangements – dormitory style, tents, private rooms for parents, or bunks for children?

6. Meeting areas.

7. Time of year – this is of importance because the weather will influence your program. It is necessary to plan activities for both indoors and outdoors, no matter when the retreat takes place.

Be sure to bring all the necessary supplies, and ritual objects. Prepare the puzzle pieces and materials in advance. Families with children under six should be encouraged to make other arrangements for these children.

**Program Description**    Below is a sample schedule for a family retreat, followed by instructions for some of the segments. Those segments of the program marked with an asterisk (*) should be assigned for advance planning to one or more participating families.

Chapter

## 33

### Schedule
Friday

| | |
|---|---|
| 3:00 | Leave for retreat. |
| 5:30 | Arrive at camp, go to cabins, set up for Shabbat. |
| 6:30 | *Kabbalat Shabbat* |
| 7:00 | Dinner and *zemirot* |

| | 8:15 | Introductory activities – *Secrets, *Match Game |
| | 9:00 | Shabbat Can Be . . . celebrating with our families |
| | 9:45 | *Oneg Shabbat* and Friendship Circle |
| | 10:15 | Children to bed |
| | | *Adults – songs and stories |

**Saturday**

| | 8:30 | Breakfast |
| | 9:30 | *Worship Services |
| | 10:30 | Free Family Time: |
| | | *Nature Walks |
| | | *Book Reviews |
| | | *Quiet Games |
| | 11:30 | *Bar Mitzvah Bowl |

Chapter

# 33

| | 12:30 | Lunch and *Shirah* |
| | 1:30 | Rest and Quiet |
| | 2:30 | Torah Study |
| | 3:30 | Round Robin: |
| | | 1. Torah Classifieds |
| | | 2. Mini-Tzedakah Fair |
| | | 3. Puzzle |
| | 5:00 | *Seudah Shleesheet* |
| | 5:15 | Free Time |
| | 6:15 | *Havdalah* (time will vary depending on the season) |
| | 6:45 | Dinner and *Shirah* |
| | 8:00 | Evening Program |
| | | *Value Prompters* (A.R.E.) |
| | | Film (*The Jazz Singer, Lies My Father Told Me*, or other film with a Jewish theme, accompanied by popcorn, hot chocolate, etc.) |
| | 10:15 | Friendship Circle |
| | | Children to bed |

**Sunday**

| | 8:30 | Breakfast |
| | 9:30 | Crafts (designing *tallitot*) |
| | 10:45 | *Olympics or Maccabiah |
| | 12:00 | Lunch |
| | 1:00 | Friendship Circle and *L'hitraot* |

## Instructions for Various Activities

1. Match Game – Prepare cards in advance which match Jewish historical figures with each other, with events, concepts, and/or literature. Distribute the cards randomly and tell people to find a match for their card. Some suggestions for cards are: Abraham, Sarah, One God; Moses, Miriam, the Exodus from Egypt; David, Holy Ark, Jerusalem; Hillel, Shammai, Talmud; David Ben Gurion, Golda Meir, May 14, 1948; Isaac Luria, Kabbalah, Safed; etc. Once everyone has been matched up, discuss the matches with the whole group.

2. Secrets – Ask everyone to fill out a "secret card," listing a secret of theirs related to Bar and Bat Mitzvah and to send it in with their camp application form. During this segment of the round robin, the secrets are shared. Shuffle the secret cards and have everyone pick one and respond to it as if it were his or her own secret.

3. Shabbat Can Be . . . – **Give** each family a copy of the book *Shabbat Can Be* by **Raymond A.** Zwerin and Audrey Friedman Marcus. Ask each **family** to read through the book and decide for themselves what "Shabbat Can Be" for them. Allow about 20 minutes for this. Once families have decided what "Shabbat Can Be," have each family share its vision. Tell them to use as many details and personal references as possible. Once everyone has shared what "Shabbat Can Be," conclude the activity by going around the group, each person responding to the sentence, "This Shabbat is special because

_____."

4. Bar/Bat Mitzvah Bowl – Use the model of the television show "College Bowl." Teams answer questions pertaining to Bar/Bat Mitzvah. The questions range from identifying commonly used terms, such as Bar or Bat Mitzvah, *tallit*, *tzedakah*, to other concepts, such as how a Torah portion is selected, the relationship between the Torah and *Haftarah*, the role of the prophetic literature in Jewish tradition, etc. Use questions relating to Jewish history and inferential questions, e.g., "What if the Sixth Zionist Congress had accepted the Uganda plan?" Or, "What would have happened to Jews in Russia if there had been no Revolution?" The teams consist of three or four people representing as many families as possible. Judges decide who gives the best answers (all very subjective, and everyone comes out a winner!).

Chapter

33

5. Round Robin – Each family goes to each of the following three activities for 20 minutes.

   a. Torah Classifieds — This is adapted from "Jewish Classifieds" in *The Jewish Experiential Book* by Bernard Reisman. The facilitator reads two or three "classified ads" which pertain to Torah portions. Participants have to identify the people, situations, etc., by finding the similar situation in the *Chumash*. Two examples of ads follow:

   Wanted: A person who likes to travel and will be keeper of a flame for a group wandering in the desert. Must be available to come to the Tent of Meeting at a moment's notice.

   Help Wanted: Individuals who are willing to help others to interpret legal jargon to improve their life styles. Should have good reading knowledge of ancient writings found on some chipped tablets.

   b. Mini-Tzedakah Fair – Set up booths or a long table with information about several charities. Have families collect the information and decide with their child which ones they would like to learn more about. Then, when they get home, they can decide where to donate *tzedakah* in honor of the child's Bar/Bat Mitzvah.

   c. Puzzle – Every person is given a puzzle piece and families put their pieces together to make a large puzzle. When the puzzle is completed, it contains pictures of things that pertain to Bar/Bat Mitzvah, but the child is missing. Families learn that the puzzle is not complete until the child becomes Bar/Bat Mitzvah. (Because this activity may not take 20 minutes for some people, have a back-up ready, such as smaller puzzles or a scrambled word game pertaining to Bar/Bat Mitzvah.)

6. Making *tallitot* — Have available double sided pieces of fabric of a medium weight that are 36″-48″ wide and 40″-60″ in length. Provide ribbons; string for *tzitzit*, strips of brocade of silk or satin; metalic threads; needles and threads, scissors, fabric glue, and Hebrew letter stencils. Have everyone select a piece of fabric to decorate. The strips of brocade may be used for an *atara* and the ribbon for stripes if they so desire. Instruct people on how to tie *tzitzit* and have them attach the

*tzitzit* to the four corners of a *tallit*. At the end of the session, teach the blessing for putting on the *tallit*. Each recites when donning the *tallit* he/she has made. For more suggestions on *tallit* making, consult *The First Jewish Catalog* by Richard Siegel, Michael Strassfeld, and Sharon Strassfeld, pp. 55-57.

**Editor's Comments**    There are several ways to vary the format of this retreat. As an example it may be held over one night — i.e., from *Erev Shabbat* to *Motza'ay Shabbat*, or *Motza'ay Shabbat* to Sunday afternoon. For a 24 hour time span, it will be necessary to eliminate several activities, such as the round robin, extended free time, and the film. On the other hand, the intensity of the experience may add to the communal feeling.

There is a variety of other activities which can be included in the program. Family interviews, for instance, may be used as an introductory activity. One family interviews another, then introduces the family they interviewed to the entire group. Prepare a list of questions families should ask each other. Still another way to open the program is to have families draw a picture of themselves doing their favorite Jewish thing. They then go around and introduce themselves to others through their picture. Or, they stand up and explain their picture to the entire group.

Chapter

33

If the retreat is being held close to a holiday, include a learning activity pertaining to the holiday. For Purim conduct a study session with particular references to the *mitzvot* of Purim and the *Megillah*. Explain some of the Purim traditions such as *Purimshpiels* and wearing masks. Participants can create *Purimshpiels* or make masks, or both.

If the retreat is close to Pesach, review the elements of the *Haggadah* and encourage families to create a family *Haggadah* to be used at their *Seder*. These *Haggadot* can be presented to the entire group, or they can be typed and reproduced for others after the weekend. Other crafts activities are: making pillow covers, *matzah* covers, *Seder* plates, cups for Elijah, etc.

*Chugim*, such as dance, music, drama, storytelling, other crafts projects, and cooking can be added to the program during the round robin or in free time. Two appropriate crafts projects are the making of *kipot* and prayer book covers. For making *kipot* have white, unlined *kipot* available, along with sequins, bangles, yarn, metallic thread, pieces of felt, and fabric glue. Have each member of the family make a *kipah* for himself/herself. For making prayer book covers, use the same materials as for *kipot*. But, in advance, cut fabric to a size which will cover the congregational prayer book, adding flaps so that the prayer book can fit into it. These may be sewn together in advance or have families glue them together after they have made the covers.

As a further idea, free time can be used for families to write a song, prepare a skit, or rehearse an evening presentation or culminating program.

**Chapter**

**33**

The retreat presented here is part of an ongoing series of family programs. It can be implemented as a one-time family event without the other one day programs. If this is the case, then it would be beneficial to include more elements that pertain to Bar or Bat Mitzvah, such as examining the *mitzvot* and personalizing them, continuing the chain of tradition through life cycle events, and intense Torah study with each family making a report about their Torah and *Haftarah* portion. Crafts can focus on the Bar/Bat Mitzvah and may include making a Torah breastplate, wimpels, or a family heirloom, such as a *mezzuzah* holder, a *Mizrach* plaque, candlesticks, or *Kiddush* cups.

**Bibliography/Resources**   See the bibliography for Chapter 8, "The Melton Bar/Bat Mitzvah Program."

# Chapter 34

 **TITLE:** God Is Alive and Well and Living At Temple Beth El

 **CONTRIBUTED BY:** Janice Alper

 **TOPIC:** God

 **TARGET AUDIENCE:** Families with children in Kindergarten and above

 **TIME FRAME:** One weekend

 **STAFF:** Overall coordinator, Rabbi, Cantor, teachers to act as facilitators, bunk counselors, junior staff, music specialist, craft specialist, dance instructor

**Overview**   This camp weekend, which took place at Temple Beth El in San Pedro, California, focuses on the theme of God with families who have children in Kindergarten and above. There are a variety of interactive segments, as well as a few parallel activities during which parents and children study separately. Both groups consider the idea of God within a Jewish framework and are helped to begin talking about God in their lives.

**Purpose**   The program has several goals:

1. To help participants think about their personal views of God.

2. To help participants realize that God has been conceptualized in many ways throughout Jewish history.

Chapter
**34**

3. To help participants bring God into their lives in a meaningful and relevant fashion.

4. To help parents find ways to talk about God with their children and among themselves.

**Preparation/Procedure**   This program requires all the normal administrative preparations pertaining to a camp weekend — site selection, meal planning, room and bunk assignments, staff recruitment, orientation, etc. As on all retreat weekends, be sure there are *Siddurim, Shironim, Chumashim,* a *Sefer Torah,* and a *Havdalah* set available. In addition, bring quiet games, sports equipment, period costumes, clay, films and projector, VCR and videotapes, and anything else that makes a retreat work.

Hold an orientation meeting with staff and review the program. If the group will be large, divide the families into several groups with a facilitator for each group. At the orientation delineate the specific cognitive elements to emphasize in the *sichot* (discussions), as well as the responsibilities of the facilitator. Bunk counselors, junior staff, and specialists need to know how they fit into the total program and what their specific responsibilities will be. If there are teen-agers in attendance, they can be utilized as junior staff and share some of the responsibilities of overseeing younger children.

Reproduce parent study materials and mail them in advance. Prepare "God Journals" for each participant. These should include guided writings pertaining to each *sichah*, several quotes about God from Jewish sources, and blank pages for additional personal comments. For younger children (K-3), the "God Journals" should be prepared on 8½" by 11" sheets of paper utilizing large print. For older children (Grade 4 and above) and parents, use smaller size paper with smaller type. Enclose the blank journals in a packet for each family that contains a schedule for the weekend, pencils, emergency procedures, and any other information participants will need.

When sending out applications for the weekend, enclose a list of things families can do to enhance the program. Ask them to check off how they would like to participate. Assign families to take charge of some of the activities, such as special interest groups, leading services, *Havdalah*, hikes, sports, etc. Let them know in advance what their assignments will be and when they will take place. If several families have signed up to do the same thing, put them in touch with each other to plan their activity. This helps to build community. Encourage families with children below the age of five to leave these youngsters at home with a babysitter.

Chapter
34

**Program Description**   The following is an outline of the weekend schedule:

**Schedule**
Friday

| | |
|---|---|
| 4:00 | Leave for camp |
| 6:00 | Arrive at camp, go to cabins/rooms/bunks and unpack. |
| 7:00 | *Kabbalat Shabbat* and dinner |
| | *Zemirot* |
| 8:30 | *Sichah* I: Concepts Of God |
| 9:30 | Israeli dancing/*Oneg Shabbat*/Friendship Circle |
| 10:00 | Children to bed |

Saturday

| | |
|---|---|
| 8:00 | Services |
| 9:00 | Breakfast |

|       |                                                                      |
|-------|----------------------------------------------------------------------|
| 10:15 | *Sichah* II: It's a Miracle                                          |
|       | Miracle Museum                                                       |
|       | Nature Walk                                                          |
|       | Shaping with clay                                                    |
| 11:45 | Free time                                                            |
| 12:30 | Lunch and *Shirah*                                                   |
| 1:30  | Quiet time                                                           |
| 2:30  | *Chugim* — Singing, dancing, drama, storytelling, etc.              |
| 3:45  | Snack                                                                |
| 4:00  | *Sichah* III: If God Exists Why . . .                               |
| 5:30  | Torah Study (optional)                                               |
| 6:30  | *Havdalah*                                                           |
| 7:00  | Dinner and *Shirah*                                                  |
| 8:30  | Evening Program                                                      |
|       | New Games: *People Pyramids, The Mating Game, Prui, Hagoo* (see *The New Games Book* by Andrew Fluegelman) |
|       | Family skits                                                        |
|       | *Chugim* Presentations                                              |
| 10:00 | Friendship Circle                                                   |
|       | Children to bed                                                     |

Sunday

|       |                                          |
|-------|------------------------------------------|
| 8:30  | Breakfast                                |
| 9:30  | Clean cabins/pack                        |
| 10:00 | *Sichah* IV: Bringing God Into My Life   |
| 11:15 | Softball game                            |
| 12:15 | Lunch/*L'hitraot*                        |
| 12:30 | Leave for home                           |

A description of the four *sichot* follows:

**Sichah I: Concepts Of God**    The purpose of this activity is to present several ways God has been thought of in Judaism and to help families develop their own views of God. Provide background materials to presenters from *midrashim*. Select three concepts of God — God as king, God as architect, God as feminine — and have someone come forward to represent each concept to the group. Have each person speak as an advocate for his/her position. Some examples follow:

I think God is like a king, because a king rules a place, protects us, and is the most important person in a country . . .

I think God is like an architect, because an architect builds things according to a plan and there is a great plan for the universe.

I think God is feminine, because the tradition teaches that wherever people gather to study, the *Shechinah* (indwelling spirit) dwells, and every day people all over the world study . . .

After the presentations, have people gather in groups of three or four families and discuss their own concepts of God. The facilitator should review the presentations and then encourage families to express other views of God — e.g., God as a president, a parent, an inventor, a team manager, a musician. When all the groups have processed their concepts of God, these are presented to everyone present.

Chapter

**34**

**Sichah II: It's a Miracle**   In a round robin fashion, families go to each of the three following activities for 30-40 minutes. It is best to divide families according to the ages of their children.

1. Miracle Museum — At this stop families view or discuss miracles in the Bible, in Jewish history, in life, and in science. Use pictures, film clips, diagrams, overhead projectors, charts, etc. Some of the miracles may be: the burning bush, the modern State of Israel, birth, the atom, space travel.

   Before doing this, discuss with the group what a miracle is. Use material about Jewish views of miracles from *A Book Of Jewish Concepts* by Philip Birnbaum. Help participants realize that miracles which occurred in the Bible may not occur today, but there are other miracles now taking place. Explain that in the museum they will see a whole range of miracles. Once the four different areas of miracles have been discussed (miracles in the Bible, in Jewish history, in life, and in science), participants are to name other things they think are miracles and talk about whether or not there are miracles in their own lives.

2. Nature Walk – Take people on a walk and talk about God's creations. Before you start the walk, ask everyone to close their eyes for a moment and listen to the sounds around

them. When they open their eyes, discuss the sounds they heard – wind, birds, animals, water running, etc. Now show them a crystal prism. Hold it up to the light and ask them what they see – there will be many colors reflected in the prism. Tell participants that they will need to listen and look very carefully at things as they proceed on the walk. Select a path that has as much variety as possible – different kinds of trees and vegetation, hills, rocks, animal life, water. When participants have completed the walk read the poem "Trees" by Joyce Kilmer.

3. Shaping With Clay – Motivate participants by reminding them that we all have God-given talents to create things. Let everyone talk about a special object that he/she has. When the discussion is completed, tell them that they are going to shape a container to hold a special object. It can be any shape they want it to be, and it can be of any size. When the clay containers are finished, suggest that they find a special object during the weekend to keep in them. If possible arrange to have the clay objects fired and glazed at a later time.

**Sichah III: If God Exists Why . . . .**     The object of this *sichah* is to help participants realize that much of what is wrong with our world can be repaired by people. For this session, divide into parallel learning activities. Parents have their own separate session and children are divided according to children's grade levels — K-2, 3-5, 6-8, 9-adult. These sessions are described below:

1. Grades K-2 – Using the book *Let's Talk About God* by Dorothy Kripke and Meyer Levin as the stimulus, talk with the children about the things God does for us. Then discuss what we do for God.

2. Grades 3-5/6-8 – The students in these grade levels put God on trial. In order to do this, they develop a job description for the ideal God. After that, each grade prepares a case against God for causing some unpleasantness in the world. There are two trials, one for Grades 3-5 and one for Grades 6-8. The students are the prosecutors and the staff members are the judges and defense attorneys.

Chapter
34

Grades 3-5 might discuss pets dying, parents fighting, or children who have no homes. Grades 4-6 might discuss world hunger, the Holocaust, or terrorism.

3. Parents
   a. Provide parents with articles written by modern Jewish thinkers, such as Eliezer Berkovits, Elie Wiesel, Abraham Joshua Heschel, Eugene Borowitz, Emil Fackenheim, Mordecai Kaplan, etc., concerning God and the People of Israel. The facilitator should be familiar with all the reading materials, have background information about the authors, and be able to guide participants.
   b. Divide parents into groups, each with one article or essay. Instruct them to read the article or essay and then, as the writer, discuss how they would respond to the question, "If God exists why was there a Holocaust?"
   c. After each group has had an opportunity to read its article and discuss their response, reconvene everyone for presentations. Tell them to summarize the article and tell about their group discussion.

Chapter

**34**

**Sichah IV: Bringing God Into My Life**   There are two parts to this *sichah*, "Bringing God Into My Life" and "Personal Prayers or Poems To God." The exercises are adapted from *God: The External Challenge* by Sherry Bissell, with Audrey Friedman Marcus and Raymond A. Zwerin. The purpose of this *sichah* is to have families find ways to bring God into their lives and to write personal poems or prayers to God.

1. Bringing God Into My Life – Distribute worksheets to everyone which contain the following statements:

   I talk to God when _____

   God talks to me when _____

   I pray to God when _____

   I know God thinks about me when _____

   Have everyone complete the worksheets individually (K-1 children may need some help from counselors or junior staff). When everyone has finished, have families come together and discuss with each other what they have written.

When this is done, ask for group responses as to how they can bring God into their lives. Make a list. Tell families to decide what they would choose from the list to bring God into their lives. Some examples may be saying the *Shema* every night, going to services regularly, helping others, taking a few moments out of the day to think about God, etc.

2. Personal Prayers or Poems To God – Play or sing the song "*Eli, Eli*" by Hannah Senesh. Translate it, then teach it to everyone. Tell participants this poem to God expresses its author's view of God. Now ask families to write a prayer or poem to God. When they are finished, ask people to share what they write. Collect all of the writings, put them into a booklet, and send it to all participating families after the retreat.

Chapter

34

**Editor's Comments**    This, like any camp program, can be varied according to the needs of the target group. One way to enhance it is to use clips from movies, such as *Star Wars* or *The Ten Commandments* to show God as a force or to illustrate some of the miracles. The film *Oh, God* is very provocative, particularly for adults.

The learning activities are designed to show how God enters our lives. The program content can be altered to include the issue of holiness and living according to divine expectations. Participants can deal with what it means to be holy, why God is holy, and what we can do in our lives to become holy.

The entire weekend can focus on God in Jewish history. Begin by discussing the God of the ancients, the God of the Bible. As the weekend progresses, look at God in the Rabbinic period, in medieval philosophy, in modern times. Compare the way God is portrayed in these perids. Develop a God lexicon which lists all the words we use for the names of God and the different words we use to describe God. Integrate prayers and blessings and how these reflect God as a part of our lives.

Another aspect of the retreat can be a discussion of what the world would be like if there were no God. Discuss the role God plays in our lives. If God did not exist for us, how would our lives be different?

An additional program can be set up for parents to deal with questions about God which they themselves have and how to answer their children's questions. Use *When Children Ask About God* by Harold Kushner as a basis for the discussion. Encourage ongoing sessions after the weekend.

### Bibliography/Resources

Berkovits, Eliezer. *God, Man and History: A Jewish Interpretation*. Middle Village, NY: Jonathan David Publishers, Inc., 1979.

Birnbaum, Philip. *A Book Of Jewish Concepts*. New York: Hebrew Publishing Co., 1964.

Bissell, Sherry, with Marcus, Audrey Friedman, and Zwerin, Raymond A. *God: The Eternal Challenge*. Denver: Alternatives in Religious Education, Inc., 1980.

Cohen, Rabbi Henry. *Why Judaism? A Search for Meaning In Jewish Identity*. New York: Union of American Hebrew Congregations, 1980.

Cone, Molly. *Hear, O Israel*. New York: Union of American Hebrew Congregations, 1973.

Fackenheim, Emil L. "The Commanding Voice Of Auschwitz." *God's Presence In History*. New York: New York University Press, 1970.

Fluegelman, Andrew, ed. *The New Games Book*. Garden City, New York: Doubleday & Co., 1976.

Gittelsohn, Roland B. *Little Lower Than the Angels*. New York: Union of American Hebrew Congregations, 1958.

Grishaver, Joel Lurie. "Family Kallah: A Program Guide." *Alternatives Magazine* 4 (Spring 1974):26-29.

Heschel, Abraham Joshua. *God In Search Of Man: A Philosophy Of Judaism*. New York: Farrar, Straus and Giroux, 1984.

Chapter
34

Kaplan, Mordecai. *Judaism As a Civilization*. Philadelphia: Jewish Publication Society, 1981.

Kripke, Dorothy K. *Let's Talk About God*. New York: Behrman House, Inc., 1963.

Kripke, Dorothy K., and Levin, Meyer. *God and the Story Of Judaism*. New York: Behrman House, Inc., 1962.

Kushner, Harold. *When Bad Things Happen To Good People*. New York: Schocken Books, 1981.

_____. *When Children Ask About God*. New York: Schocken Books, 1971.

Markowitz, Samuel H. *Adjusting the Jewish Child To His World*. New York: National Federation of Temple Sisterhoods, 1961.

Plaut, Gunther. *Judaism and the Scientific Spirit*. New York: Union of American Hebrew Congregations, 1962.

Reisman, Bernard, and Abraham, Harriet. *Jewish Families Together: A Model Weekend Retreat for Family Life Enhancement*. New York: William Petschek National Family Center, American Jewish Committee, 1986.

Soncino, Rifat, and Syme, Daniel B. *Finding God*. New York: Union of American Hebrew Congregations, 1986.

Chapter

34

# Chapter 35

 **TITLE:** Passport To America

 **CONTRIBUTED BY:** Ronald Isaacs and Leora Isaacs

 **TOPIC:** Immigration to America

 **TARGET AUDIENCE:** Families with junior high and high school children

 **TIME FRAME:** One evening (2-2½ hours) and one day (3-5 hours); 2-3 months preparation

 **STAFF:** Classroom teachers, volunteers for the various stops

**Overview**   At Temple Sholom in Bridgewater, New Jersey, junior high and high school age students with their families reenacted the immigration experience in America. The program began on a Saturday night and ended on Sunday morning. It was an extension of the students' curriculum and allowed them to actualize their experiences by portraying one of their forebears. This simulation involves a great deal of preparation and cooperation among students and parents and the school.

**Purpose**   The intent of the program is to bring the Jewish immigration experience to life for the students and to make it relevant. The program can also help students to appreciate the experiences of their ancestors as they arrived in America.

Chapter

35

**Preparation/Procedure**   Classrooms are transformed into the American Consulate, the Great Hall at Ellis Island, a ship, and the Lower East Side of New York. One area is made into a *shtiebl* (one-room synagogue) with a *mechitzah* (separation between men and women).

During the two months preceding the event, students in the 7th and 10th Grades make an in-depth study of the third wave of immigration (the Jews who came from Russia 1881-1924). The material is reviewed briefly with 8th and 9th Grades, and with 11th and 12th Grade students. Adult volunteer participants are briefed and receive outlines of their roles and a list of suggested readings. In addition, each participant is instructed to choose an ancestor to portray and to research his/her family history. Teachers and parents are involved in helping students with this preparation. Any student who is unable to fulfill the task is assigned an identity. Each student is also instructed to prepare a wardrobe for the journey and a *peckele* filled with carefully selected possessions to take along.

**Program Description**   An overview of the program follows:

**Saturday Evening**   The event begins on Saturday night, with an orientation event from 8-11:00 P.M. For this session, students do not come in costume. Following *Havdalah*, the movie *Hester*

Street is shown. To insure that participants pay close attention to relevant details in the film and to maximize its impact, hold a contest. A series of three question sheets, one for each third of the film, is prepared and handed out. Students are given a few moments to familiarize themselves with the questions before each third, and time afterward to complete each sheet. A number of trivia-type questions are *not* printed in advance, but read after each third to add to the suspense and fun, and to diminish the "test" aspect. Prizes are awarded for the top three scores overall.

The evening ends with an old fashioned make-your-own-sundae ice cream social. Background music for dancing and listening can be arranged by high school students who also act as DJs and play a mixture of contemporary and *Klezmer* records.

**Sunday**   Students arrive at the synagogue at 10 A.M. for the *Shacharit* service dressed in turn of the century costumes. They are greeted by the Rabbi and the faculty, who are also in costume. The library-chapel is transformed into a *shtiebl* with a *mechitzah*. Participants *daven* using Ashkenazic Hebrew, traditional *nusach*, and no modern melodies. Parents, also in costume, play an integral role in the simulation.

Chapter

# 35

After services, the reenactment continues. Each "immigrant" is required to pass through four stations. The stations, which are described below, are:

Station I:   American Consulate Office at a port city in Western Europe

Station II:   Ellis Island

Station III:   Night School

Station IV:   Lower East Side

**Station I: The American Consulate Office**   Immigration manifests and passports are distributed. "Immigrants" fill them out using their prepared identities. Some, including Cabbage Patch children, come as family groups; others as individuals. Passport photographs are taken with an instant camera and appended to the passports. Students retain these as mementos of the event. The completed manifests and passports are checked by the United States Consular Official (who wears an appropriate and imposing uniform), then approved with rubber stamps, and a visa issued. Some officials seem to be corrupt and extort bribes from individuals whose papers are not in order.

The group finally proceeds to the point of embarkation. The very cramped ship is simulated by placing long tables on their sides. Immigrants crowd in, sit on the floor, and rock back and forth. Portions of the Charlie Chaplin film entitled *The Immigrant*, which humorously depicts an ocean voyage, are screened.

**Station II: Ellis Island**   Upon arrival, participants get a view of a facsimile of the Statue of Liberty. Passengers disembark to the Great Hall at Ellis Island. They are given landing cards to complete and lapel tags so that officials can mark their status after each examination. Their first stop is at the desk of the Immigration Officer who interrogates each family group separately and collects their landing cards. The immigration officer, after verifying which language the immigrant speaks, asks questions in a different foreign language. This simulates the communication problems actually encountered. Immigrants are asked such questions as:

1. What is your name?

2. With whom have you come?

3. What work do you do?

4. Who paid for your passage?

5. Is anyone meeting you? Do you have a sponsor?

6. With whom are you staying? Do you have any relatives?

7. How much money do you have? Show it to me. Can you provide for yourself? Where did you get the money?

8. Are you an anarchist? Have you ever been in prison?

9. Do you have promised employment?

The Immigration Officer is instructed to **arrange** for certain individuals to be denied immigration. Immigrants are forced to solve such dilemmas as:

1. Female with no sponsor, denied admittance. (Solutions include marrying a HIAS official, or another immigrant who had a sponsor, right at Ellis Island.)

2. Less than $20 (insufficient funds). Robberies and borrowing occur.

3. Anarchist discovered/criminal record

4. Name changes occurred for many immigrants.

5. An immigrant admitted to having been promised employment, and was denied admittance due to the law prohibiting slave labor arrangements.

Immigration officials are instructed to "hang tough," not to suggest solutions, and to make immigrants solve their own problems. Officials speak foreign languages whenever possible.

Chapter

**35**

Upon passing the initial cross-examination, immigrants wait in line to be examined in the medical examination booth by the doctor and his nurse. Using a child's medical kit, they question and examine each immigrant. Of course, some are sent to be deloused. In a family group a young child is denied admittance and the family is required to decide what to do. Another adult is placed in quarantine, and still others are denied admission due to mental and physical handicaps.

As they leave Ellis Island, immigrants are met by HIAS representatives. They receive copies of the column "Bintel Brief" from the *Forward* and circulars for job openings, most of which deny employment to Jews. There is a hubbub of noise as immigrants share experiences and comments about discrimination, etc.

**Station III: Night School**   Once in America, the process of acculturation begins. Students study a lesson in English and hear a selection from *The Education of H\*Y\*M\*A\*N  K\*A\*P\*L\*A\*N* by Leo C. Rosten.

They also prepare for and take their citizenship exams. Upon completion of the exam, a robed judge enters to administer the oath of citizenship and immigrants are awarded "green cards," which are coincidentally meal tickets on the Lower East Side.

**Station IV: Lower East Side**   Immigrants are treated to a "Lower East Side Pushcart Hot Dog Lunch," including a "pickle for a nickle," and have the opportunity to wander about viewing media booths set up around the room. In one are continuous showings of a student-made slide-tape presentation on the immigration of their grandparents. In another booth, there are continuous showings of the filmstrip *Inside the Golden Door*. In a third booth *Klezmer* music and songs, such as "World Of Our Fathers" from the album *Sons Of Safam*, are broadcast. In a fourth booth, a videotape of presentations by residents of a Jewish home for the aged relating their actual experiences at Ellis Island is aired.

**Synthesis**   If desired, document the entire event on slides and tapes or on videotape. Debrief and complete the follow-up the following week in the classrooms led by the respective teachers.

Chapter

## 35

**Editor's Comments**   This program serves as a culminating event to a course of study and involves older students and their families. It can be scaled down to a one-day event and a shorter period of time by eliminating the film *Hester Street*. It can also be revised to focus on the Sephardic experience only. Whatever the approach, it requires thoughtful preparation and cooperation from all the families involved.

Karen Sobel and Terry Bookman at Congregation Sinai in Milwaukee have developed a less intense program for the sixth grade called "Immigration To America." Their program involves a group activity with three stations among which families all rotate:

Station I:    Oral histories

Station II:   Comparison of American value system to Jewish value system

Station III: Jewish objects and concepts: a legacy for the future

Visits to the three stations are followed by a culminating session which focuses on the future.

For Temple Beth El, San Pedro, California, I developed a sixth grade program called "Tracing Your Family Roots" as an introduction to a class genealogy unit. Families fill out a questionnaire in advance of the program which prepares them for the day. They are instructed to bring the questionnaire and a Jewish object belonging to their family with them on the day of the program.

The program begins with introductions and talks about the objects. Then families work independently to trace their immigration routes. Atlases, *shtetl* finders, globes, and maps are provided. When a family has located their route, it is plotted on a large wall map. Other activities include sharing of recipes, telling a favorite story, or interviewing parents. The program concludes by examining the trends on the map and sharing something new that was learned. There is follow-up work in class.

If "Passport To America" is adapted for a family retreat weekend, all of the activities described above can be integrated into the retreat. Worship services can be conducted first as if everyone is on a ship going to America. The next day services can be held on Ellis Island. Assign some families the roles of people who are in America already. These veteran immigrants can greet the newcomers, provide jobs, housing, and other necessities. The Saturday evening program can focus on a reenactment of the Yiddish theater. Be sure to decorate the retreat site with pictures and posters and have costumes available which can be used throughout the weekend.

Chapter

## 35

## Bibliography/Resources

Howe, Irving, and Libo, Kenneth, eds. *How We Lived: A Documentary History Of Immigrant Jews In America.* New York: New American Library, 1979.

Howe, Irving. *World Of Our Fathers.* New York: Simon and Schuster, 1976.

Hutchins, Hapgood. *The Spirit Of the Ghetto: Studies Of the Jewish Quarter Of New York.* New York: Schocken, 1976.

Kranzler, David. *My Jewish Roots: A Practical Guide to Tracing and Recording Your Genealogy and Family History.* New York: Sepher-Hermon Press, 1979.

Kurzweil, Arthur, *From Generation To Generation: How to Trace Your Jewish Genealogy and Personal History*. New York: Schocken, 1982.

————. *My Generations: A Course In Jewish Family History*. New York: Behrman House, 1983.

Manners, Ande. *Poor Cousins*. New York: Coward, 1972.

Rochlin, Harriet. *Pioneer Jews: A New Life In the Far West*. Boston: Houghton Mifflin, 1984.

Rosten, Leo C. *The Education Of H\*Y\*M\*A\*N  K\*A\*P\*L\*A\*N*. By Leonard Q. Ross (Pseudonym). New York: Harcourt, Brace & World, Inc., 1965.

Rottenberg, Dan. *Finding Our Fathers: A Guidebook To Jewish Genealogy*. Baltimore: Genealogical Publishing Co., Inc., 1986.

Schoener, Allon. *The American Jewish Album: 1654 To the Present*. New York: Rizzoli, 1983.

Schoener, Allon, ed. *Portal To America: The Lower East Side, 1870-1925*. New York: Holt, Rinehart and Winston, 1967.

Shepard, Richard F. *Live and Be Well: A Celebration Of Yiddish Culture In America From the First Immigrants To the Second World War*. New York: Ballantine Books, 1982.

Stein, Conrad. *The Story Of Ellis Island*. Chicago: Children's Press, 1979.

*Toledoteinu: Finding Your Own Roots: An Activity Book*. Milwaukee: Arbit Books, 1978.

Weidman, Jerome. *Fourth Street East: A Novel Of How It Was*. New York: Pinnacle Books, 1970.

**Chapter**

**35**

### Mediated Materials

*Hester Street*. Almi Cinema 5, 1 Lincoln Plaza, New York, NY 10023, 1974. (film, 89 min.)

*Inside the Golden Door*, Part 2. Anti-Defamation League, 823 United Nations Plaza, New York, NY 10017. (filmstrip, 101 frames)

*The Immigrant*. Budget Films, 4590 Santa Monica, Los Angeles, CA 90029, 1917. (film, 20 min.)

*Sons of Safam*. Safam, c/o Dan Funk, 36 Hamlin Rd., Newton Centre, MA 02159, 1980. (record)

## Organizations/Museums
American Jewish Archives
Hebrew Union College-Jewish Institute of Religion
3101 Clifton Avenue
Cincinnati, OH 45220

American Jewish Historical Society
2 Thornton Road
Waltham, MA 02154

Museum of American Jewish History
Independence Mall East
Philadelphia, PA 19106

Chapter
**35**

# Introduction To Jewish Family Life Education

## Fradya Rembaum

**Overview**   In ever increasing numbers, families are turning to Jewish agencies for Jewish identity enrichment, for assistance with family life cycle needs, and for education in Jewish family rituals. In response to this and other perceived needs, Jewish agencies are beginning to offer more and more Family Life Education programs. The following section is a description of some of the factors in contemporary life which motivate families to seek such assistance and a delineation of characteristics unique to this program form.

**The Contemporary Jewish Family**   Sociologists point to a number of factors which indicate the changing nature of the modern Jewish family:

1. Later marital age, postponed childbearing, and, some fear, potential lower birth rate.

2. Rise of divorce and increase in single parent and blended families.

3. High mobility and distance from the support and reinforcement of the extended family and traditional neighborhood.

4. A growing rate of intermarriage which is bringing into the Jewish community a large group of spouses with non-Jewish backgrounds for whom Jewish life is alien and filled with challenges.

While the more recent social research is lifting the doom and gloom predictions about the strength and staying power of the Jewish family, today's Jewish families are developing new patterns of adjustment to the exigencies of modern life which propel them to seek new forms of support.[1]

In addition to reflecting changes resulting from the current sociological climate, today's Jewish families differ from their forebears in other significant ways:

*Many contemporary Jewish families view themselves as poorly prepared to transmit their cultural heritage adequately to their children.* Despite the irony of living in a country which promotes religious tolerance and an appreciation of Judaism, today's Jewish families have limited Jewish knowledge and have to "work at Judaizing their lives."[2] Most Jews who have partaken of some level of Jewish education cease their studies prior to or at Bar or Bat Mitzvah age, and are left in adulthood with pediatric images of Judaism. Their memories satisfy neither their own questions nor those of their children. When these families enter Jewish agencies and institutions for their children's Jewish education or for assistance in parenting problems, they recognize these moments as opportunities to enrich their own Jewish education as well.

*Contemporary Jewish adults do not affiliate with Jewish institutions as automatically as in earlier generations. However, their need for belonging is heightened when they marry and have children.* While many singles demonstrate their yearning for spiritual and communal support by joining synagogues and participating in a plethora of cultural, social, and leadership development programs, most Jews affiliate as they enter family life.[3]

Modern Jewish family life, then, with its changing structures and experiences, and its awareness of the need for Jewish knowledge reinforcement, has created a readiness on the part of families to participate in programs which meet their life style, family situation, and educational needs. These young families, regardless of their previous educational backgrounds, are confronted with new Jewish options afforded to them by a variety of threshhold experiences. For some, Family Life Education programs enable them to strengthen that which was already strong. For others, these programs enable them to go back and pick up the pieces of observance and affiliation which had lapsed or lain fallow for years; and for yet others, they provide an opportunity to learn and participate in that which their own parents had minimized or rejected. Many of today's Jewish families are taking charge of their Jewish lives in ways in which their parents and grand-parents did not want to do or did not have to do.

**Family Programming By Jewish Communal Agencies and Organizations**   Family Life Education programs which respond to the needs of families searching for Jewish meaning and community provide Jewish communal agencies with a special opportunity to reach beyond their agency walls. Such programs enable agencies to serve families who might not otherwise seek their assistance and to serve existing clientele in new ways.

Agencies which are providing family programming include such traditional providers as Jewish Family Service and Jewish Big Brothers; Jewish educational or religious institutions, such as Bureaus of Jewish Education and synagogues, larger community organizations, such as Jewish Federations and Jewish Centers; and membership groups, such as the American Jewish Committee.

Family Life Education for these communal agencies is both "out-reach" and "inreach." As "outreach," the effectiveness of such programs may be measured in the response and participation of those who are peripherally affiliated with the Jewish community and who seek a Jewish means of addressing their concerns. As "inreach," family programs and workshops enable institutions, organizations, and agencies to respond with relevancy to the changing needs of members.

As an added benefit to the agency, Family Life Education creates and reinforces Jewish content and commitment. Offering Family Life Education that is truly Jewish creates a responsibility for agencies and staff to examine Jewish resources and values as they relate to the cutting-edge concerns of contemporary Jewish families. Jewish institutions, in offering co-sponsored programs, build bridges between themselves as community service providers and between their staffs as co-workers. This Jewish reinforcement is both an opportunity and a challenge. Integrating Jewish values in a process of helping families with contemporary life issues confronts Jewish agencies with questions not easily answered. This will be further discussed below.

**Program Characteristics** Family Life Education, as a program category, is distinguished from other family education programs which are utilized in a religious school setting and linked to a particular graded curriculum. The category includes a broad range of programs and workshops related to life cycle or contemporary family situations, among which are the following:

1. Marriage preparation, such as "Making Marriage Work" for engaged, newly married, second marriages, and even marriages of long-standing.

2. Jewish childbirth preparation which combines childbirth education, such as Lamaze instruction, with discussion about Jewish identity and Jewish birth-related rituals.

3. Support groups for Jews by Choice.

4. Groups for interfaith couples or groups for parents of interfaith couples which combine ethnotherapy, marital counseling, and Jewish learning.

5. Parenting groups assisting families with issues related to children of all ages, ranging from infancy to adolescence to preparation for college and to parenting adult children.

6. Special needs parenting for single parents, blended families, adoptive parents, and parents of disabled children.

7. Mid-life programs for adults described as "the sandwich generation" or "empty nesters."

8. Widow or widower support groups.

Despite the broad range of content issues and populations seen in this list, Family Life Education programs have certain common characteristics:

*Programs are life cycle or crisis-of-transition related.* Crisis theory describes how families experiencing life cycle transition are open to re-examining and learning new attitudes and behaviors. This openness applies to family as well as to religious issues. As discussed earlier, these transition moments are special opportunities for Jewish communal institutions to provide support to families experiencing these normal crises and to strengthen family coping skills by offering the enrichment of Jewish resources.

*Programs are entry or re-entry points for families into Jewish communal life.* Participation in these programs often may be a family's first attempt to cross the threshhold into Jewish practice and affiliation. For this reason, institutions offering programs must handle inquiries with sensitivity and be concerned with follow-up if the entry is to be sustained. Follow-up might include assistance with joining a *bavurah* or referral to other Jewish communal resources for continuing education or affiliation. This is especially important for families whose tie to the Jewish community is very tentative, such as single parents or interfaith couples.

*Family Life Education programs serve a normal, healthy population.* Programs designed to enable families to deal with life cycle issues generally serve a population seeking guidance for universal life experiences. Families who are in need of more intensive support are better assisted by referral for counseling.

*Family Life Education, in concept and technique, combines the two disciplines of group or family therapy and adult education.* Programs which help participants to deal with life's problems concurrently with issues of Jewish identity and Jewish observance blend elements of group therapy, ethnotherapy, and Jewish education. As a type of group therapy, these programs are time-limited and structured according to an established agenda which may include input from the group. As a form of adult education, programs are not taught in a formal, frontal manner, but rather are a combination of presented didactic material and group discussion. Potential resources for both the discussion and didactic elements can be found in experiential exercises, life scripts, trigger plays, and Jewish texts, some of which are referenced in the bibliography of this book. Since there is no formula for determining the precise amount of therapy and educational content, the combination will be determined by staff skills and training, agency orientation, and available resources.[4]

*Group facilitation skills as well as Jewish knowledge and comfort are important criteria in staff selection and are factors to be considered in training facilitators for the special needs of the program.* Common among the variety of staffing models for family life education programs are dual facilitation (one leader is trained in group work and the other is a Judaic resource), or facilitation by one person who is capable of both, or facilitation by one person skilled in one area and augmented by guest facilitators. Again, it is important to emphasize that an effective balance depends on pre-planning and prior discussion with the agency leadership, program planners, and involved facilitators. Since these programs are designed to evoke emotional and religious issues, and since it is difficult to predict the balance between group discussion and didactic content, it is essential to select staff who can be flexible and comfortable with each other's skills. Not every social worker or other mental health practitioner is comfortable with Jewish practice and not every Jewish educator or Rabbi can tolerate adverse expressions about Judaism or the Jewish community. It is also important to give attention to the messages, however subtle, conveyed in the selection of the Jewish facilitator. A Rabbi or educator who is a sensitive, open person may be ideal for enabling participants to rework previous negative experiences. However, a Jewishly knowledgeable therapist may present a role model whose Jewish life style is more accessible to the group.

*Jewish Family Life Education, by definition, has Jewish content and is Jewish value-based and not value-free.* This is a strong statement which, at first, may seem to contradict the non-judgmental value system underlying family service agencies. However, on further consideration, mental health practitioners are trained to recognize their own values and those of their clients and to help clarify values as they assist clients in making choices. While families may turn to private practitioners and other non-Jewish agencies for assistance through crises-of-transition, their selection of a Jewish agency frequently indicates a readiness on some level for Jewish reinforcement. Participants need to ventilate emotions, explore solutions to problems, and clarify their Jewish values. Specially trained and Jewishly knowledgeable group leaders can effectively respond to these needs. They are also advocates for Jewish perspectives and values, while at the same time accepting their clients' right to choose. This is a delicate balancing act and reinforces the earlier discussion of the importance of staff selection and training which includes not only the facilitators, but also the program planners and agency leadership. To be non-judgmental and yet based in a religious value system requires careful consideration of program goals. The agency must establish its expectations, define its values, articulate them in staff training, and be up front with group participants. The importance of this is most clearly seen when dealing with groups for intermarried families.

*Programs are appropriately offered by, and conducted in, many types of Jewish institutional settings.* Any of the types of programs listed above can be offered effectively by Jewish Family Service agencies, synagogues, Jewish Community Centers, and other community agencies, either alone or in co-sponsorship. Staff skills, financial resources, agency policies, and community politics are all factors which determine which agency or setting offers a particular program. Perceived sensitivities can also influence site selection. In some communities, for example, parenting programs or interfaith couples' groups might best be offered in a clinical setting. This is in response to a concern that families might hesitate to seek help in a synagogue because of previous religion-based anxieties. Or, conversely, such programs might especially be offered in religious settings in response to a concern that families would not enter a clinical agency for fear of being identified as "having emotional problems."

*Recruitment of program participants requires an active outreach approach to publicity.* Design and distribution of flyers and brochures and use of press releases and paid advertising involves sophisticated planning. To recruit families seeking to cross the threshhold into Jewish life, publicity must reach beyond internal Jewish community resources. A successful program must be marketed to a community-wide and population-specific audience through use of press, radio and television, as well as to family activity locations — parks, family gyms, pediatricians' offices, etc. Too many quality programs fail to attract sufficient participants because the publicity reached a population already being served, or it reached the wrong audience. A marketing or active outreach approach also utilizes market research techniques in eliciting program content from potential participants and in designing publicity materials which appeal to the needs and sensitivities of the specific population.

*The costs of staff training, curriculum development, and effective publicity require budgetary and agency leadership* commitment. While costs may vary, Family Life Education programs have built-in additional cost factors which may exceed the budgets set for traditional agency services. Agency co-sponsorship is an effective way to reduce expenses.

**Summary**   Jewish Family Life Education programs present opportunities to agencies and families to respond to the needs of contemporary life within a Jewish context. These programs represent a trend in service which is highly successful and which strongly reinforces Jewish values and community. This book contains examples of a number of successful Jewish Family Life Education programs, reflecting the fact that such programs and resources are growing in both popularity and scope.

## Endnotes

1. Steven M. Cohen, "Vitality and Resilience In the American Jewish Family," in *Response: A Contemporary Jewish Review*, no. 48 (Spring 1985): 21-27.
2. Bernard Reisman, "Jewish Family Education," in *Pedagogic Reporter* 27, no. 3 (Spring 1977).
3. Steven M. Cohen, "Vitality and Resilience," 25.
4. Kathryn Apgar and Jennifer Kan Coplon, "New Perspectives on Structured Education Groups," in *Social Work* 30:2 (March-April 1985): 138-143.

# Chapter 36

 **TITLE:** Lecture Series for Engaged and Newly Married Couples

 **CONTRIBUTED BY:** Dr. Leo Davids

 **TOPIC:** *Halachic* and interpersonal aspects of marriage and family life

 **TARGET AUDIENCE:** Engaged and newly married couples

 **TIME FRAME:** Five to six 2 hour sessions

 **STAFF:** Coordinator to recruit a lecturer for each session and to head publicity/recruitment group; volunteer speakers/facilitators; organizing committee

**Overview**   The "Lecture Series for Engaged and Newly Married Couples" is an ongoing project of the Jewish Marriage Education Committee of Toronto, Canada. The committee — which is composed of community volunteers and several Rabbis — has been sponsoring the series since 1970 twice a year, in the fall and spring. The series helps couples to prepare to bring the Jewish tradition into their new homes, and also introduces practical topics relevant to beginning families.

**Purpose**   The purpose of the program is to present traditional aspects of Jewish marriage and family life to young couples in order for them to adopt a Jewish lifestyle. A further purpose is to minimize the frictions and conflicts that occur for most new couples.

Chapter

36

**Preparation/Procedure**   This program is open to any Jewish couple. Publicity should extend to synagogues and Jewish centers, as well as Jewish organizations. Advertising in the Anglo-Jewish press is also advised, as well as close contact with Rabbis who perform weddings.

Recruit personnel for the lectures three to six months in advance of the series. Let each lecturer know when he/she will be speaking and what each aspect of the series covers, so that there will be little repetition. The lecturers should be role models who are willing to share their knowledge and who are in touch with current trends regarding marriage and family life.

This series is generally held in a local synagogue. It is advisable to rotate the site among the different synagogues in the community. Usually 15 to 25 couples participate in this program each year, thus 7 to 12 couples per series. The fee or donation is minimal, and no distinction is made for those affiliated or unaffiliated with synagogues.

**Program Description**   The program consists of five or six evening lecture-discussions and a *mikvah* tour. The speakers include congregational Rabbis, a professor of sociology, a social worker, and a financial consultant. The typical schedule is as follows.

## Schedule

Week 1
    Introduction:                    Congregational Rabbi
    The Marriage Ceremony

Week 2
    Love Day In/Day Out:        Social Worker from
    Essential Communication   Jewish Family Service
    Skills

Week 3
    The Extended Family:        Sociologist
    Parents and In-laws

Week 4
    Sunday: *Mikvah* Tour
    and Discussion
    Lecture Night: The Sum and   Congregational Rabbi
    Substance Of Jewish Marriage

Week 5
    Financial Strategies        Financial Consultant
    for a Young Couple

All the lecture-discussions are informational in nature, and there is no formal syllabus or bibliography. During the course, couples may receive a book, such as one of those listed below in the Bibliography/Resources section, so that they can review the material covered in the lectures after the course. If couples wish to pursue further study, they are referred to adult education classes and other course offerings available in the community.

**Editor's Comments**   The program as presented here utilizes lecturers from various disciplines. It may also be facilitated by one person alone who has the skills and knowledge to speak on the various subjects.

Other topics that would be of interest to this target audience are: the role of women in Jewish tradition and how that role is defined today; two career families and the effects of this phenomenon on the structure of the traditional family; communal

Chapter

36

resources, agencies, and institutions; family planning, and the place of children in a marriage.

Since the purpose of the program is to present traditional aspects of marriage and family life in order to promote a Jewish life style, it is important to provide opportunities to study and to participate in traditional Judaism. Encourage participants to attend Shabbat *minyanim*, to gather together for Shabbat lunch and/or *Seudah Shleesheet* on Shabbat afternoon, and to try out existing classes/*shi'urim* to see which suit them best. Make others in the community aware of the group so that they may be invited for Shabbat and holiday celebrations.

This program is designed as a "talk-then-dialogue" series, providing information about Jewish tradition to the participants. In addition to the lecture, some part of the evening might be set aside for actual text study. While this would extend the time frame for each program about a half an hour, it would allow the couples a more in-depth look into the basis of the Jewish tradition.

Chapter

36

## Bibliography/Resources

Donin, Rabbi Hayim Halevy. *To Be a Jew: A Guide To Jewish Observances In Contemporary Life*. New York: Basic Books, 1972.

Kaplan, Aryeh. *Made In Heaven*. New York: Moznaim Publishing, 1983.

_____. *Waters Of Eden*. New York: N.C.S.Y. – Union of Orthodox Jewish Congregations, 1982.

Kitov, Eliyahu. *The Jew and His Home*. New York: Shengold Publishers, 1963.

Lamm, Maurice. *The Jewish Way In Love and Marriage*. San Francisco: Harper and Row, 1982.

# Chapter 37

 **TITLE:** Tzores and Success: Jewish Singles and Jewish Single Parents

 **CONTRIBUTED BY:** Marilyn E. Stoumen

 **TOPIC:** Coping with being a Jewish single in a non-single society

 **TARGET AUDIENCE:** Single and 25 to 40; any size audience

 **TIME FRAME:** One 1-1½ hour session

 **STAFF:** One trained facilitator

**Overview**   This one-time program provides an opportunity for singles in their upper 20s to mid 40s to discuss issues of concern in a non-threatening environment. It was developed at the Jewish Family and Community Service of Chicago, Illinois. The facilitator sets the agenda, focuses the discussion, and prepares a list of Jewish community resources for the group. This program is usually a first step toward ongoing group programs or toward a mechanism for singles to network with each other.

**Purpose**   The program is designed to encourage networking among singles and to provide them with resources, both Jewish and non-Jewish, that will serve as a support system. One of the goals is to encourage singles to change their focus from finding the "one and only" to finding themselves as they engage in personal growth.

Chapter

37

**Preparation/Procedure**   Publicize this program through the local press, synagogue bulletins, community agency news-letters, and in the work place. The program can be offered through a Jewish Family Service as one of a series of programs dealing with Jewish singles and Jewish single parents.

The facilitator assesses the audience and its needs, then prepares a talk with three clear points or themes in mind which are appropriate for a one-time program. He or she needs to be sensitive to the group and to be flexible enough to switch the focus as necessary. The facilitator prepares resources and suggestions for participants listing where they can go for help or for personal growth. The list may include Jewish communal agencies, as well as museums, Jewish organizations, university classes, political organizations, etc.

**Program Description**   Allow about one hour for the facilitating talk and an additional half hour for discussion. Be sure to provide refreshments.

This format is a lecture-discussion program. Some points to be considered in the lecture are as follows:

1. Isolation, loneliness, alienation

2. Various groups of single parents — divorced, widowed, foster, adoptive, homosexual

3. The single person as parent — issues of visitation, co-parenting, discipline, time management, dating

4. Developing oneself — knowing oneself, one's skills, interests, strengths, reaching beyond oneself and risking

5. Resources in the Jewish community or the community at large for help and personal growth

6. Single by choice as a way of life — the implications for relationships with parents, family, couples, married, and unmarried friends

Chapter

37

**Editor's Comments**    Since one of the goals of this program is to provide for networking among singles, it may be useful to include some social time before or after the talk, along with some structured ice breakers.

The discussion segment may be managed in several different ways, depending on the size of the group. If desired, divide into smaller groups and ask people to react to the talk. If this method is chosen, a facilitator will be needed for each group and someone to take notes. Provide time to get feedback from each of the groups.

If you want to keep the group together, but make the discussion more focused, ask individuals to write their comments or suggestions. Appoint people to collect them and organize them to avoid repetition. Questions can be complied into categories, e.g., those pertaining to coping with being a single parent, where to go for help in a crisis, taking steps for self-improvement. Having questions written down eliminates long personal stories and different wording of the same questions.

This is a one-time workshop. However, some people may want to continue to meet to discuss their concerns or just to get together. Have sign-up sheets so that participants may be contacted for any future activities.

**Bibliography/Resources**

Apgar, Kathryn, and Callahan, Betsy Nicholson. *Four One Day Workshops.* New York: Resource Communication, Inc. with the cooperation of Family Service Association of America, n.d.

Barnes, Beverly C., and Coplon, Jennifer K. *The Single Parent Experience.* New York: Resource Communication, Inc. with the cooperation of Family Service Association of America, n.d.

Chapter
# 37

# Chapter 38

 **TITLE:** In the Beginning . . . Jewish Preparation for Childbirth

 **CONTRIBUTED BY:** Karen Lebow

 **DESIGNED BY:** Karen Lebow; materials written by Fradya Rembaum

 **TOPIC:** Preparing for childbirth

 **TARGET AUDIENCE:** 4-10 couples who are expectant parents

 **TIME FRAME:** Ten 2 ½ hour sessions

 **STAFF:** Birthing instructor, Judaica coordinator, and consultants (*mohel*, Rabbi, Jewish educator, couples from past classes)

**Overview**    "In the Beginning," originally developed in 1980 by the Bureau of Jewish Education, Department of Parent and Family Education in Los Angeles, combines Jewish content along with training in the latest methods of giving birth. Through participation in a program such as this, new parents focus on the Jewish aspects of birthing and child rearing. They share and reflect on the joys and challenges of becoming Jewish parents.

**Purpose**    The purpose of this program is to strengthen the Jewish identity of the participants and to help them become part of a supportive Jewish community.

Chapter

# 38

**Preparation/Procedure**    Publicize the program through local synagogues, Jewish Centers, and preschools. It is also effective to distribute publicity to local obstetricians and birthing and maternity centers. Send press releases to the Anglo-Jewish press and local secular newspapers. Submit public service spot announcements to local radio stations.

Make arrangements for a *mohel* and for couples who were former class participants to come to the class for the appropriate sessions.

**Program Description**    "In the Beginning" consists of ten 2½ hour classes. Approximately ninety minutes of each class is devoted to preparation for childbirth. The remaining hour is focused on discussion of Jewish material. Participants are expected to keep a journal in which they record the meaningful experiences that occur as they anticipate and prepare for the birth of a child. Participants are asked to share their entries during classes. An outline of the Jewish content for each session follows.

**Suggested Jewish Content**
Session I: Introductions and Sharing Of Leaders' and Participants' Expectations
    A. *Shehecheyanu* blessing
    B. Jewish values of life, birthing, and parenting

C. Journal — "Letter To a Loved One"
D. Assignment: Research Hebrew names and family tree.

Session II: Exploring Your Jewish Heritage — What Does It Mean to Be Jewish?
    A. The many facets of Judaism
    B. Baby naming
    C. Share family trees
    D. Journal: "Who Am I?"

Session III: Jewish Values In Parent-child Relationships
    A. Obligations of parents and children
    B. Journal: "The Kind Of Parent I Hope to Be"

Session IV: It's a boy!
    A. *Brit Milah* — its spiritual and historical significance
    B. Review of ceremony
    C. Visit by *mohel*
    D. Journal: "Feelings About Baby's Gender"

Session V: It's a Girl!
    A. Traditional and alternative ceremonies — synagogue baby naming ceremony, *B'rit Banot* ceremonies
    B. Feelings about ceremonies
    C. Journal: "Traditions and Rituals In My Life"

Session VI: Jewish Response
    A. "*Gomel*" blessing
    B. *Pidyon HaBen/HaBat*
    C. Journal: "Baby's Name"

Session VII: Rituals
    A. Sharing of baby names
    B. Creative birth announcements
    C. Wimpel
    D. Journal: "One Thing I Like Best and One Thing I Like Least About Pregnancy"

Session VIII: Developing Jewish Rituals for Your Family
    A. Values clarification
    B. Resources for adult education
    C. Jewish weaning ceremony

Chapter

# 38

D. Issues of *kashrut* and *halachah* related to breast feeding
E. Journal: "The Jewish Things I Do"

Session IX: Coping As a New Parent —
"The Kind of Parent I Hope to Be"
A. Jewish values in parenting
B. Consumer advocacy
C. Community resources
D. Journal: "Continuing the Chain Of Tradition"

Session X: "Is There Really a Baby After All This?"
A. Normal newborn
B. Discussion: "Supermom – Myth or Reality"
C. Visits with couples from past classes and their babies
D. Evaluation

Chapter

## 38

**Editor's Comments**   Just as participants of past classes come to share their experiences, it may be beneficial to set up a mechanism so that all participants can remain in touch with each other. There can be an annual reunion. Often the groups can come together to celebrate Shabbat and holidays, or even form a *havurah* (see Chapter 4, "How to Start a Synagogue Havurah Program"). Efforts should be made to have participants attend the *Brit Milah* and naming ceremonies of each other's babies.

**Bibliography/Resources**   See the bibliographies for Chapter 39, "Lamaze Childbirth and Jewish Parenting Class," and Chapter 40, "Having a Jewish Baby."

# Chapter 39

 **TITLE:** Lamaze Childbirth and Jewish Parenting Class

 **CONTRIBUTED BY:** Miriam Feinberg

 **TOPIC:** Helping expectant Jewish parents to prepare for childbirth, and new and expectant Jewish parents to create a Jewish home

 **TARGET AUDIENCE:** 4-10 couples who are expectant parents

 **TIME FRAME:** Six sessions of Lamaze Training (90-120 minutes each); three 2 hour Judaic content sessions; additional social evening

 **STAFF:** Instructor trained in prepared childbirth, Judaica facilitator, Jewish parenting educator

**Overview**   The "Lamaze Childbirth and Jewish Parenting Class," sponsored by the Board of Jewish Education of Greater Washington, provides couples with Lamaze childbirth training by a certified Lamaze instructor, and separate classes concerning Jewish parenting issues. There are nine sessions in all: six consecutive weekly sessions on childbirth and three two hour sessions dealing with Jewish content. The Jewish content sessions are facilitated by a professional educator in the Jewish community. It is possible for expectant couples who have arranged to take a separate Lamaze or prepared childbirth course, as well as for new parents, to enroll solely in the three session Jewish parenting section of the course.

Chapter

# 39

**Purpose**   The purpose of this program is to provide expectant couples in the Jewish community with training for a specific method of prepared childbirth. In addition, it is designed to educate them about Jewish rituals, traditions, and practices associated with childbirth.

**Preparation/Procedure**   Secure the services of a certified Lamaze instructor, as well as a Jewish parenting educator who will facilitate the Jewish content sessions. Since there are only three two hour Jewish content sessions, it is essential to define the topics for discussion so that they are meaningful to participants. Select an evening on which to have the classes and set a fee. Since the Jewish content sessions are concurrent with the childbirth training classes, these may be set up every other week, so that everything takes place within a six week time frame. An additional final session is a social occasion.

Publicize the program in local newspapers, synagogues, preschools, maternity centers, and on the radio. Write letters and send flyers to local obstetricians, pediatricians, and Rabbis.

**Program Description**   The three Jewish content sessions consist of structured discussions about Jewish heritage and Jewish educational choices. The following topics are covered:

Jewish values regarding parenting

What does Jewishness mean?

Rituals and customs of baby naming

*Brit Milah*

Traditional and alternative ceremonies — *Brit HaBat, Simchat Bat, Pidyon HaBen/HaBat*

What makes a home Jewish?

The value of rituals in family life

Resources for Jewish education

As a follow-up to the discussion sessions, the Jewish content facilitator arranges for a subsequent session during which participants spend an evening or a Sunday morning at brunch socializing and learning from Jewish professionals in the community about community resources. If desired, participants can be invited to a Shabbat dinner in the facilitator's home.

Chapter

39

Participants who wish to continue to meet as a group, as well as couples who have not previously participated are invited to participate in a three part series (2 hours per session) led by the Jewish parenting educator. The content for these sessions is as follows:

1. Dealing with changes as new parents: learning to cope

2. Growing babies: sharing concerns and milestones

3. Developing as a Jewish family through the celebration of Chanukah, Passover, and Shabbat

**Editor's Comments**    This program trains expectant parents in a specific method of prepared childbirth. Having the Jewish content at a separate time allows for in-depth discussion of the topics. Since the Jewish content areas are pertinent for all young families, these sessions are opened up to couples who already have young children, but who did not have the opportunity to participate in a program of this nature when they were expecting. Couples who are new parents can also share their pregnancy and childbirth experiences with the couples who are expecting.

As an enhancement of this program, and also of the program described in Chapter 39, "In the Beginning . . . A Jewish Lamaze Experience," consider setting aside one or two sessions for *parents* of expectant couples to come together with their children to discuss the rituals and traditions connected with childbirth, particularly *Brit Milah, Brit HaBat* and naming, as well as the role of grandparents in the raising of a Jewish child. Engaging in dialogue together often helps to clarify values and feelings and helps to preserve the chain of tradition.

## Bibliography/Resources

Donin, Hayim Halevy. *To Raise a Jewish Child.* New York: Basic Books, 1977.

Fridman, Masha, and Fishel, Rachel. *Mazal Tov: Baby's First Record.* Jerusalem: Geffen Publishing Co., 1981.

Greenberg, Blu. *How to Run a Traditional Household.* New York: Simon and Schuster, 1983.

Kolatch, Alfred J. *The Name Dictionary: Modern English and Hebrew Names.* Middle Village, NY: Jonathan David Publishers, 1967.

Strassfeld, Michael. *The Jewish Holidays: A Guide and Commentary.* New York: Harper and Row, 1985.

Strassfeld, Sharon, and Green, Kathy, eds. *The Jewish Family Book.* Toronto: Bantam Books, 1981.

"Life Cycle: In the Beginning." In *The Second Jewish Catalog.* Sharon Strassfeld and Michael Strassfeld, eds. Philadelphia: Jewish Publication Society, 1976.

Weintraub, Selma, and Ravich, Elaine. *Welcome To the World: Jewish Baby's Record Book.* New York: Women's League for Conservative Judaism, 1985.

Chapter

39

# Chapter 40

 **TITLE:** Having a Jewish Baby

 **CONTRIBUTED BY:** Arlene Eisenberg

 **TOPIC:** Preparation for pregnancy; history of naming practice in Judaism; raising a young Jewish child

 **TARGET AUDIENCE:** Couples who are expecting a baby and couples who hope to expect a baby in the near future

 **TIME FRAME:** Six 1 hour sessions

 **STAFF:** Facilitator knowledgeable about physical and psychological factors related to pregnancy; facilitator well versed in Jewish naming practice and in raising a Jewish child (and/or guests with such expertise)

**Overview**   "Having a Jewish Baby" is a six session program which prepares expectant parents for the physical and psychological changes that are a part of pregnancy. The course consists of a series of talks that cover the time span from before pregnancy up to delivery. The last two sessions deal with issues of Jewish practice that confront expectant parents. The program is facilitated by Arlene Eisenberg and Heidi Eisenberg Murkoff, authors of the book *What to Expect When You're Expecting*, by a *mohel*, and by congregants knowledgeable about naming and raising a Jewish child. The program is listed in a brochure as part of an adult education program sponsored by eight synagogues and the Jewish Association for Services for the Aged (JASA) in New York City. The brochure reaches the constituency of all participating agencies. Whatever the audience, it is necessary to print and distribute flyers describing the program and to send out well prepared press releases.

Chapter

# 40

**Purpose**   The program is designed to help both expectant parents deal with all aspects of having a baby. It serves several functions:

1. To give expectant mothers and fathers a chance to meet others like themselves who share the goal of raising Jewish children.

2. To allow couples to ventilate their worries in an environment where most everyone will feel the same way.

3. To encourage optimum medical care coupled with self-care for the mother with the goal of healthier Jewish babies and families.

4. To provide a place where sound medical information is available on subjects, such as circumcision, that expectant couples may not feel comfortable discussing with their doctors.

5. To help Jewish parents look upon their synagogue and community as sources of assistance in important, if not specifically Jewish, aspects of their lives.

**Preparation/Procedure**   Arrange for a guest speaker who is well versed in Jewish aspects of childbirth and child rearing to facilitate the last two sessions. A *mohel* should also be invited to discuss *Brit Milah*.

When setting fees, consider offering a two for the price of one rate for couples.

**Program Description**   The topics for each of the one hour sessions are:

Session I: Preparing for pregnancy: What you need to know and do – from quitting tobacco and caffeine to getting thorough medical checkups before conception – so that you can conceive a healthy baby.

Session II: What to eat when you're expecting: How to feed yourself, your spouse, and your baby correctly from conception to delivery, including kosher cooking tips and recipes. The goal: a healthy Jewish family.

Session III: Pregnancy worry clinic: Bring your worries; leave without them. You'll have the chance to ask questions (some you may hesitate to ask your doctor) about the things that worry you about any aspect of pregnancy.

Session IV: Childbirth worry clinic: Answers to worries about recognizing labor, about pain, medication, episiotomies, Caesarian sections, fetal monitors, and more.

Session V: Jewish decisions: What's *Brit Milah*? Who should do it? When? How to deal with those who say, "How barbaric!" What about naming the baby? What's the Jewish thing to do?

Session VI: Raising a Jewish child (It's probably easier to go through labor!): What can parents do to make a Jewish home for their expected baby? How can what we do, say, and think, influence our child to follow a Jewish life style? (We don't answer the questions as much as discuss possibilities.)

The first four sessions utilize the book *What to Expect When You're Expecting* by Arlene Eisenberg and Heidi Eisenberg Murkoff. (This book contains a comprehensive month-by-

Chapter

# 40

month guide to pregnancy and responds to all the worries of prospective parents.) The facilitators introduce the evening's topic for discussion. They refer to the material in the book and draw on their own personal experiences as well. The participants have an opportunity to react to the material and to present personal views and concerns. The format is an informal dialogue between the facilitators and the participants.

In Session V, on Jewish decisions in pregnancy, the discussion centers around selecting Jewish names. The facilitator uses himself/herself as an example and tells the groups what his/her name means, for whom he/she was named, and why the name was chosen. Participants then share what they know about their names. There is a brief overview on the history of naming practice in Judaism and the decisions involved in naming a Jewish child. Finally, there are questions about the history of naming practice, for whom the child should be named, how to select the name, etc.

**Chapter**

# 40

In the final session, on raising a Jewish child, participants look to the future. The discussion is geared to creating a Jewish home and to the child's Jewish education. Jewish day care and Jewish preschools are considered in terms of viable options for the child's first formal Jewish educational experience. Concrete suggestions are made for Shabbat and holiday celebrations and how to make the child aware of his/her environment from the earliest years.

**Editor's Comments**   This program is geared to expectant parents and those hoping to be expectant parents. It does not cover training in one particular method of prepared childbirth; it centers rather on pregnancy as a family experience. The discussion of the Jewish subject matter may vary depending on the group and the skill and knowledge of the facilitators. As an enhancement of this program, consider setting aside one or two sessions for parents of expectant couples to come together with their children to discuss some of the rituals and traditions connected with childbirth, particularly *Brit Milah*, *Brit HaBat* and naming, *Pidyon HaBen*, the chain of tradition, as well as the role of grandparents in the raising of a Jewish child.

Ms. Eisenberg and Ms. Murkoff offer a subsequent program entitled, "What to Expect the First Year As a Jewish Parent." The six sessions of that program cover parental concerns, such as a discussion of circumcision; crying and colic; feeding the baby, sleep habits, and illness; separation anxiety and other fears; and introducing the baby to Jewish life.

For additional follow-up suggestions, see the Editor's Comments for Chapter 38, "In the Beginning," and Chapter 39, "Lamaze Childbirth and Jewish Parenting Class."

## Bibliography/Resources

Browder, Sue. *New Age Baby Name Book*. New York: Workman Publishing Co., 1978.

Cardozo, Arlene Rossen. *Jewish Family Celebrations: The Sabbath, Festivals and Ceremonies*. New York: St. Martin's Press, 1982.

Eisenberg, Arlene, and Murkoff, Heidi Eisenberg. *What to Expect When You're Expecting*. New York: Workman Publishing Co., 1984.

Gottlieb, Nathan. *A Jewish Child Is Born*. New York: Bloch, 1960.

Hertz, J. H., ed. *The Pentateuch and Haftorahs*. London: Soncino Press, 1973.

Klein, Issac. *A Guide To Jewish Religious Practice*. New York: Jewish Theological Seminary of America, 1979.

Kolatch, Alfred J. *The Name Dictionary*. New York: Jonathan David, 1967.

Kurzweil, Arthur. *From Generation To Generation: How to Trace Your Jewish Genealogy and Personal History*. New York: Schocken Books, 1982.

Plaut, W. Gunther; Bamberger, Bernard J.; and Hallo, William. *The Torah: A Modern Commentary*. New York: Union of American Hebrew Congregations, 1981.

Chapter

# 40

Rubin, Garry and Sheila. "Preserving Tradition By Expanding It: The Creation Of Our Simchat Bat" *Response* (Fall-Winter, 1982): 61-68.

Schauss, Hayyim. *The Lifetime Of a Jew Throughout the Ages Of Jewish History*. New York: Union of American Hebrew Congregations, 1950.

Strassfeld, Sharon, and Green, Kathy, eds. *The Jewish Family Book*. New York: Bantam Books, 1981.

Strassfeld, Sharon, and Strassfeld, Michael, eds. *The Second Jewish Catalog*. Philadelphia: Jewish Publication Society, 1976.

Trepp, Leo. *The Complete Book Of Jewish Observance*. New York: Behrman House, 1980.

Chapter

# 40

Write for *Simchat Bat* ceremonies to:
Jewish Women's Resource Center
9 East 69th Street
New York, NY 10021

# Chapter 41

 **TITLE:** Jewish Parenting Centers

 **CONTRIBUTED BY:** UAHC Department of Education

 **TOPIC:** The establishment of Jewish Parenting Centers in order to: Enable parents to discuss Jewish parenting issues, to feel better prepared for the various stages of parenthood; and to attain support for their personal decisions, values, and choice of life styles; and to introduce young children to the Jewish world through age appropriate sensory experiences.

 **TARGET AUDIENCE:** Primarily families with infants and/or children of preschool age; may be adapted for families with older children.

 **TIME FRAME:** Year round

 **STAFF:** 1-2 trained facilitators; 1-2 trained assistants

**Overview**   The Union of American Hebrew Congregations has initiated a national program of Jewish Parenting Centers to respond to the changing needs of young Jewish families and to involve them in congregational life. Along with the many family education programs now being sponsored by many Reform congregations throughout the country (many of which are described in this volume), these Jewish Parenting Centers serve to:

Strengthen and enrich the Jewish nuclear family.

Introduce children to Jewish education.

Outline the first step of the UAHC's William and Frances Schuster Curriculum.

Chapter

# 41

Offer information and guidance to adults during the challenging years of raising infants and toddlers.

Create a feeling of belonging to an extended family at the synagogue.

Encourage the active participation and affiliation of young families with their local congregation.

**Background**   The dramatic changes in the traditional nuclear family; the loss of the extended family unit; the increased rates of separation, divorce, and inter-marriage; as well as today's economic pressures, have had a profound impact on the daily lives of adults who are raising infants and toddlers. New parents often report feeling isolated, primarily because they no longer live near their extended family. In the past, the extended family unit provided rich resources. Family members offered each other support, guidance, and child care during the early stages of family development. In today's modern society, adults are now turning toward their peer group and community institutions for this information and support, and also to recreate a feeling of belonging.

**Program Development**   This new program model defines three main areas of focus:

1. Judaism
    a. Creating a Jewish home with young children
    b. Introducing children to the Jewish world around them
    c. Exploring Jewish identity, life style, and practice
    d. Celebrating the holidays, Shabbat, and life cycle events
       with other Jewish families

2. Child Development
    a. Learning about normal child growth and development
    b. Observing variations in children's growth and stages of
       maturation
    c. Understanding children's behavior

3. Parenting and Family Issues
    a. Building parenting skills
    b. Increasing the pleasure between parents and their children
    c. Strengthening and enriching family relationships.

Chapter

41

**Parenting, Parenthood, and Jewish Parenting**   The
current research in infant development and the subsequent
published reports in the mass media, have focused national
attention on early childhood and parenting issues. Magazine
covers now highlight subjects relating to the challenges facing
the American family in the 1980s. These include such issues as:
the economic pressures adults experience when raising young
children, the delicate balance between family and career,
startling new discoveries regarding the capabilities of infants and
toddlers, profound concerns about child care, and shocking
reports about child abuse.

The terms "Parenting" and "Parenthood" refer to the active role
a mother and father assume during the formative years of raising
young children. It is acknowledged that these very early familial
relationships and experiences help shape a child's personality
and view of himself/herself in the world. Yet, there is another
important issue which is of concern to our Jewish community:
how these early experiences influence a child's Jewish identity
and cognition.

"Jewish Parenting" refers to the way parents introduce their
infants, toddlers, and preschoolers to the Jewish world around

them; help them to develop a sense of Jewish self-esteem and identity; and enable them to feel a part of a Jewish family, community, and rich heritage. The Jewish Parenting Centers provide an arena in which adults can discuss these issues with each other, one in which they can feel better prepared for the various stages of parenthood, and attain support for their personal decisions, values, and choice of life style.

The research in child development demonstrates that infants and toddlers are sensitively attuned to their environment. During the earliest stages of life, a child is capable of observing and integrating their personal world of sights, tastes, smells, textures, sounds, and objects. Interactions with parents, siblings, adults, and peers become familiar and anticipated. In the Jewish Parenting Centers, we utilize this knowledge and introduce children to Jewish references through age appropriate sensory experiences. With parents as partners, we encourage children "To See the World Through Jewish Eyes."

Chapter

41

## The UAHC William and Frances Schuster Curriculum

The early childhood component of the William and Frances Schuster Curriculum outlines a fully integrated and continuous process of Jewish early childhood education. Jewish experiences introduce children to holidays, life cycle events, symbols, rituals, Hebrew, music, art, stories, and food. Structured activities in the infant and toddler groups and preschool class-rooms are designed to promote in children self-esteem and to build skills in physical, social, cognitive, language, and emotional development.

Through the curriculum process, parents participate with their children as they begin the first step of their Jewish education, the infant and toddler groups. At 2½-3 years, the children are ready to progress to the next step, the preschool classroom, and discover the objectives and learning activities of *The Guidelines for the Pre-School Years*. Adults have an opportunity to parti-cipate in the PATT program, which outlines family and home enrichment activities to do with their preschool child. The early childhood section of "Parents Are Teachers Too" is co-sponsored by the National Federation of Temple Sisterhoods and the Department of Education.

**Program Activities: The Models** One of the most important aspects of implementing a successful program is the choice of the model or format. We recognize that each congregation has a different set of needs and goals; has a variety of existing programs and directions for future planning; and also has differing financial resources, varying building facilities, and unique demographic trends. As a result, the staff of the Department of Education has created a broad range of program models. Each format is considered to be an integral part of the Jewish Parenting Center concept.

The basic Jewish Parenting Center services are as follows:

Weekly parent-infant groups

Weekly parent-toddler groups

Weekend family sessions

Weekend father-child groups

Adult education seminars

Holiday-oriented family groups

Jewish resource center

Chapter

41

The parenting groups are conducted by any of the following individuals: synagogue staff members; professionals in the field of infant/toddler development, early childhood education, Judaic studies, social work, and psychology; volunteers; or the parents themselves (the traditional co-op model). The groups meet once a week or once a month, depending on the model.

**Editor's Comments** Jewish Parenting Centers can attract people to the synagogue preschool and religious school and provide an entry point for them into congregational life. If a congregation is not prepared to make a full-time commitment to such a Center, short-term programs of 6-10 sessions may be instituted instead. Groups of parents with children of similar ages may also be formed.

A Jewish Parenting Center can also sponsor events and special worship services which attract people to the congregation.

An example is a "Tot Shabbat Service" — a separate worship experience for families with preschool children before a Friday evening or Shabbat morning service. An *Oneg Shabbat* or *Kiddush* can follow a brief service that includes singing, a story or puppet show, and birthday blessings for the children.

Other programs which may be sponsored under the auspices of a Jewish Parenting Center include "Daddy and Me" and "Mommy and Me" programs (once or twice a week classes during which toddlers and their fathers/mothers engage in play activities, music, stories, and snacks), one-time presentations and lectures on parenting, participatory holiday workshops, parent discussion groups, and support groups. The staff of the Center can provide resources and information on Jewish views of childrearing and family to those who participate in the various programs, as well as to the congregation at large. They can also act as a referral service for the various social service agencies in times of family crisis.

Chapter

41

**Bibliography/Resources**   The following materials are available through the Union of American Hebrew Congregations, Department of Education, 838 Fifth Avenue, New York, NY 10021:

Reshotko, Deborah. "Parent Activity Guide for the PATT Program." New York: Union of American Hebrew Congregations-National Federation of Temple Sisterhoods, 1985.

*Guidelines for the Pre-School Years*. New York: Union of American Hebrew Congregations-Central Conference of American Rabbis Joint Commission on Jewish Education, 1981.

# Chapter 42

 **TITLE:** The Holiday Workshop Series™

 **CONTRIBUTED BY:** Patricia Singer Golden

 **TOPIC:** Hands-on, Jewish consciousness raising program using the study and practice of Shabbat and Jewish holidays as a vehicle

 **TARGET AUDIENCE:** Adults who want to begin or enhance their home observances of Shabbat and the cycle of Jewish festivals

 **TIME FRAME:** 8 months, almost weekly, total of 30 class sessions (23 2½ hour sessions and 7 sessions of varying duration) synchronized with Jewish and school calendars

 **STAFF:** One person specially trained to teach The Holiday Workshop Series™

**Overview**  "The Holiday Workshop Series™" is an eight month long program which utilizes a step-by-step approach to teaching about Shabbat and the Jewish holidays. The presentation of material begins with a traditional, historical perspective. From a variety of suggestions, students choose what they are ready to do in their own homes. Teachers are especially trained to facilitate the course. There are approximately 30 sessions (23 regular classes of 2½ hours each and seven special events of varying duration). This time frame allows students to make dramatic changes in attitudes and life style and to integrate into their lives many of the practices they learn in class. It permits the teacher to reinforce values and concepts from previous lessons and to shape the class into a support group.

Chapter

# 42

**Purpose**  The overall purpose of the program is described by one of its mottos: to teach a person how "To Live Joyously As a Jew." Specifically, the most obvious goal is to enable adults to have meaningful and enjoyable celebrations of Shabbat and the Jewish holidays in their own homes. Thus, the program helps participants to:

1. Understand the background, values, and symbolism of Shabbat and Jewish holiday celebrations.

2. Feel secure and comfortable about their Jewish practices.

3. Gear their observances to the changing needs of their families.

Of even greater significance are the less obvious goals of the program: to raise Jewish self-esteem and deepen Jewish commitment. In these regards the program helps to:

1. Strengthen children's Jewish identity by teaching their *parents* how to live Jewish lives.

2. Improve Jewish education in the classroom by providing home reinforcement of the Jewish values and observances taught in the school.

3. Strengthen Jewish families by uniting them in home holiday celebrations.

4. Increase and activate synagogue membership by familiarizing students with the staff and site of the synagogue.

5. Increase involvement in the Jewish community.

**Preparation/Procedure**   The teachers play a key role in this program. In addition to disseminating information, they act as facilitators and role models. As the facilitator of the class, the teacher needs to be warm, sensitive, and open to diversity in students' backgrounds, attitudes, and family structures. As role models, teachers customarily express personal feelings and opinions and relate anecdotes about their own families and their own home holiday experiences. While teachers should be bright, articulate, enthusiastic people with leadership ability and some basic knowledge of Judaism, they do not need to be trained educators. Like the students, the teachers make a commitment to the program. First year instructors in this program devote 10 to 15 hours a week to the class, the training, and the necessary preparation. In the Los Angeles area, trainees attend training sessions on a weekly basis and then implement in their own classrooms what they have learned. Outside L.A. trainees participate in two intensive short courses with follow-up by local Jewish educators.

Chapter

# 42

Students are recruited by the teachers with the assistance of community professionals. Teachers receive an extensive publicity packet which includes sample press releases, flyers, and letters to prospective students, as well as sample announcements to be made at meetings and synagogue services. Financially, the program is self-sustaining. Tuition fees are set to cover the operating costs of the program.

To encourage affiliation and to help activate existing members, it is advisable to offer the class at a synagogue. For the same reasons and to ensure that sensitive subjects are taught in accordance with synagogue philosophy, Rabbis, Cantors, or Directors of Education may be invited to be guest speakers or to lead particular class discussions. Coordination with synagogue and community calendars is important for special events, such as the class Shabbat dinner and the graduation.

The classroom should be sufficiently large to accommodate students seated at tables in an arrangement that fosters group interaction. Refreshments are brought by students who volunteer to prepare at home selected recipes found in the classroom materials. Purchases from synagogue approved bakeries provide an alternate method of enabling students to see and sample typical holiday fare. For each session, teachers arrange for a display of books which pertain to the subjects to be discussed.

**Program Description**    The program begins with an intensive study of Shabbat, with emphasis on the home ceremony for Friday evening. Each holiday is covered in depth as it occurs during the cycle of the year. Because the program begins after the High Holy Day season, the Tishre holidays are taught out of sequence. In addition to holiday study, there are introductory sessions on the Bible, God concepts, and life cycle events. Discussions about basic Jewish concepts and values are interwoven into holiday and introductory lessons.

Chapter

42

The special events include: An *Erev Shabbat* class family dinner at the synagogue, a *Havdalah* ceremony and a *Chanukat Habayit* in a participant's home, and a tour of local Jewish agencies and the Jewish community building with participants from all "The Holiday Workshop Series™" classes. Whenever circumstances permit, there is a graduation ceremony as part of a synagogue service and a *Shabbaton* which includes *Seudah Shleesheet* and a study session of the portion of the week.

An important characteristic of the "Holiday Workshop Series™" is the warm and accepting atmosphere in the classroom. The sharing of experiences, exchanges of strategies for incorporating Jewish observances in the home, and other group discussions create bonds and build community among the students. Special relationships also develop between teachers and their students.

**Materials**    The student notebook contains preparations for each holiday, home ceremonies, bibliographies, songsheets, and recipes. Priorities are indicated in the notebook to assist students in choosing how to begin or enrich their home holiday observances. Novices are further aided by transliteration of the Hebrew throughout and by detailed instructions for preparing for and observing holidays in their homes. There are tape recordings of blessings and songs for Shabbat, Chanukah/Purim, and Passover.

The Teachers Manual has comprehensive information for inaugurating, administering, and teaching the program. For each session there are: a detailed lesson plan, goals and objectives, instructions to the teacher for class preparation, and recommended timing.

**Editor's Comments**   Training for the "The Holiday Workshop Series™" is done by its creator and founder, Patricia Singer Golden. Ms. Golden can be contacted to discuss the training of teachers for communities or synagogues wishing to introduce this program. She is constantly updating and refining the materials and the processes. The Teachers Manual and student materials are purchased only from her. These copyrighted materials are available only to trainees and students enrolled in the program.

Since its inception in 1973, "The Holiday Workshop Series™" has attracted mixed marrieds, Jews by Choice, and those born Jewish, but with little or no Jewish knowledge or experiences, as well as those *with* Jewish background. Primarily the program has been offered by Reform, Conservative, and Reconstructionist synagogues. It has also been held at day schools and Jewish Community Centers.

A longitudinal study of the impact of the program on people who have participated in "The Holiday Workshop Series™" revealed that, as a result of having taken the course, participants became more involved in the Jewish community in a variety of ways. They continued Jewish study, celebrated Shabbat in their homes, and most had begun to celebrate *all* the Jewish holidays. Additionally, many were working in the Jewish community and most had joined a synagogue. Many of the participants also reported on increased closeness in their family relationships.

Overall, this program is a catalyst for people to seek more Jewish education and involvement, to solidify their own Jewish identities, and to strengthen their family life.

**Bibliography/Resources**  For each holiday and subject studied in "The Holiday Workshop Series™," there is an extensive list of books recommmended for adult students and their children. The following is a sampling of these:

Bamberger, David, adapter. *My People: Abba Eban's History Of the Jews.* Vols. I and II. New York: Behrman House, 1978, 1979.

Gersh, Harry. *When a Jew Celebrates.* New York: Behrman House, 1986.

Schauss, Hayyim. *The Jewish Festivals.* New York: Schocken Books, 1976.

Prager, Dennis, and Telushkin, Joseph. *The Nine Questions People Ask About Judaism.* New York: Simon and Schuster, 1981.

*Tanakh: A New Translation Of the Holy Scriptures According To the Traditional Hebrew Text.* Philadelphia: Jewish Publication Society, 1985.

Chapter

42

# Chapter 43

 **TITLE:** Mishpacha — Family Learning Experiences ("FLEX")

 **CONTRIBUTED BY:** Karen Lebow

 **DESIGNED BY:** Diane Baxter; sample lesson by Karen Lebow

 **TOPIC:** Parent/child interactional workshops

 **TARGET AUDIENCE:** Parents with children in a Jewish school

 **TIME FRAME:** One 1½-3 hour session

 **STAFF:** Jewish parent educator, social worker/psychologist or facilitator with Judaic background, and classroom teachers

**Overview** "Mishpacha — Family Learning Experiences" consists of a series of lessons on various topics which mesh with the child's Jewish school experience. Each session focuses on lessons to be learned about Jewish parenting through holidays and Jewish concepts. Each session includes three components: a parenting discussion, a children's classroom lesson, and a family learning experience. Parent handouts, teacher's outlines, and materials are included in each package.

The Tu B'Shevat lesson of the program, summarized below, is an example of a "FLEX" program. Like the other holiday programs, it provides families with an opportunity to learn facts and history, and to explore their feelings about some of the concepts and ideas pertaining to the holiday. The program should be facilitated by an individual who is skilled in group dynamics and who has a strong background in Judaism. Classroom teachers lead the children's classroom lesson.

Chapter

# 43

**Purpose** "FLEX" was designed to be easy to implement, inexpensive, and highly successful in bringing parents to schools on a regular basis. The program, while enabling families to connect with each other, provides a specific time for parents and children to learn about Judaism and to be Jewish together. The program designer hopes that parents will begin to think about and apply some of the childrearing wisdom demonstrated in Jewish concepts and holiday observance. She also hopes that "FLEX," by its very nature, will relay the message to children that their parents care very much about their offspring's Jewish education.

**Preparation/Procedure** To ensure the success of "FLEX," survey the particular characteristics and dynamics of the school, Community Center, or congregation. A meeting and discussion with a few parents, teachers, and leaders can help to outline goals and focus on their achievement. For example, it is very important to assess accurately the following:

1. What kind of program will attract a good attendance?

2. What time structure will work?

3. What topics are relevant?

4. When should publicity be distributed?

At least two working days prior to the "FLEX" lesson, make the final arrangements. List and procure materials, walk through traffic patterns, confirm seating arrangement set-ups, make sure there is plenty of space in which participants can move around, confirm food and type of food service, and make a time sheet (see sample below).

At the beginning of the lesson, be sure to mention the overall purpose of "FLEX" and the objective of the selected lesson. Also, give participants a general overview of the agenda.

**Program Description**   Following is an outline of the schedule used for the "FLEX" Tu B'Shevat program. A sense of how time is budgeted is illustrated by the time sheet which follows the schedule.

Chapter

**43**

### Schedule
Parents' Portion
(Children go to regular classrooms; adults gather in a large meeting room.)

I. Introduction
  A. Purposes and goals
    1. Learn about parenting as it relates to Jewish celebrations and concepts.
    2. Gain information about the significance of Tu B'Shevat.
    3. Have a shared experience – with your own family and other families.

  B. Narrate the history and purpose of this celebration. Explain how we find meaning and how traditions and customs have been adapted through the ages.
    1. Suggested group exercises
      a. Break large group into smaller groups of eight people. Provide an easel, newsprint, and crayons or markers for each group. Ask one person in each group to be a recorder. Pass out printed story of Tu B'Shevat. Ask each group to list those values and attitudes reflected

in the story which they want to pass down to their children.

b. Ask recorders to tape each list to the wall in front of the room. The instructor will lead a brief summary discussion with the whole group about the content of the lists, commenting on such things as similarities, differences, and the relevancy of this festival as it relates to Jewish parenting.

2. Internalizing values and attitudes through personal experiences

a. Pass out large index cards and pencils. Ask participants to think about a childhood experience relating to trees or plants. Ask them to reflect on this for a moment or two. Ask each participant to jot down notes about their experience on the index card (not to be collected). Divide the large group again into the original small groups. Ask each group to divide itself into two groups. Provide, or have parents bring, tape recorders. Give each group a chance to share their stories with each other and to comment on the stories. Each group records their stories.

b. Lead a summary with the group as a whole about what was learned and experienced during this session. Include themes about the ebb and flow of life and the seasons, the change over time in our relationships to the earth, the factors in nature over which we do and don't have control (which shall flourish and which shall shrink), *Tikun Olam* (repairing the world), caring about future generations and being grateful and appreciative of what took place before us, the use and the esthetics of this celebration, and what all of the above mean to Jewish families.

**Family Time – Suggested Activities**

1. Parents tell their own stories to children in small groups. Children select two favorite parts of the story to illustrate with crayons and paper. Drawings are then captioned by parents and stapled together so that each child brings home a book.

2. A parent reads a related story such as *The Giving Tree* by Shel Silverstein, *A Tree Full Of Mitzvos* by Dina Rosenfeld, *Tu Bi-*

Sh'vot by Sophia Cedarbaum, or *The Birthday Of the Almond Tree*. Children select and illustrate their two favorite sections.

3. Conduct a family Tu B'Shevat *Seder.*

## Children's Program: Objectives and Activities

1. Suggested Objectives – Children learn about Tu B'Shevat, the name of this holiday, and age appropriate concepts or themes.

2. Suggested Classroom Activities
   a. Make tissue paper trees.
   b. Plant citrus trees in large pots.
   c. Learn a song with a Tu B'Shevat theme.
   d. Tell a flannel board story with the children, showing how growth of a fruit tree proceeds from seed to fruit.
   e. Engage in a dramatic/musical experience about growing plants.
   f. Play a sorting game using fresh fruits, dried fruits, and nuts.
   g. Join in a cooking experience.
   h. Make and decorate individual planters.

Chapter

43

## Time Sheet

Children go to regular classrooms.

| | |
|---|---|
| 10:00-10:15 | Adults check in and gather in meeting room 1. |
| 10:15-10:20 | Rabbi Donnell welcomes everyone, introduces program and Karen Lebow. |
| 10:20-10:25 | Karen Lebow reviews agenda and states goals and purposes of "FLEX" and of lesson on Tu B'Shevat. |
| 10:25-10:35 | Rabbi Donnell describes the festival of Tu B'Shevat, its purpose, and history. |
| 10:35-11:05 | Karen Lebow – group exercises |
| 11:05-11:15 | Karen Lebow – summary |
| 11:15-11:20 | Children walk from classroom to meeting room 1 and join parents. |
| 11:20-11:25 | Paul Roberts sings. |
| 11:25-11:40 | Story – "Birthday Of the Almond Tree" by Joshua Margolin |
| 11:40-11:45 | Marla Bemel – instructions to parents and children |

| 11:45-11:50 | Parents and children go to back of meeting room 2. |
| 11:50-12:05 | Children make illustrations and receive handouts. |
| 12:05-12:25 | *Seder* |

**Editor's Comments**   A parent orientation session should precede the implementation of the "FLEX" program. Parents need to learn what the program is about and the issues that will be confronted. If some parents are unable to participate, it is important to have an option for their children on days when the program itself takes place. If an orientation session is not practical for your group, send a detailed letter home describing the program, along with a schedule and a response card for the first session.

Chapter

43

For each session of "FLEX," a list of books should be sent home. These resources can be on display during the session. For some of the holiday and life cycle programs, objects and artifacts can be included in the display.

Refreshments will add to each session. Plan a brunch, lunch, or snack. Ask parents to participate in bringing the food, as appropriate.

The "FLEX" programs may be integrated into a school setting in several ways. Each lesson stands on its own, so you may decide to select one or more "FLEX" lessons on holidays, life cycle, or Jewish concepts to program and implement sometime during the school year. Another way is to select a specific grade level and use the entire body of programs.

A list of all the "FLEX" programs follows:

Group I
    Introductory Unit

    Shabbat: The Orchestration Of Family Values Through the Use Of Family Time

            Chanukah: Conformity and Conflict —
            The Role Of the Peer Group vs. the Family

Blessings and Prayers: The Meaning and Importance Of Ritual for Children

Pesach: The Struggle to Parent a Child To Freedom

Shavuot: The Relationship Between Rules and Family Values

Talking To Children About God

Group II
Jewish Attitudes Toward Family

Life Cycle: Birth, Bar/Bat Mitzvah, Marriage, Death and Mourning — The Special Way Jewish Celebrations Touch All Points Of Our Lives

Celebrating the Holidays Together

The Jewish Community Support

Education — Exploring the Options — for Kids and You

Chapter
43

Group III
Judaism and Parenting: Contemporary Challenges

Judaism and the Larger Community

The Changing Jewish Family

Exploring and Transmitting Jewish Values

## Bibliography/Resources
Cedarbaum, Sophia. *Tu Bi-Sh'vot: The New Year's Day for Trees.* New York: Union of American Hebrew Congregations, 1961.

Rosenfeld, Dina. *A Tree Full Of Mitzvos.* Brooklyn: Merkos L'Inyonai Chinuch, Inc., 1985.

Silverstein, Shel. *The Giving Tree.* New York: Harper and Row, 1964.

## Mediated Materials
*The Birthday Of the Almond Tree.* Union of American Hebrew Congregations, 1967. (filmstrip, 24 frames)

See also the bibliography for Chapter 18, "Intergenerational Tu B'Shevat Seder."

Chapter

43

# Chapter 44

 **TITLE:** Rainbow Connection

 **CONTRIBUTED BY:** Harlene Winnick Appelman

 **TOPIC:** Providing Jewish enrichment resources to families

 **TARGET AUDIENCE:** Families with children in Grades K-2

 **TIME FRAME:** Varying, depending on the specific workshop or program

 **STAFF:** One overall coordinator, teachers, Rabbi, other professional staff at the synagogue

**Overview**   "Rainbow Connection" is an ongoing Jewish family life education program which was developed at Congregation Shaarey Zedek in Southfield, Michigan. It provides families with children entering Grades K-2 with opportunities to broaden their knowledge about Shabbat and the Jewish holidays and to become acquainted and cultivate friendships, particularly through the synagogue. "Rainbow Connection" includes discussion groups and workshops for Shabbat and holidays. Families are also encouraged in a variety of ways to attend Shabbat services.

**Purpose**   The purpose of the "Rainbow Connection" is to provide Jewish enrichment and resources that will strengthen family units and create a strong bond between the family, the religious school, and the synagogue. The program provides adults and children with the skills and knowledge to participate in a meaningful way in Shabbat and holiday observances. It fosters social bonds for families with mutual interests.

Chapter

# 44

**Preparation/Procedure**   Monetary incentives are an integral part of this program. Prior to publicizing this program, a synagogue should decide upon the nature of these incentives. At Shaarey Zedek, members' children in Grades K-2 receive free tuition.

It is also necessary to form a committee of lay leaders and parents. These individuals are needed to assist with recruitment and to encourage new families to become involved.

Here are the suggested steps that make this program successful:

1. Recruit families from preschools. Prepare a presentation for them in May which provides an explanation of the unique possibilities for family involvement that this program has to offer.

2. Repeat this process in August, calling it a Kindergarten roundup.

3. One-on-one contact is a must. Members of the lay committee should call potential families and invite them to be part of this program.

Since they may be required to participate in the planning and implementation of enrichment activities, teachers need to be involved with the ongoing planning. You may need to consider the possibility of providing these teachers with additional compensation.

Prepare a brochure which contains program goals, a curriculum outline, and a calendar of events. Implement an advertisement campaign in the local Jewish press. Have the Rabbi invite all potential candidates to an informational coffee with the professional staff. Be sure to provide child care.

**Program Description**   "Rainbow Connection" includes the following programming:

Chapter

**44**

1. Kindergarten Round-up – This is a gathering of all parents enrolling their children in Kindergarten. A separate activity is planned for the children (i.e., magician, puppet show, movie), while the "Rainbow Connection" concept is presented and explained to the parents.

2. Rainbow Connection Kindergarten Coffees – Coffees introduce "Rainbow Connection" to families who are interested in participating. Such get-togethers provide an opportunity to meet with the Rabbi to discuss the program. Schedule coffees at different times of the day and evening to guarantee that every parent who is eligible attends. Distribute a questionnaire (see below) to everyone. This can become the basis for a discussion lasting approximately 45 minutes. Invite families who are veterans of the program to offer practical suggestions and encouragement to families who are interested in becoming more involved in Judaism.

QUESTIONNAIRE
Rainbow Connection Kindergarten Coffee

What rituals, ceremonies, etc., do you remember from your childhood that revolved around Shabbat?

What Shabbat rituals do you observe with your family today?

Do you observe these in your home or in the home of parents, grandparents?

What Shabbat celebration or observance have you been meaning to introduce into your life?

What steps can you take to make this celebration or observance a part of your family's Shabbat?

3. First Day of School – Distribute bookbags and binders with the "Rainbow Connection" logo to all children in K, 1, and 2 to help them feel that they belong to a special group. Take instant photographs of students with their teachers and parents to emphasize the point that beginning religious education is a significant act and should be celebrated.

4. Sukkot Family Luncheon in Honor Of Aleph Inductees – On Shabbat morning in the synagogue, present first grade children with a book of blessings. Again, this is a way to let these families know that they are special.

5. Three Sundays In October – The theme of the informational series which takes place on three Sundays after the coffees is "The Magic Of Shabbat." The one simple goal of the series is to encourage everyone to light candles on Shabbat. However, the information transmitted includes the Shabbat home rituals, tactics to encourage spouses and children to be together for Friday night dinner, and suggestions as to how to spend family time throughout the Shabbat. There is ample time for individuals to share past and present experiences and to ask questions about customs and observances that the Rabbi can answer. A sample of one Sunday session follows:

Session I: Growing Into Shabbat: A Sometimes Gradual Experience (1½ hours)

A. *Shabbat Shalom* – Show *Shabbat Shalom*, a 6 minute trigger film produced by the Toronto Jewish Congress, which centers on a Mother's decision to celebrate Shabbat for the first time. Her family's negative reaction shocks and dismays her.

B. Trying Again – Shabbat has received poor P.R. It has always been an all or nothing proposition.

C. The Image Of the Wheel – Show a diagram of a wheel with hub, spokes, and rim. Explain that this image is the model proposed for developing the observance of Shabbat. At the hub is the commandment to observe Shabbat. The spokes represent the major categories (central *mitzvot*) of Shabbat observance. Your ever-widening observance is like the rim.

D. Taking Time for Shabbat – It takes time to build meaningful home observances and rituals. Start with simple modest goals. It is only after one learns to love the Shabbat that one wants to embrace it and do more.

E. Sustain Your Child's Delight With Jewish Learning – A classic scenario regarding a commitment to observe Shabbat or any holiday begins with sending your child to a Jewish school. The child learns about Shabbat ritual and the young child is especially delighted by the ceremony and splendor of candles, wine, and special bread. He/she then looks to you. Perhaps you visit his/her class for a special Shabbat program and you see how delighted the child is. You want to sustain that delight. How?

Chapter

44

1. Learn.
2. Get support – Shabbat celebration is easier in a group of family and friends.
3. Realize the limits of your commitment.
4. Go slowly.
5. Other ideas to consider:
   a. The necessity of dealing with your own anger or discomfort — (are you rejecting prayer or the person who first made you pray?)
   b. Realizing that observance at any level is not an all or nothing proposition
   c. Child-centered Judaism — bringing a ritual down to the level of the children. You want to involve children in what interests you. If your only motive is that it's for the sake of the children, then is it worthwhile?

F. Developmental Receptivity To Ritual – Children in Grades K-2 are developmentally receptive to ritual. Participating together in meaningful ritual celebration provides an opportunity for families to experience closeness, warmth, and a mutually satisfying endeavor. Repeating blessings regularly each Shabbat will enable a child to know the words and say them. The meaning to the child of the words and actions will depend on the context. Is it a joyful, loving, fun, or sad experience?

G. The Wheel Again – Return to the image of the wheel. At the hub are the following texts:

Exodus 31:16-17
"The Israelite people shall keep the Sabbath, observing the Sabbath throughout the ages as a covenant for all time: it shall be a sign for all time between Me and the people of Israel."

Exodus 20:8, 11
"Remember the Sabbath day and keep it holy . . . For in six days the Lord made heaven and earth and sea and all that is in them, and He rested on the seventh day; therefore, the Lord blessed the Sabbath day and hallowed it."

Deuteronomy 5:12, 15
"Observe the Sabbath day and keep it holy . . . Remember that you were a slave in the land of Egypt and the Lord your God freed you from there with a mighty hand and an outstretched arm; therefore, the Lord your God has commanded you to observe the Sabbath day."

H. Pair & Share Shabbat – This is a supplemental session for "Three Sundays In October." Preparation for this segment takes place during the last discussion session of "Three Sundays In October." Families are encouraged to invite one other family for Shabbat dinner on a designated Sabbath. It is significant and effective for participating families to share Shabbat with others in the group.

I. The Magic Of Shabbat – This is a hands-on workshop during which families make *challah* trays, *challah* covers, and decorate *kippot*. If families make ritual objects together, it is likely that they will use them. The finale of this program is a magician who keeps trying to produce

Chapter
44

the Shabbat Magic. He is unsuccessful because only a family sharing Shabbat can produce such a miracle.

J.  Havdalah Workshop – During this session families come together for a *Seudah Shleesheet*, followed by *Havdalah*. Families then make their own *Havdalah* candles by twisting together long thin tapers that have been dipped in hot water. Everyone is given a small spice box made from filmstrip canisters. Singing, eating, and the beauty of *Havdalah* make this program a beautiful experience.

K.  Sticker Shabbat Incentive – Children in Grades K-2 are given stickers for attending Saturday morning services.

L.  Holiday Packets – At the appropriate time during the year, holiday packets containing home observance guides for Chanukah, Tu B'Shevat, Purim, and Pesach are sent out. All of these include games and puzzles for the children and an instructive message for the parents. The Passover pack contains Passover family task cards and the guarantee of winning a prize. Participants receive a certificate and a "Rainbow Connection" pen for their efforts.

Chapter

# 44

**Editor's Comments**   "Rainbow Connection" has been very successful for Shaarey Zedek Congregation as demonstrated by the fact that, in the last several years, the Kindergarten class has doubled in size. It is a program that can be implemented at any level of Jewish school education. Other congregations may wish to use the program as it is outlined here or adapt parts of it to fit their particular needs. In order to make such a program work, a synagogue needs to determine the parameters: i.e., financial arrangements, the time commitment of professional staff, grade level of the children.

Harlene Winnick Appelman and her staff have produced a booklet which describes the "nuts and bolts" of the program in detail. It includes discussion outlines, pointers for Shabbat, and Shabbat blessings and songs. There is a whole section entitled "When Your Child Asks About Shabbat" which contains questions and answers on Shabbat. The booklet is a valuable resource for those who are contemplating such a program.

## Bibliography/Resources

Appelman, Harlene Winnick. "J.S.L.E. and the Synagogue." *Journal of Jewish Communal Service* 62, no. 2 (Winter 1985).

### Mediated Materials

*Shabbat Shalom*. Canadian Jewish Congress, 4600 Bathurst Ave., Willowdale, Ontario M2R 3V2, Canada, 1981. (trigger film, 6 min.)

For other references, see the bibliography for Chapter 7, "The Joy Of Shabbat."

Chapter

# 44

# Chapter 45

 **TITLE:** When Parents Grow Old

 **CONTRIBUTED BY:** Deborah Fins and Alan W. Harris

 **DESIGNED BY:** Alan W. Harris

 **TOPIC:** Issues of concern for children of aging parents

 **TARGET AUDIENCE:** Adults who are faced with aging parents who may need special help

 **TIME FRAME:** Three 1½-2 hour sessions

 **STAFF:** One facilitator trained in group work/social work and/or gerontology

**Overview**   This program, targeted for middle aged adults, was developed at the Jewish Family Service of Worcester, Massachusetts. It provides a forum in which people may express their cares and concerns about their aging parents in a supportive environment. It allows participants to discuss how to care for an aging parent while caring also for themselves. It also provides participants with information about community resources that are available for senior adults.

**Purpose**   The purpose of the program is to provide information and promote discussion about issues arising in caring for elderly relatives. An additional purpose is to impart to participants the sense that they are not alone with their problems.

Chapter

45

**Preparation/Procedure**   Publicize the program throughout the community through flyers and letters to agencies which come into contact with senior adults and their families, and through press releases to the Anglo-Jewish and secular press and synagogue and community newsletters. Request that Rabbis announce the program from their pulpits. Send personal letters from the agency to families of senior adult clients. Post notices in senior citizen centers, senior housing complexes, and in convalescent and nursing homes. If there is a university nearby with a department of gerontology, inform them of the program as well.

Offer the program as often as is needed in the community. The optimum size of a group is 15. Structure the fee schedule so that there is a discounted price for a couple.

**Program Description**   The following is an overview of the three sessions:

Session I: Film and Discussion
Show the film *When Parents Grow Old*. Use the film as a trigger for a discussion of common issues and concerns. Utilize a brainstorming technique to list the issues and problems, then prioritize them. Some of the topics which will most likely come up are: mid-life crisis, role reversal, stress, guilt, anger, and responsibility.

Session II: Community Resources
Provide participants with the list of issues developed for
discussion at the previous session. Since the focus of this session
is on community resources, have available information about a
variety of agencies that can be of assistance to participants, such
as Jewish Family Service, legal counsel, Social Security Administration, medical services, etc., and how participants go about
securing the assistance of each. Also compile a list of senior
centers, senior adult housing complexes, and senior adult
groups. Other information to disseminate might include some
guidelines on how to go about selecting a board and care facility,
or a convalescent/nursing home, should the need arise.

Session III: Problem Solving
At this session there is directed discussion about the issues and
concerns of the group which were developed during the first
session. Participants discuss how they might use the community
resources available to them to assist in solving some of their
problems. In addition, the facilitator can develop role plays or
present case histories to help participants to focus on the
problems and work through them. In order to make maximum
use of the time, it is best to subdivide the group. Each sub-group
can work on a specific problem and solution which is later
presented to the entire group. Discussion follows.

Chapter

45

**Editor's Comments**   This program can be augmented by
including Jewish content material, such as Jewish views of death
and mourning practices, and Jewish views of aging and caring
for the aging.

Since participants come to this program for support, it may be
beneficial for the sponsoring agency to help the group continue
on a less formal basis after the three structured sessions are over.
The continuation of the group is encouraged by the Jewish
Family Service of Worcester, and one such group has been
meeting for a year and a half. A group of this type can meet
without a professional, with various participants assigned to lead
specific discussions. If a problem requires professional help,
the agency could be called upon to sit in. The agency could
provide the meeting place or meetings could be in the homes
of group members.

Claire Nussbaum of the Jewish Family Service of Charleston, South Carolina, offers a similar program. Using the book *Your Aging Parents* by John Deedy as a teaching manual, there are structured discussions based on the text. The program consists of five 1½ hour sessions. The topics are: Changing World, Expanded Life Span; Coming To Terms With the Death Of Loved Ones and Of Oneself; The Extended Family and Its Role; When to Help and When to Encourage Independence; Health, Sickness, Alzheimers Disease. Ms. Nussbaum has also presented the program as one 2 hour session for adult children of aging parents who reside in a senior apartment complex adjacent to the Jewish Community Center.

Programs of this type can also be offered by hospitals, homes for the aged, synagogues, hospice organizations, Jewish Community Centers. They can be designed to include a Jewish value component, giving participants an opportunity to learn about Jewish attitudes toward aging.

Chapter

45

## Bibliography/Resources

Azoff, Judy, and Nacman, Edith. *Trigger Plays On Aging.* Jewish Family Life Education Department, Jewish Family Service of Rochester, Inc., 441 East Avenue, Rochester NY 14607.

Deedy, John. *Your Aging Parents.* Chicago: Thomas Moore Press, 1983.

Olitzky, Kerry M., and Olitzky, Lee H. *Aging and Judaism.* Denver: Alternatives in Religious Education, Inc., 1980.

Otten, Jane, and Shelley, Florence P. *When Your Parents Grow Old*, New York: Funk & Wagnalls, 1976.

Rushford, Pat. *The Help, Hope and Cope Book.* Old Tappan, NJ: Revell, 1984.

Silverstone, Barbara, and Hyman, Helen Kandel. *You and Your Aging Parent: The Modern Family's Guide To Emotional, Physical, and Financial Problems.* New York: Pantheon Books, 1975.

Workshop Model, "Aging Parents – Whose Responsibility?"
    Human Communication Resources. Available through
    Family Service Association of America, Family Life Educa-
    tion Department, 44 E. 23 Street, New York, NY 10010.

**Mediated Materials**

*When Parents Grow Old*. Learning Corporation of America,
    1350 Avenue of the Americas, New York, NY 10019, 1971.
    (film, 14 min.)

Chapter
45

# Chapter 46

 **TITLE:** Trigger Plays On Aging

 **CONTRIBUTED BY:** Alan Shapiro

 **TOPIC:** Common problems confronting the elderly as shown through drama

 **TARGET AUDIENCE:** Senior adults, adult children of seniors, school age children

 **TIME FRAME:** Two 2 ½ hour sessions

 **STAFF:** One facilitator who is familiar with the scripts and who can involve the audience

**Overview**   This is a program of the Jewish Family Life Education department at the Jewish Family Service of Rochester, New York. It is comprised of a series of brief vignettes, written by Judy Azoff and Edith Nacman, which depict common problems situations confronting the elderly and their families. The scenarios are designed to trigger discussion in the audience on the subject of aging. The format is informal and discussion-oriented. Participants open up to share ideas and problem solving techniques after seeing the plays.

**Purpose**   The program provides a safe non-threatening environment in which individuals and families can look at the controversial issues that surround aging, as well as the normal changes that take place during the aging process. Other objectives are:

Chapter

46

1.  To stimulate the elderly to express some of the concerns and problems they face with their peers and family members in a non-threatening, comfortable format and a supportive environment.

2.  To provide a means of group problem solving for the elderly.

3.  To help other age groups in the community, especially young people, to begin to understand some of the concerns of the elderly.

4.  To help the adult children of elderly parents understand, and cope more effectively with, their aging parents, and to receive emotional support from others who are in similar situations.

5.  In terms of community education, to make the community aware that aging is a natural process, and to identify resources available in the community for the elderly and their families.

**Preparation/Procedure**   This program requires a trained facilitator who is familiar with the plays. The scripts are available, with a Leader Guide, from the Jewish Family Service of Rochester, Inc., 441 East Ave., Rochester, NY 14607. The program is appropriate for any community group, including school age children and seniors. Any or all of the plays can be presented during a program, depending on the size and needs of the audience and the time parameters.

Publicize the program through synagogue and organizational newsletters.

**Program Description**   The facilitator introduces the program and the scripts. He/she describes the purpose of the plays to the audience. Recruit volunteers from the audience to act in one or two of the plays. (Let as many people as possible participate.) Describe the characters and the setting, using simple props, such as a telephone, chairs, etc. Volunteers read the scripts (which are typed in large print to accommodate the needs of the elderly) to the rest of the group. At the conclusion of each script, the facilitator leads a discussion that is triggered by the issues raised in that script.

Chapter

46

A synopsis of each script follows:

*Long Distance* depicts the problems that arise when adult children do not live in the same city as their aging parents.

*The Weekend* depicts different expectations for family involvement which often exists between aging parents and their grown children and grandchildren living in the same city.

*The Date* explores the issues of dating, sexuality, and friendly jealousies, which are just as complex and important for senior adults as for younger people.

*Getting Around* shows how one can keep active while living independently.

*The Home* demonstrates the difficulty for aging parents and their families of coping with a residential placement.

**Editor's Comments**   The presentation of these plays can be accompanied by specific information about caring for the aged in the community. The discussion can also be expanded to include intergenerational relationships, particularly those between the elderly and grandchildren and great grandchildren.

Jewish content should be included in the discussions following the plays. If the program is geared to school age children, it would be appropriate to compare the situations depicted in the plays with some texts with which they are familiar – e.g., the aging Patriarchs; the communal response to specific groups, such as orphans, etc. Values clarification exercises and lessons in instant aging would add to the youngsters' understanding. For ideas on an instant aging lesson, see Chapter 5, "Bridging the Gap."

**Bibliography/Resources**     See the bibliography for Chapter 45, "When Parents Grow Old."

Chapter

46

# Chapter 47

 **TITLE:** Bridge To Understanding

 **CONTRIBUTED BY:** Karen Lebow

 **DESIGNED BY:** Felice Andiman, Kyla Epstein, and Fradya Rembaum

 **TOPIC:** Discussion of concerns regarding Judaism and Jewish practice, as well as information about the Jewish community in general

 **TARGET AUDIENCE:** Interfaith couples

 **TIME FRAME:** Six 2 hour sessions

 **STAFF:** One facilitator

**Overview**   This communal program was developed by the Family Life Education Department of the Bureau of Jewish Education of the Jewish Federation Council of Los Angeles. It is open to couples with only one Jewish partner. Couples are married or about to be married. "Bridge To Understanding" helps participants survey the dilemmas which intermarried couples face as they attempt to raise Jewish children. It prepares them to deal with these problems and to gain information about and insight into Judaism. The series usually features one Jewish celebration. The format includes guided discussions about a particular topic and a question-answer segment concerning any and all aspects of Judaism. It is time limited and there is a fee.

**Purpose**   The purpose of the program is to bring couples closer to the Jewish community and to provide them with a Jewish support network with which to connect when confronted with issues relating to family relationships and child rearing. It is also designed to provide a Jewish group experience during which interfaith couples can confront and reconcile the place of religious identity and observance in their lives, and to promote a sense of ownership by the Jewish partner of his/her Jewish identity.

**Preparation/Procedure**   Recruitment for this program takes place throughout the community. Couples may be referred by Rabbis, Directors of Education, Preschool Directors, and other Jewish professionals; or, they may be drawn to the program by public announcements, press releases, and flyers.

The facilitator should be a person who is a knowledgeable Jewish role model. This person must be sensitive to the needs of the participants. The facilitator must have training in group dynamics, psychology, teaching, or social work, as an inter-marriage issue is sometimes a "cover" for some deep pathology. He/she also needs referral skills, as this is not a psychotherapy group.

**Program Description**   "Bridge To Understanding" is a series of six two-hour sessions and one subsequent, hands-on celebratory experience. Each session includes guided discussion on a set topic. Agenda items are determined from the needs of the group and the input of the facilitator. They are presented at the first or second session. A sample agenda for the discussions is as follows:

Session I    Overview of the program, setting group and individual goals, and introductory activities

Session II   The component of Jewish identity for you, your non-Jewish spouse, your children

Session III  Components of Jewish identity, continued

Session IV   The role of the Jewish parent as educator; the value of ritual as an educational tool

Session V    Relationships with the extended family; celebratory experience

Session VI   Community resources; where to go from here; evaluation

Chapter

47

**Editor's Comments**   This is a communal program which cuts across denominational lines. It is important for participants to know that there may be differing views about the issues which are brought up for discussion, e.g., holiday rituals, *kashrut*, matrilineal and patrilineal descent, etc.

Depending on the group, you may wish to introduce Jewish texts through a brief *D'var Torah* at the start of each session, or study the portion of the week on a regular basis. Texts may be selected which address some of the issues under discussion, such as child rearing, Jewish education, honoring father and mother. This helps to put problems into a Judaic perspective by showing that many of the concerns people have are not new to Jewish thought.

A subsequent program may be developed which focuses on community involvement. The sessions, then, would acquaint participants with the community at large and what it means to be a part of a community. Perhaps you could invite leaders from the local synagogues, Federation, B'nai B'rith, Hadassah, ZOA, and other community organizations and agencies to talk about their identity as Jews and what being Jewish means to them. Continuing this concept, this could be integrated this with on-site visits to area synagogues, a Jewish museum, and/or a Jewish bookstore. If neither of the latter two exist in your community, ask individuals who own Jewish art and ceremonial objects and have a good Judaica library whether the group may spend an evening at their home(s) talking about these collections.

## Bibliography/Resources

Aron, Melanie W., and Zucker, David Jeremy. "The Structure, Fruition, and Organization Of a Mixed Marriage Support System." *Journal of Reform Judaism* (Summer, 1984).

Einstein, Stephen J., and Kukoff, Lydia. *Introduction To Judaism: A Course Outline.* New York: Union of American Hebrew Congregations, 1983.

Kukoff, Lydia. *Choosing Judaism.* New York: Union of American Hebrew Congregations, 1981.

Mayer, Egon. *Love and Tradition: Marriage Between Jews and Christians.* New York and London: Plenum Press, 1985.

Sandmel, Samuel. *When a Jew and Christian Marry.* Philadelphia: Fortress Press, 1977.

Syme, Daniel. *The Jewish Home Series.* New York: Union of American Hebrew Congregations, 1976-1981.

Winer, Mark L. "Sociological Research On Jewish Intermarriage." *Journal of Reform Judaism* (Summer, 1985).

Winer, Mark. "When Americans Intermarry." *Reform Judaism* (Spring 1984).

Chapter

47

# Chapter 48

 **TITLE:** My Other Grandma Isn't Jewish

 **CONTRIBUTED BY:** Cynthia Himmelfarb

 **TOPIC:** Dealing with the problems and conflicts that arise in intermarried families

 **TARGET AUDIENCE:** Families in which there are close relatives who are not Jewish

 **TIME FRAME:** One 2-2½ hour session or four 2 hour sessions

 **STAFF:** Facilitator

**Overview**   This program is sponsored by the Jewish Family Service of Santa Clara County, California as part of an ongoing series of Jewish Family Life Education programs. It is designed to help interfaith families deal with the problems and conflicts that arise as a result of multi-religious practices by family members.

**Purpose**   The primary purpose of the program is to heighten awareness and improve coping skills in a potential problem area by focusing on the positive opportunities that diversity provides.

**Preparation/Procedure**   Staff members of the agency are trained each year in the "what, why, and how" of the program. At this particular agency, each staff person and supervisor is responsible for planning and implementing Jewish Family Life Education in his/her particular area of practice. Local Jewish organizations and agencies are contacted and are largely responsible for the publicity. With regard to this particular program, the Family Service Agency must decide whether it will be a one-time program or part of an ongoing series for intermarried families.

**Program Description**   The program begins with a values clarification questionnaire. Participants complete the questionnaire to the best of their ability and the forms are then collected. The following questions appear on the questionnaire, which was prepared by the author for the Jewish Family Service of Santa Clara County. Participants check their responses under the headings Always True, Sometimes True, or Never True.

1. The most important thing to me is that I maintain a close and loving relationship with my child regardless of who he or she marries.

2. I would tell my child how I really feel about his or her intended mate even though I think he/she would be hurt.

3. If my grandchild was being confirmed in a faith different from mine, I would not attend the ceremony even though my child wanted me to.

4. I'm comfortable in participating in non-Jewish celebrations such as Christmas and Easter in my child's home.

5. I try to expose my grandchildren and non-Jewish son-in-law or daughter-in-law to Jewish activities and events, such as Jewish holiday celebrations in my home.

6. I am pleased to participate in ecumenical celebrations, such as a Christmas/Chanukah party in someone else's home.

7. I enjoy having such ecumenical celebrations in my own home.

8. I believe the most important thing is a belief in God. It's less important how a person worships.

9. I think the Jewish relatives of an intermarried couple should try to get the non-Jewish person to convert to Judaism.

10. I think my synagogue should make an effort to welcome anyone who wants to participate in the services, regardless of whether or not they are Jewish.

11. Intermarriage is a threat to Jewish survival.

12. Intermarried couples have to decide whether to live as Jews or Christians, because they can't really live as both.

13. I feel uncomfortable when I'm with my non-Jewish relatives.

14. The religion of a person is unimportant to me. What is important is the kind of person he or she is.

15. I think the increase in intermarried couples will ultimately bring about a reduction in anti-Semitism.

Chapter

# 48

The members of the group then express what they want from the program. The question is posed, "If this group is successful, what will you have that you do not have now?" The answers are written down and serve as points of reference for future discussions.

The second session consists of a mini-lecture on the increased incidence of intermarriage and why it is an issue today. The facilitator discusses what other communities are doing about it. It is noted that there is not a large body of knowledge on the subject of intermarriage from which to draw, so that anything learned in the group can be used to teach others. The information is constantly updated, and intermarriage is looked at as a universal problem in the Jewish community. A discussion follows based on the data presented in the mini-lecture and on the values clarification questionnaire.

During the last two sessions, participants share personal experiences. In these discussions reference is always made back to what people wish to get from the program. Many people have specific situations which they present to the group, such as a Bar/Bat Mitzvah that is coming up, Christmas celebrations, a child at an age to enter religious school, an impending birth.

At the final session, the same questionnaire used in the first session is distributed and everyone is asked to answer it again. Participants then receive back their original questionnaires so that they can compare the two sets of answers. An evaluation form is also distributed and collected at this session.

Chapter

# 48

It is possible to facilitate this program in one session; however, doing so may preclude discussion about specific situations or personal experiences. In the shortened version, distribute the questionnaire at the outset and then discuss it. The mini-lecture then follows.

**Editor's Comments**   This program is also appropriate for seniors, many of whom have children who are intermarried and grandchildren who are not Jewish. Conversely, there are non-Jewish senior adults who have children married to Jewish partners and have Jewish grandchildren. This population often feels a need to explore its role in relation to interfaith marriage – where they fit in at life cycle celebrations, how to handle the December holidays, and what values are particularly important to transmit.

A less formal way of dealing with the problems of interfaith couples is through ongoing "rap" groups. One Jewish Center sponsors a weekly group for women who are intermarried. The women come and go in the group as they are able; there is no registration and no attendance requirement. The Center provides the facilitator and the room. The group meets regularly, every week, from September through June.

**Bibliography/Resources**   See the bibliography for Chapter 47, "Bridge To Understanding."

# Additional Programs
# In Brief

This section contains brief synopses of programs for Jewish families developed by and implemented through synagogues, Jewish Family Service agencies, Jewish Centers, etc. For additional information, write the contact person directly. The five categories of programs are as follows:

# Ongoing Programs

**Jewish Education Family Style**   This program provides an alternative to the traditional Sunday School program for parents who have children in third, fourth, and fifth grades. Parents accompany their children to Sunday School every other week. The first part of the day, parents study with the Rabbi. The subject matter is the same as that which the children study, but on an adult level. This is followed by an interactive classroom experience which can be incorporated into a family's life at home. The general curriculum remains constant: Grade 3 – Shabbat and Holidays; Grade 4 – Israel; Grade 5 – Life Cycle Observances. The experiences vary from year to year, depending on the needs and interests of the families involved.

Contact:
Mardee Costa
Temple Sholom Religious School
3480 Lake Shore Drive
Chicago, Illinois 60657

**Parent PACAJE**  Parent and Child Activities for Jewish Enrichment was developed by the staff of the Creativity Center of the Milwaukee Association for Jewish Education for parents of children aged 3-7. It is a subscription program, operating on a two year cycle, which includes stories and activities relating to Israel, Hebrew language, Bible, and *Midrash*. There are audiotapes, magnetic story boards, Hebrew games, books to make about Israel, puzzles, puppets, matching games, stories, toys, recipes, and individual handicraft projects. Two packets a year are distributed at workshops where the staff introduces the projects, explains how best to use and assemble the materials, and shows the finished products. Each PACAJE comes with all materials and instructions for assembling them at home. The cost is $25 a year.

Contact:
Alice Jacobson
Milwaukee Association for Jewish Education
4650 North Port Washington Road
Milwaukee, Wisconsin 53212

**Mishpachah**    This program is for young Jewish families and their preschool age children. Sponsored jointly by the San Francisco Bureau of Jewish Education and the Jewish Community Federation in conjunction with area synagogues, it is limited to 20 families at each of five locations. Participation includes Shabbat morning sessions and services once a month, October through June; two Shabbat family dinners; Tu B'Shevat tree planting; and adult discussions. The program allows participants to share Shabbat and holiday celebrations in a meaningful way. Families learn appropriate blessings, songs, customs, and other skills pertaining to Shabbat, holidays, and *tefillah*. They acquire a repertoire of stories, games, music, and recipes to enrich their lives Jewishly.

Contact:
Bureau of Jewish Education
639 Fourteenth Avenue
San Francisco, California 94118

**Ongoing Parent Participation for K-1**  As part of a program to reach out to parents, parents are required to work in the class six times during the year. They are expected to participate in meaningful ways — tell a story, teach a Hebrew lesson, prepare for a holiday, etc. Materials are provided for them. If they have special skills in music, dance, art, or anything else, they work in those areas. Parents are also invited for major holiday celebrations in the class.

Contact:
Buzz Hellman
Baltimore Hebrew Congregation
7401 Park Heights Avenue
Baltimore, Maryland 21208

**Family Education Council**   The Council consists of a group of concerned educators and lay leaders who meet monthly to share materials and ideas and to solve problems related to family education. Together the council plans programs that are needed in the community on such subjects as teen-age self-esteem and sexuality, choosing a mate, pre-marriage workshops, etc.

Contact:
Dr. Betsy Katz
Bureau of Jewish Education of Metropolitan Chicago
618 South Michigan Avenue
Chicago, Illinois 60605

# Multi-Session Programs

**Home Start Workshops**   This is a series of workshops for
parents of four to six-year-old children designed to introduce
families to Jewish holiday celebrations and to augment the
*Home Start* materials (New York: Behrman House, 1983). Each
program includes songs, a puppet show, and a craft project.
Time is set aside to meet separately with parents to review the
*Home Start* materials, to discuss background about the holiday,
and to share ways of celebrating the holiday in the home. Each
workshop lasts 1½ hours. Refreshments are served and the
room is decorated to reflect the holiday under discussion.

Contact:
Carol K. Ingall
Bureau of Jewish Education of Rhode Island
130 Sessions Street
Providence, Rhode Island 02906

## Mishpachah: Experiences In Jewish Family Living

Families participate in planned monthly experiences centered around Shabbat, holidays, and events in the Jewish life cycle. Families are divided into clusters (10 families each) in which they may participate in several optional activities. These activities might include:

Preparatory Activity Options:
Shopping for fruits
Preparing a Tu B'Shevat *Seder*
Learning Israeli songs and dances
Preparing a bird feeder for *Shabbat Shirah*

Mishpachah Family Experiences:
Tu B'Shevat *Seder*
Eating Israeli fruits
Singing and dancing

Follow-up Activity Options:
Buying a family tree through Jewish National Fund
Planting a tree at home or in a nearby place

Contact:
Jo Kellman
Board of Jewish Education of Greater New York
Department of Early Childhood Education
468 West 58th Street
New York, New York 10019

**My Family: A Roots Project**   This oral history program
consists of 10 units during which students explore their roots by
interviewing family members. Through the use of charts which
are provided, students compare findings and discover general
trends and cultural patterns relating to history, human geography,
folklore, and values. The project promotes self-directed work,
interviewing skills, creative writing, role play, and the involvement
of family members in the curriculum. Included are a Teacher's
Manual, a student workbook containing "Parent Pages," and
*Alpaim* value cards (seven card games designed to help students
discuss biblical values and apply them to social dilemmas).
Materials are available for purchase through the authors.

Contact:
Sylvia Stipelman, Batia Bettman, and Phyllis Pinchuk
Jewish Education Council of Greater Montreal
5151 Cote St. Catherine Road
Montreal, Quebec H3W 1M6
Canada

# One-Time Programs

**Kindergarten Family Education Day: Shabbat**   This program helps participants to develop the skills necessary for introducing Shabbat into their homes. Families come together for an interactional activity. They introduce themselves to each other via a family picture or creative name tags. They then proceed to a series of stations where they learn several Shabbat skills, such as the blessings over the candles, wine, and *challah*; make things for their Shabbat tables at home, such as candlesticks, *challah* covers or *challah* boards; and gather a repertoire of songs and stories about Shabbat. The songs are on tape and the stories are reproduced so that parents can take them home to read at the Shabbat table. The day ends with a *"Kabbalat Shabbat"* celebration during which everyone practices the blessings, displays the artifacts they have made, and sings the songs they have learned.

Contact:
Rabbi Terry Bookman and Karen Sobel
Congregation Sinai
8223 North Port Washington Road
Fox Point, Wisconsin 53217

**My Me Book**   This program focuses on the Jewish self for Kindergarten children and their families. There is a 12 page booklet with four headings: My Physical self, My Pretend Self, My God Self, and My Jewish Home. During the course of a morning, families rotate to four stations where they participate in activities to complete and personalize their children's books. A description of the activities for each of the four stations follows:

My Physical Self: Children are weighed and measured, and parents and children are fingerprinted. They paste Hebrew word body parts onto a large drawing of a body.

My Pretend Self: Parents read stories about two Jewish heroes to the children. The children dress up as the heroes/heroines and, with an instant camera, pictures are taken that are pasted into the book. The families answer a series of questions about the heroes/heroines, which are also included in the book.

My God Self: At this station there are parallel activities. The classroom teacher works with the children to create wishes using the first letter of their English names. The Family Education Coordinator works with the parents to create a blessing or prayer for their child using the child's Hebrew name in conjunction with Psalm 119. The children's wishes and the parents' blessings are put into the book.

My Jewish Home: Each family brings a Jewish object from home. Families walk through a museum created from the objects. The children paste pictures of Jewish objects into home scenes provided in their books.

Contact:
Rabbi Terry Bookman and Karen Sobel
Congregation Sinai
8223 North Port Washington Road
Fox Point, Wisconsin 53217

**Values and Moral Development**   This is a three part program for third grade students and their parents.

Part One: Values Fair – Parents are led to an area decorated to simulate a fair. Parents select one value from a list which they will try to "sell" to the children. They make posters, buttons, etc., with slogans about the value.

Students are given $40 each and told that they will be given a chance to support personally the values most important to them by distributing the money in $10 increments at the fair.

At the fair a "candyman" enters and competes with the sale of values by selling candy bars for $20 each. Once all the money is distributed, a discussion is held to talk about the decisions the students made and the parent's reactions to their choices.

Part Two: Moral Dilemmas – Students work on a moral dilemma from *Moral Development: A Practical Guide for Jewish Teachers* by Earl Schwartz (Denver: Alternatives in Religious Education, Inc., 1983).

Parents are involved in a lecture/discussion on Kohlberg's "Theory Of Moral Development." There is particular emphasis on the nine-year-old.

Part Three: Problem Solving – Families identify a real problem they face in one of the following areas:

1. Sibling rivalry

2. Respecting and/or caring for older family members

3. Disagreeing with and/or disobeying a parent

4. Together each family describes the values involved and creates a skit about the problem. The skit is performed for the entire group and solutions are offered from the audience.

Contact:
Rabbi Terry Bookman and Karen Sobel
Congregation Sinai
8223 North Port Washington Road
Fox Point, Wisconsin 53217

**Tu B'Shevat Together Workshop**   This program utilizes as its basis "Issue Six: Trees" of *Together: A Parent Child Kit*. The workshop helps families with children in Grades K-4 learn more about the holiday of Tu B'Shevat and celebrate it together. This program represents a partial alternative to the Tu B'Shevat *Seder* as the only activity for Tu B'Shevat. It may be feasible to include a Tu B'Shevat *Seder* in a modified form as a culmination to the day.

Tu B'Shevat is introduced by reading passages from "People Need Trees" and "Trees Need People" in *Together Magazine*. Then there are family activities:

1. "Ecology Check List – Taking Care Of the Earth" (from *Together Magazine*). Families complete the check list and add personal items. They then regroup to share the additions to their family lists.

2. Activity Centers – Three tables are set up at which families can participate in one, two, or three of these activities:
   a. Spatter painting leaves on T-shirts
   b. Laminating leaves and making leaf mobiles
   c. Planting parsley

3. Snacks – Snacks representing the seven species are prepared. They are introduced separately and the appropriate *brachah* is recited before eating each food.

4. Games and Singdown
   a. "Botany" – based on the game "Geography" in which you name things in nature.
   b. Singdown – groups sing songs which relate to nature, e.g., "You Are My Sunshine," "Everything's Coming Up Roses," etc.

Contact:
Zelda Goodman
9760 Blackgold
La Jolla, California 92037

**The Jewish Home**   This two hour program is designed to help parents and children identify and appreciate the Jewish elements of their homes. Families stay together for projects and activities and are divided for study by grade level — K-3, 4-7. All participants join together for culminating activities.

Every family participates in cooking and making crafts. The study sessions focus on what makes a Jewish home. For the youngest group, there is a puppet show about moving to a new home. For the intermediate group, there is a skit about inviting non-Jewish friends to one's home. For the adults there is text study and discussion. The culminating activities include music, drawing a family symbol, and listening to a story to tie everything together.

This program requires a staff to facilitate the cooking and craft activities and the learning sessions. In addition to the Rabbi, Director of Education, and the program facilitator, the classroom teachers should be involved, as well as assistants and specialists.

Contact:
Marsha Grazman
Shaare Emeth Religious School
11645 Ladue Road
St. Louis, Missouri 63141

**The Jewish Family: An Endangered Species**   This is a two-hour family day for fifth and sixth grade classes where the focus is on what constitutes a family, particularly a Jewish family, and what a family does.

The program includes the following components:

Discussion – The Jewish Family: An Endangered Species — based on an ad from the New York times.

Videotape – *Our Family Our People* (Denver: Alternatives in Religious Education, Inc., 1983). List adjectives that describe your family, your people.

"My Jewish Family" – A worksheet which describes what a Jewish family does, from *Proud and Jewish* by Zena W. Sulkes (Denver: Alternatives in Religious Education, Inc, 1980, p. 12).

Create a Social Action Diary – Each family is furnished with a booklet. There is a heading on each page (helping people help themselves, *pikuach nefesh*, visiting the sick, feeding the hungry, etc.). Families decide what they have done during the past week that fits the topic heading and write it down on the appropriate page. There are blank pages for additional items.

Family Traditions – What is a tradition in your family? How did it begin? Is it Jewish? Will you continue to do it? Everyone depicts their family traditions on mural paper.

Shabbat Tradition: Lighting candles – This is a connection to Judaism in which we can all participate.

Contact:
Robin Eisenberg
Temple Beth El
333 Southwest 4th Avenue
Boca Raton, Florida 33432

**Mitzvah Magic**    This program is for families with children in Grades K-6. It is designed to help families become aware of a variety of *mitzvot*, and how these *mitzvot* apply to their lives. Its purpose is also to create an awareness of those *mitzvot* that are performed on a daily basis.

Twelve classrooms are set up as different *mitzvah* stations. The *mitzvot* to be studied are selected by the teachers. Families, after receiving a list of the *mitzvot* that are being studied in each classroom, can go into as many classrooms as time allows. Each family also receives a bag in which to collect all the projects they made, information, and miscellaneous materials. As families move in and out of the classrooms, a magician performs in the hallway to add to the magic of the day. The day ends with everyone gathered together for a closing activity and refreshments.

Contact:
Marsha Grazman and Janice Sanders
Shaare Emeth Religious School
11645 Ladue Road
St. Louis, Missouri 63141

**Grandparents Day**  This program is designed to broaden children's awareness of their grandparents' outlook on Jewish education and, conversely, to help grandparents become more aware of what it is like to be involved in religious education today.

Prior to the actual program, grandparents are extended a special, written invitation for a particular school day. The children prepare a bulletin board on "A grandparent is . . ." The teacher hangs up pictures of grandparents doing things with their grandchildren.

On the special day, grandparents and children follow the normal school routine. The major part of the class time is a dialogue between grandparents and grandchildren on how their respective religious schooling differs, the importance of Jewish education, and personal thoughts and feelings. At the end of the day, there is a simulated Shabbat experience.

Contact:
Regina Schur
Am Shalom
840 Vernon
Glencoe, Illinois 60062

**The People Of Israel**   This is a one-time program for fourth grade students and their families. For the first part of the day, the class is divided into two groups. Each group has an opportunity to cook Israeli foods and to participate in an activity to identify the country of origin of various Israelis. After the group activities, families come together to listen to the song "Just Another Foreigner" (on the album *Safam Bitter Sweet*, available from Safam, 36 Hamlin Road, Newton Centre, MA 02159) and to discuss the ideas expressed in the song. Each family unit completes a worksheet which deals with expectations of Israel. The program concludes with a group discussion about Israel as the homeland for all Jews and the *mitzvah* of supporting and traveling to Israel. Everyone eats the foods that were prepared.

Contact:
Rabbi Terry Bookman and Karen Sobel
Congregation Sinai
8223 North Port Washington Road
Fox Point, Wisconsin 53217

**Parent Involvement At Home and At Religious School**  Buzz Hellman, a teacher at Baltimore Hebrew Congregation, has been most successful in involving parents in her programs at Religious School. Some of her ideas require active class participation; others require parents and children to do things at home which are followed up in class. A few of these programs are described below:

1. Recipe Book – Parents send in family Passover recipes. Children write silly recipes. A recipe scrapbook is compiled containing the family recipes with a separate section of silly recipes.

2. Pesach Presentations – Using the book *But This Night Is Different* by Audrey Friedman Marcus and Raymond A. Zwerin (New York: Union of American Hebrew Congregations, 1980), families are given a section of the book and instructed to develop a presentation about it. Families come together in class the following week and give their presentations.

3. Mitzvah Munchies At Chanukah Time – Focusing on *mitzvot*, parents are expected to come to class with admission of *mitzvah* munchies (dried fruit or nuts). The food is packaged and gift cards are made by the children. After gift wrapping, packages are sent to a senior center as *Shalach Manot*.

4. Personalizing Mitzvot – Parents and children outline *mitzvot* they can do. Each *mitzvah* is written on a card and each child picks a card. The parents take a picture of the child and together they write a summary of when and how the child will fulfill his/her *mitzvah*.

Contact:
Buzz Hellman
Baltimore Hebrew Congregation
7401 Park Heights Avenue
Baltimore, Maryland 21208

# Extended Time Program

**Ewok Adventure Day**   This program focuses on the high holidays and the fall festivals. Parents and children go on a treasure hunt for the blessings and symbols of the holidays. At some stops there are things to be learned or reviewed, such as the blessing over the *lulav* and *etrog* or the *"Al Chayt"* prayer. At other stops there are things to make, such as New Year cards for Soviet Jewish families or flags for Simchat Torah. At still other stops, there are discussions on topics such as, "What comes to mind when you hear the sound of the *shofar?*" Participants follow a tape recorded script which takes them from place to place. The script may begin at different stops so that people are not crowded together in one place.

Contact:
Sharon Katz
Congregation B'nai Jehudah
712 East 69 Street
Kansas City, Missouri 64131

# Family Life Education Programs

**Teen Suicide** Educating parents and teens about teen suicide is the focus of this one time program. Facilitated by a psychiatrist, the purposes of the program are to educate parents about depression and suicide, to teach teen-agers how to help a friend who may be troubled, and to encourage parents and teens to seek help when needed. Following a formal presentation, participants ask questions. Those in attendance receive information about community agencies which are available to assist with suicide prevention. The program lasts from 1½ to 2 hours.

Contact:
Claire K. Nussbaum
Jewish Family Service
1645 Wallenberg Boulevard
Charleston, South Carolina 29407

**They Are Our Children Too**    This is a one-time community forum and panel discussion which addresses questions and misunderstandings about homosexuality, as well as possible disruptions of family relationships. There is also a presentation on Jewish views of homosexuality. Panel participants include a Rabbi, a Jewish gay man, a Jewish lesbian, the straight Jewish parent of an adult homosexual child, and the straight adolescent child of a homosexual parent.

Contact:
Vivien Benjamin
Family Life Education
Jewish Family Service
1214 Boylston Avenue
Seattle, Washington 98101

**Living With Your Adult Child At Home**   This is a three session program for parents of children 21 and older who have returned home after living away for several years. Discussions focus on the added responsibility of an adult child returning to the family residence. Other topics include parent/child expectations and strategies for adjusting/adapting behavior. As a result of the program, participating parents often become a support group for each other.

Contact:
Natalie Merkur Rose
Tampa Jewish Family Services
112 South Magnolia
Tampa, Florida 33606

**The Family With Special Needs**   The Jewish Family and
Children's Service of Baltimore offers three programs for the
family with special needs:

1. For Parents Of Mentally Retarded Children (six sessions) –
   This program consists of discussions on the special problems
   a retarded child brings to a family, the effects of this child on
   the family, where to find help, trained baby sitters, and appropriate schools; how to set appropriate behavioral rules; legal
   rights of parents and retarded children. There are
   discussions about communicating Jewish values and
   integrating the retarded child into the Jewish community.

2. For Parents Of Mentally Retarded Adults (six sessions) – These
   sessions help parents of mentally retarded adults cope with
   the unique situations with which they are confronted as the
   retarded person matures. The group discusses such issues as
   community resources, behavioral management, appropriate
   social behavior, financial planning, and living arrangements.

3. Parenting the Learning Disabled Child (8 sessions) – These
   workshops serve as a support system for parents of learning
   disabled children. Discussion centers on what a learning
   disability is and how the parent and child can adjust to it. The
   workshops demonstrate how to communicate with a learning
   disabled child and how to set reasonable expectations for
   him/her. Parents learn about school and community
   resources as well as vocational training options.

Contact:
Joan Ephross
Jewish Family and Children's Service
5750 Park Heights Avenue
Baltimore, Maryland 21215

**Jewish Families Talking About Sex**   This program, contributed by Dr. Cecile Jordan, is geared to students 10-12 years old and their parents. There are four 2 hour sessions. The purpose of the program is to increase family communication and knowledge about sexuality, and to teach families about the Jewish laws and values pertaining to sexuality. The topics covered are:

1. Importance of sexuality in Jewish tradition

2. Importance of the family as the primary sex educator

3. Anatomy and physiology of pubescent males and females

4. The need for increased communication between parent and adolescent

5. Sexual myths

6. Values and decisions about sex

7. Questions adolescents have about sex

8. Preventing sexual abuse

The activities include parent-student interviews, values clarification exercises, and problem solving situations. Several films from the local branch of Planned Parenthood are shown. Materials prepared by Meryl Cohen, a certified sex educator, are the basis for the course.

Contact:
Beth Yeshurun Day School
4525 Beechnut Boulevard
Houston, Texas 77096

**Gesher LaBayit — Bridge To the Home**   This multi-session series, developed by the Jewish Family Life Education department of the Bureau of Jewish Education of Los Angeles, is designed to help parents come to terms with their own Jewish identity. The program takes place in the warm atmosphere of the participants' homes. Often the small groups of participants evolve into *havurot*. "Gesher LaBayit" is neither a lecture series nor a how-to course. The agenda emerges naturally from the needs of the group and from the expertise of the facilitator. A formal agenda consisting of a variety of topics is presented to the group at the end of the first or the second session. Pre and post evaluation are an integral part of the program. Through the years a variety of specific populations have been identified and programs have been developed to meet their needs. These have included the following programs:

1. Gesher LaBayit — Bridge To the Home for Couples (4-8 session series)

2. Gesher LaBayit — Bridge To the Home for Single Parents and Their Children (6 session series)

3. Gesher LaBayit — Bridge To the Home for Parents/Teens (4 to 6 session series)

4. Gesher LaBayit — Bridge To the Home for Russian Families (6 session series)

5. Gesher LaBayit — Bridge To the Home for Blended (Remarried) Families (4 to 8 session series)

Contact:
Karen Lebow
Jewish Family Life Education
Bureau of Jewish Education
6505 Wilshire Boulevard
Los Angeles, California 90048

**Choosing Judaism**  The Jewish Family Service of Worcester, Massachusetts facilitates this follow-up to a class in basic Judaism. The Family Service worker conducts three discussion sessions about personal and familial issues surrounding contemplated conversion to Judaism and/or upcoming interfaith marriage. The content of the sessions is as follows:

Session I (1 hour)
- A. What Is Conversion?
- B. Issues Around Conversion (to be discussed in greater detail in Sessions II and III)
- C. Involvement Of Spouse
- D. Family and Friends

Sessions II and III (2 hours each)
- A. Ethnic vs. Religious
- B. What About Your "Old Ethnicity"?
- C. Will the New Group Accept You?
- D. Becoming Integrated Into the Jewish Community
- E. *Mikvah*/Circumcision
- F. After Conversion

Contact:
Deborah Fins
Jewish Family Service of Worchester, Inc.
646 Salisbury Street
Worcester, Massachusetts 01609

**Times and Seasons**  This is an 8 session program for people who are in interfaith marriages or in serious interfaith relationships. The series helps couples to explore some of the issues with which they have to deal, such as child rearing, holiday celebrations, in-laws, etc. The content of the program includes background information about Jewish practices with regard to holidays, life cycle, and creating a Jewish home, as well as focused discussions on issues of the participants' choice.

Facilitators for "Times and Seasons" receive special training under the auspices of the Commission on Reform Jewish Outreach of the Union of American Hebrew Congregations-Central Conference of American Rabbis. Facilitators receive a manual to assist them in structuring the program.

Contact:
Lydia Kukoff
Commission on Reform Jewish Outreach
UAHC-CCAR
6300 Wilshire Boulevard, Suite 700
Los Angeles, California 90048

**On Being a Jewish Kid In a Christian World**   This is a program for pre-teens and teen-agers which addresses a variety of issues Jewish children confront as members of a minority living in a Christian world. The program uses role play, values clarification, and discussion to teach young people how to respond to specific situations in which they are clearly in the minority. It also teaches them pride in being Jewish. Some of the issues dealt with include what it is like to be a minority in public school, conflicts that arise in school when there are Jewish holidays (e.g., tests on Yom Kippur or field trips on the first day of Pesach), responding to anti-Semitic remarks, dating.

Contact:
Mishka Luft and Ben Goldberg
Jewish Family Services
930 Madison Avenue
Albany, New York 12208

**Explaining Christmas To the Jewish Child**  The material covered in this workshop is based on a booklet *Explaining Christmas To the Jewish Child* by Lois Miller Weinstein. It is appropriate for parents and for religious school teachers who deal with children in Grades 1-6. The entire workshop lasts 90 minutes. After a 40 minute presentation of the material, the remaining time is devoted to questions and answers concerning the topic. The several sections of the booklet are:

Introduction – Background information about the program and cognitive material covered.

Six lessons, each containing an introduction and a guide for explaining the material:

Lesson I: Holidays and Symbols

Lesson II: The *Shema* Prayer, Chanukah and Christmas.

Lessons III-VI: Explaining Christmas to the Jewish Child – Detailed information about Jesus, the time in which he lived, and the Jewish concept of Messiah. Participants complete a worksheet on understanding Christmas which contains several paragraphs based on the information presented in the lessons.

Contact:
Lois Miller Weinstein
Bureau of Jewish Education
2640 North Forest Road
Getzville, New York 14068

**Strengthen Your Marriage**   This is a six session seminar for recently married couples (less than three years) and for newlyweds. The sessions are facilitated by a social worker from the Jewish Family and Vocational Service. A Rabbi, an attorney, and a financial advisor share their expertise. The sessions are:

I. Marriage: The Give and the Take – Expectations and realities of marriage and Jewish perspectives on marriage

II. Did you Hear What I Thought I Said? – Effective means of communication

III. Dual Careers/Dual Responsibilities – Legal, financial, and career concerns

IV. You and Family – Parents, in-laws, children

V. Sex and Intimacy In Marriage – Developing intimacy, the role of sex in marriage, and Jewish perspectives on sexuality

VI. Living Under the *Chupah*: Creating a Jewish Home – Rituals, symbols, observances

Contact:
Judy Freundlich Tiell
Jewish Family and Vocational Service
3640 Dutchmans Lane
Louisville, Kentucky 40205

**When Your Married Children Divorce**    This is a four session series which deals with the effect of separation and divorce on the parents of the divorcing couple. The topics include loss of expectations and dreams; your grandchildren, including the possibility of coping with the added responsibility of caring for them while the single parent goes to work; and being supportive to your son or daughter while helping him/her to move on in life.

Contact:
Joan Ephross
Jewish Family & Children's Service
5750 Park Heights Avenue
Baltimore, Maryland 21215

**Being An Adoptive Parent**   This is a four session program for parents who already have adopted children and for those hoping to adopt a child. One session is a discussion with a panel of parents who have older adopted children. Other sessions deal with the legal rights of the adoptive parent/child, and questions adopted children ask. Participants also have the opportunity to learn about the Jewish view/attitude toward adoption.

Contact:
Judy Freundlich Tiell
Jewish Family and Vocational Service
3640 Dutchmans Lane
Louisville, Kentucky 40205

**Living With Irreconcilable Differences** This is a program for teen-agers which meets for four sessions of 2 hours each. It focuses on family relationships, living arrangements, step parents, and "blended families." The teen-agers in attendance also help to focus some of the discussions based on their own needs and agendas.

Contact:
Natalie Merkur Rose
Tampa Jewish Family Services
112 South Magnolia
Tampa, Florida 33606

**The Men's Club**  This is an ongoing support group for divorced or separated men. During each 2 hour session, participants focus on personal issues. It is primarily a self-help group designed to serve as a network for support and to assist single men with socialization.

Contact:
Jewish Family Service
1035 Newfield Avenue
Box 3038
Stamford, Connecticut 06905

**Contemporary Jewish Life Styles**   This is a one-day conference for singles which addresses current issues of Jewish identification. It begins with a keynote address for everyone. Participants then attend a variety of workshops. Some of the workshop topics are:

Effectively Single: Alone But Not Lonely

The Jewish Connection: Spiritual, Social, and Organizational Options

Jewish Identification In the Workplace

Homosexuality and Judaism

Maintaining Jewish Values in Relationship, Marriage, and Intermarriage

The Modern Single Life Style: Legal, Social, and Jewish Perspectives (including pre-nuptial agreements, adoption for the single, post divorce, custody support)

Contact:
Debbie Aron
Jewish Family and Child Agency
1610 Spruce Street
Philadelphia, Pennsylvania 19103

**Life Planning for Women**   This is a four session series for women in the middle years of life. The series examines the feelings, responsibilities, and joys of the middle years and explores ways of enriching these years, particularly within the Jewish community.

Contact:
Sheila Freeman
Jewish Family and Child Service of Metropolitan Toronto
4600 Bathurst Street
Willowdale, Ontario M24 3V3
Canada

**Motherhood Today: It's Okay to Stay Home**   This is a four session program for women who choose to stay home to care for children, husband, and family. The 90 minute programs are held during the day and babysitting is provided for participants. The topics discussed are: Challenges and difficulties faced by women who choose to remain home; feelings of wives, husbands, and society toward the homemaker; and how to keep one's mind alert when most of each day is spent with children.

Contact:
Judy Freundlich Tiell
Jewish Family and Vocational Service
3640 Dutchmans Lane
Louisville, Kentucky 40205

**Jewish Women's Day** This one day, extended time program, is designed to provide Jewish women in the community with a means of learning about themselves and their families under the auspices of a Jewish communal agency. The program consists of several workshops focusing on family issues, personal issues, and Jewish identity issues. The luncheon session includes a keynote address. All the facilitators are women. Topics include:

Sexuality and the Jewish Woman

Issues Our Parents Never Thought About: Homosexuality, Sexual Diseases, Sexual Abuse, Abortion

The Identity Of the Child Of Intermarriage/Relating To Two Cultures

The Identity Of the Adopted Child

When Children Divorce: Relations Of Parents, Children, Grandchildren

Self-Worth Without a Paycheck

Jewish Women In Literature: Are We What Authors Say We Are?

Tensions Among Jews: The Convert, the Orthodox, the Conservative, the Reform

Being Jewish In a Non-Jewish World: The Effects On Parent and Child

Children Of Successful Parents

Teen's Growing Independence: The Struggle With Family Values and Control

When Children Aren't Having Children/Always a Mother But Not a Grandmother

Mothers and Grandmothers: An Intergenerational Dialogue

Stress and Burnout: Examining Our Self-Image to Manage Our Life Styles

Keynote Address: "All the Women We Are"

Contact:
Tema Rosenblum
Jewish Family and Community Service
210 Skokie
Highland Park, Illinois 60035

**Adult Jewish Identity Program**    This program has six formal sessions of 1½ to 2 hours each and three informal sessions. It is aimed at adults from the early 20s to the early 40s. The purposes are to help them feel less ambivalent about being Jewish, to help parents pass on positive feelings about Judaism to their children, to help parents find ways to celebrate Judaism with their children at home, and to help adults feel identified with and part of the Jewish community.

The six formal sessions consist of discussions which range from instruction in the life cycle, to adapting traditional Judaism, to personal feelings about being Jewish, to socializing within Jewish circles. The informal sessions include participation in such community events as Israel Solidarity Day, or a Jewish community fair, attending services together, or getting together on a Shabbat afternoon for study, *Seudah Shleesheet*, and *Havdalah*.

Contact:
Helen Victor Turk
Federation Day Care Services
Paley Branch
Strahle and Horrocks Streets
Philadelphia, Pennsylvania 19154

## New Americans: Communicating American Style

The Coordinator of Resettlement for the Jewish Family Service of Dallas facilitates a three session program for new immigrants. Each session lasts 2 hours. The sessions provide New Americans with an opportunity to explore communication methods. The facilitator helps participants to bridge the gap between their old culture and their new with emphasis on colloquial expressions, humor, authority, child rearing, and other life tasks.

Contact:
Lorraine Stevens
Jewish Family Service
7800 Northaven Road
Dallas, Texas 75230

**Getting On With the Rest Of My Life**   This is a four session program which explores the challenges facing adults in the later middle years. It helps participants deal with some of the issues which will confront them as they enter the senior years. The sessions are as follows:

Session I:   Setting Goals for the Next 20 Years – Assertiveness

Session II:  My Adult Children – My family for better or for worse, the dependent child, the uninvolved child, grandchildren

Session III: Alone Now Or Maybe Later – Feeling alone in a crowd, making new friends, divorce in the later years, widowhood, dealing with death

Session IV: Getting On With It – Financial planning, insurance, having fun, support groups

Contact:
Jewish Family and Children's Service
525 South Mill Avenue, #204A
Tempe, Arizona 85281

**Blazing New Trails**   This is a three session program on coping with life changes and isolation for senior adults. Each session lasts 1½ hours and is conducted in the early afternoon on weekdays. Participants may sign up for one session or for the entire series. There is a modest fee. The sessions are as follows:

Session I: Getting Around Town – Ways for senior adults to cope with restricted mobility due to physical or emotional barriers

Session II: Social Skills and Networking – How to make friends now that you are in later life

Session III: Maintaining Quality Long-distance Relationships – A discussion on maintaining good communication between older parents and middle-aged children residing in different cities

Contact:
Natalie Merkur Rose
Tampa Jewish Family Services
112 South Magnolia
Tampa, Florida 33606

**Coping With the Stress Due To the Severe Illness Of Spouse or Parent**  This six session program helps the participants cope with the new relationship that evolves as a result of a loved one's debilitation. It is designed to have participants deal with their feelings of sadness, guilt, anger, helplessness, and anxiety. It also helps participants to understand the importance of caring for one's own needs at this time of stress.

Contact:
Joan Ephross
Jewish Family and Children's Service
5750 Park Heights Avenue
Baltimore, Maryland 21215

**Marvelous Middle Years**   This is a six session program for individuals or couples to explore "middlessence," the middle years, as a stage of life marked by physical and emotional changes. It helps participants to investigate new interests and career opportunities. Those who participate in the program learn to deal with the "empty nest syndrome" and to understand changing family relationships and changing expectations in marriage.

Contact:
Joan Ephross
Jewish Family and Children's Service
5750 Park Heights Avenue
Baltimore, Maryland 21215

**Surviving a Loss**   This eight session support group for those who are struggling with the death of a loved one is open to adults of all ages. (The loss does not necessarily have to have been recent.) Participants focus on their experience of coping with grief. The group is limited to eight participants and is offered as an adjunct to individual counseling provided by the agency.

Contact:
Yona Kollen
Jewish Family Service, Southern Region
Jewish Federation Council of Greater Los Angeles
22410 Palos Verdes Boulevard
Torrance, California 90505

**Widowed To Widowed**   This six session discussion series is for people who are widowed less than two years. The sessions focus on coping with grief and helping participants to confront the issues of living alone, coping with changing relationships, and creating a new identity. Participants begin to develop into a support network for one another.

Contact:
Sheila Freesman
Family Life Education Department
Jewish Family and Child Service of Metropolitan Toronto
4600 Bathurst Street
Willowdale, Ontario M2R 3V3
Canada

# Annotated Bibliography
# On the Jewish Family

Barbara Eidelman Wachs

## General Background

*About the Jewish Family: Its Values and Relevance In Israel and In the Contemporary Jewish World*. Edited by the Center for Programming, Department of Development Services. New York: World Zionist Organization, 1982.

Collection of articles by Avraham Aderet, Shmuel Avigdor Hacohen, Leah Handelman, Sergio Della Pergola, Yochanan Peres, Zeev Shafrir, and Eliezer Schweid. Topics include: Sanctity and Family, Education and Family, Characteristics Of the Life Cycle, Family and School Achievement, Life In Israel, Characteristics Of Jewish Families.

Blidstein, Gerald. *Honor Thy Father and Mother: Filial Responsibility In Jewish Law and Ethics*. New York: KTAV, 1975.

Excellent book analyzing some of the norms that help form the concept of what a family ought to be. The book emphasizes the significance and scope of filial responsibility, as well as some problems inherent in these areas, such as support and respect. The author makes use of Talmudic, biblical, and *Responsa* literature. The cases he cites, which have been studied for generations, have had a major influence on normative views.

Cantor, Aviva. *The Jewish Woman 1900-1980*. Fresh Meadows, NY: Biblio Press, 1982.

A comprehensive bibliography of material concerning Jewish women, this is a companion guide to *Jewish Women and Jewish Law*. An excellent and invaluable research tool.

Cohen, Burton, and Lukinsky, Joseph. *Religious Institutions As Educators*. Chicago: University of Chicago Press, Yearbook of National Society for the Study of Education, 1985.

The authors conclude that American schools help students understand what it means to be a member of the American Jewish community when the students are helped to understand their own traditions.

Cohen, Steven M. *The American Jewish Family Today.* In *American Jewish Yearbook.* New York and Philadelphia: Jewish Publication Society, 1982, pp. 136-154.

> Using comprehensive data, Cohen examines the extent to which American Jews have participated in the larger society. In addition, he notes how family status (being single, childless, or divorced) affects family life style. Cohen also assesses the extent to which recent changes in the family, especially among young people, have been linked to diminished Jewish identification. Finally, he considers alternative communal policies in the light of research.

Epstein, Louis M. *The Jewish Marriage Contract: A Study In the Status Of Women In Jewish Law.* New York: Arno Press, 1973.

> Subjects include: marriage, women, law, legal status, *ketubah*, divorce. Useful for general background.

Fuchs, Lawrence. *The Jewish Father for a Change. Moment* 1, no. 3 (1975): 45-50.

> Good popular review of the role of father in the past, as well as an analysis of problems in modern day America. Fuchs makes suggestions for renewal of some aspects of the traditional father's role. Classical Jewish texts indicate that, in the Jewish tradition, authoritative love and teaching are necessary for the well-being and healthy development of youth.

Feldman, David M. *Birth Control and Jewish Law.* New York: N.Y.U. Press, 1968.

> Fine classic on the subject. Feldman makes extensive use of sources. Many useful comparisons are made to Christian beliefs.

Gertel, Elliot B. *Jewish Views On Divorce.* New York: American Jewish Committee Institute of Human Relations, April 1984.

> A review of evolving Jewish views on marriage and divorce up to the present time. Gertel discusses the contemporary

challenge of adapting Jewish divorce law to current needs while retaining the "spirit of tradition." He stresses that "while Jewish tradition was liberal about granting divorce its ethos stresses the sanctity of marriage and the importance of keeping families together." The other theme traced is the ongoing effort to protect the rights and privileges of the woman. Liberal use of classical sources and *Responsa*. Bibliography.

Goldscheider, Calvin. *Jewish Continuity and Change: Emerging Patterns In America*. Bloomington, IN: Indiana University Press, 1986.

An important demographic study based on information obtained in Boston. Study indicates that despite assimilation and intermarriage, Jews have developed distinctive patterns of marriage, residence, and affiliation. Goldscheider explores these new patterns of ethnic community identification.

Goldstein, Sydney. "Jews In the U.S.: Perspectives From Demography." In *American Jewish Yearbook*. New York and Philadelphia: American Jewish Committee and Jewish Publication Society, 1981, 3-59.

Updates to 1980 of Goldstein's definitive study of *American Jewry 1970: A Demographic Profile*. The author focuses on size, composition, distribution, and components of change (fertility, mentality, migration, and intermarriage).

Goitein, S.D. *A Mediterranean Society*. Vol. 3, *The Family*. Berkeley: University of California Press, 1978.

Good description of Sephardic family patterns, customs, and traditions.

Gordis, Robert. *Love and Sex: A Modern Jewish Perspective*. New York: Women's League for Conservative Judaism, 1978.

Excellent popular summary with references to traditional sources. Topics included: Sex and Judaism, Woman In Jewish Life and Law, Sexual Ethics, Intermarriage, and Abortion. The modern material is written from a Conservative perspective.

Green, Kathy, and Strassfeld, Sharon, eds. *The Jewish Family Book*. New York: Bantam Books, 1981.

Uneven series of articles written by authors and contributors about life cycle events and bringing up Jewish children. Very good articles about single parents, new ceremonies for leaving home, and letting go. Pluralistic in approach, functions as a resource guide.

Grossman, Lawrence, ed. *For the Jewish Family: Goals, Programs, Accomplishments 1979-1986*. New York: The American Jewish Committee, Institute of Human Relations, 1986.

A summary and description of the conferences, research papers, and projects undertaken by the William Petschek National Jewish Family Center. Very useful for students and teachers of the modern Jewish family. Lists all the publications of the Center.

*The Jewish Family: An Annotated Bibliography*. New York: Jewish Education Service of North America, 1984.

This useful bibliography, prepared for the General Assembly meeting in Toronto, features material that focuses on the family in transition. Subtopics include: About and for the Jewish Family; Converts To Judaism; Divorce, Singles, and the Single Parent Family; Genealogy: Tracing Our Roots; Parent-Child Education; and The Special Child.

*Jewish Women's Resource Center*. 3 East 69th Street, New York, NY 10021.

Fine source for annotated bibliographies on women's issues – e.g., women in the Middle East, women in Israel, women's legal status in Israel, women in leadership positions in Jewish communities in Federations, women in the Rabbinate, Jewish mothers, Jewish American Princesses, Jewish women in the early 20th century, Jewish feminism, divorce, battered women, *mikvah*, prayers to be said during pregnancy, etc.

Kaganoff, Ben Zion. *A Dictionary Of Jewish Names and Their History*. New York: Schocken Books, 1977.

Popular history of origin of Jewish surnames which became common in the 10th century. Includes list of most common names. Useful for courses on the Jewish heritage.

Katz, Jacob. *The Traditional Jewish Family In Historical Perspective*. New York: William Petschek National Jewish Family Center, American Jewish Committee, March 1982.

Good, short, clear historical survey.

_____. "Marriage and Sexual Life Among the Jews At the End Of the Middle Ages." *Zion* X (1945): 21-56. (Hebrew)

Good article to be used for contrast to modern period.

Kranzler, Gershon. *The Changing Orthodox Family: Dimensions Of Orthodox Judaism*. New York: KTAV, 1983.

After analyzing changes affecting families in America, Kranzler discusses the effect of these changes on Orthodox Jewish families. He points out "the return to ghetto phenomena," as well as the development and expansion of Torah education from preschools to post graduate levels. Other characteristics mentioned are consistency between what is learned in school and what is seen at home, high birth rate, study in Israel, and the status of the Rabbi. Although a bit chauvinistic in tone, the book provides a good overview of the topic. No bibliography is provided.

Lasch, Christopher. *Haven In a Heartless World*. New York: Basic Books, 1979.

Good description of the role of the family in the modern world.

Lerner, Stephen P. *The Jewish Family: A Background Paper On Jewish Views Of the Family*. New York: William Petschek National Jewish Family Center, American Jewish Committee, 1982.

Contains many classical Jewish sources which exemplify such basic values in Jewish family life as *Sh'lom Bayit, Kid-*

dushin, *Taharat Hamishpacha*, etc. Lerner also deals with
the problems encountered while raising children. Can be
used for study groups.

Leichter, Hope Jensen. *Some Perspectives On the Family As
Educator.* New York: Columbia University Press, Teachers
College, 1975.

Review of literature on family as educator. Topics included:
Education within the nuclear family, models of the family
as an educative system, conception. of education, and
process of education.

Liebman, Charles S. *The Ambivalent American Jew: Politics,
Religion, and Family In American Jewish Life.* Philadelphia: Jewish Publication Society, 1973.

An excellent analysis of the factors that determine the
American Jewish identity. The book traces the evolution of
American Judaism from its European roots. The author
focuses on showing how the efforts to overcome the
integration-survival tension led to a particular conception
of reality and to the redefinition by the Jews themselves of
their religion.

Forms of religious behavior, such as public and elite
religion, are included, with coverage given to all of the
movements. The unique position of Israel, which the
author feels provides the major symbolic content of the
Jewish religion, is also treated. The rest of the book concentrates on special segments of the community, Jewish
youth, Rabbis, college students, and political liberals. The
effort of American Jews to reshape their political environment to minimize the survival-integration tension is
described. Many insights are provided for educators
working on Jewish identity programs. Important resource
for courses on the American experience.

Linzer, Norman. *The Jewish Family: Authority and Tradition In
Modern Perspective.* New York: Human Science Press Inc.,
1984.

Linzer attempts to rehabilitate the significance of the family
in modernity by offering ways to make the Jewish family

a vital and viable institution. The author creates an inter-disciplinary frame of reference (social values, political thought, *halachah* and *aggadah* are interwoven), while showing that important psychological and political categories are not unfamiliar to *halachah*. He focuses on the relationships between tradition and its institutions and the individual's need for self-assertion. An integrative model is provided which makes use of cases from the Jewish classical tradition. His model recognizes the inevitability of tension between obligation and needs. He also offers a means for reducing the tension through mutual interdependence. Linzer also develops approaches and services for the Jewish family in the Jewish Community Center. Recommended for adults, social workers, Rabbis, teachers, and Center workers.

Linzer, Norman. *The Jewish Family*. New York: Federation of Jewish Philanthropies, 1972.

The book provides *halachic* sources so that social workers can gain a Jewish perspective on various aspects of family life. With this information available, it is hoped that they will be sensitized to the Jewish dimension in their profes-sional work. Topics include: husband-wife relationships (marriage, sexuality, birth control, abortion, and divorce), parents and children (adoption, foster care, drugs, Holocaust survivors, and aging).

Litwak, Eugene, and Meyer, Helen. *School, Family and Neigh-borhood: The Theory and Practice Of School Community Relations*. New York: Columbia University Press, 1974.

Standard reference on topic.

Mayer, Egon. *Love and Tradition: Marriage Between Jews and Christians*. New York: Plenum Publishers, 1985.

Popular book based on extensive interviews addressing marriage between Jews and Christians. Who are intermar-ried couples? How do they deal with their family heritages? How do their children view their relationships with their dual heritage? In 1985 this represented the most current information on the subject. Very helpful for sessions on Jewish identity, intermarriage, and assimilation.

Mitchell, William E. *Mispokhe, A Study Of New York City Jewish Family Clubs*. Hawthorne, New York: Aldine Paperback, n.d.

The book studies the formation of cousin clubs, which began in the early 1900s. Mitchell suggests that their formation might have developed to counteract social atomization in the big city. Helpful when teaching about community and kinship.

Monson, Rela Geffen. "The Graying Of the American Jewish Congregation" *Conservative Judaism* 34, no. 6 (July/August, 1981): 51-56.

The author makes a series of practical programming suggestions based on the realities of the graying of the "Baby Boomers" in our congregations.

Monson, Rela Geffen. "The Jewish Family In America Today: Is It Jewish?" In *Perspectives On Jews and Judaism*. Arthur A. Chiel, ed. New York: The Rabbinical Assembly of America, 1978.

The author makes use of Nahum Glatzer's typology of the classic Jewish family — patriarchal, three generations, encompassing all aspects of life, shaped by Jewish calender, committed to the ideal of non-goal oriented perennial learning. In addition, she discusses the concepts of *kiddushin*, family purity, *sh'lom bayit*, *derech eretz*, and *nachas fun kinder* as referrents for a description of the American Jewish family as of 1978. Very helpful for family educators and teachers of Jewish values.

Patz, Naomi. *Family and Community Models Of Age Old Tensions Among Jewish Leaders*. Milwaukee: Board of Jewish Education, 1981.

Author uses Moses, David, Maimonides, and Don Isaac Abravanel as examples of those who either failed or succeeded in keeping the balance between family and community responsibility. Good for use with young leadership families.

*William Petschek National Jewish Family Newsletter.* Lawrence Grossman, ed. American Jewish Committee, 165 East 56 St., New York, NY 10022.

Excellent source of current studies and issues dealing with the Jewish family — e.g., "Jewish Divorce and American Law," vol. 3, no. 3, Fall 1983;; "Spouse Abuse," vol. 3, no. 2, Summer 1983; "Jewish Population Growth," vol. 4, no. 1, Winter 1984.

Phillips, Bruce A. "Los Angeles Jewry, A Demographic Profile." In *American Jewish Yearbook, 1986.* New York: American Jewish Committee; Philadelphia: Jewish Publication Society, 1986, 126-196.

Most recent demographic information which correlates with Goldscheider's information on the demographics of Boston. Compares Los Angeles to New York, Chicago, and Philadelphia. A good article which enables the reader to see the most recent trends. Useful for planning activities which target specific populations.

Ritterband, Paul, and Cohen, Steven M. "Why Contemporary American Jews Want Small Families: Inter-Religious Comparison Of Graduate Students." In *Modern Jewish Fertility: Studies In Judaism In Modern Times*, Vol. I. Paul Ritterband, ed. Leiden, Netherlands: Brill, 1981.

Interesting attitudes; good for course on modern Jewish family.

Rosenthal, Gilbert. *New Directions In the Jewish Family and Community.* New York: Commission on Synagogue Relations and the Federation of Jewish Philanthropies, 1974.

Anthology of articles and essays on such topics as Jewish youth and Jewish families.

Schlessinger, Benjamin. *The Jewish Family: A Survey and Annotated Bibliography.* Toronto: University of Toronto Press, 1971.

A comprehensive review of literature and articles.

Singer, David. *Focus On the American Jewish Family: A Selected Annotated Bibliography 1970-1982*. New York: American Jewish Committee, 1984.

This bibliography is intended to give a well rounded perspective on the state of contemporary American Jewish family life. Includes 100 articles which report data, offer theological viewpoints, and share an adumbration of Jewish communal perspectives.

Spiro, Melford E. *Children Of the Kibbutz: A Study Of Child Training and Personality*. New York: Schocken Books, 1965.

This book presents a structural description of *kibbutz* socialization with particular emphasis on collective education. Contains chapters on middle childhood, adolescent personality, and high school. Discusses role of nurse, nursery teacher, parents, and parent surrogates. Most interesting is chapter on the *sabra* personality and the author's problem with Jews and Judaism. Although he tends to focus on the negative aspects of the *sabra* personality, the book is quite useful when developing programs on Jewish identity.

Talmon, Yonina. *Family and Community In the Kibbutz*. Cambridge, MA: Harvard University Press, 1972.

Collection of essays on major aspects of family life on the *kibbutz*. Based on findings of research programs begun in 1955 under the direction of the author and sponsored by Hebrew University and the Federation of Kivutzot and Kibbutzim. Topics include: The family in collective settlements, social structure and family size, the family evening meal, children's placement, mate selection, and elite formation. Standard text for topic. Useful for comparative study.

Tufte, Virginia, and Meyerhoff, Barbara. "Observation: The Contemporary American Family." Chapter 3 in *Changing Images Of the Family*. Virginia Tufte and Barbara Meyerhoff, eds. New Haven: Yale University Press, 1979, 194-231 and 297-315.

Excellent general background. Helps place Jewish issues in contemporary perspective.

Wall, Susan. *Jewish Family Education In the United States: Assessment and Application*. Paper presented at Jerusalem Fellows Colloquium, June 1985.

A good analysis of the current state of the field as of 1985. Includes suggestions for developing a more comprehensive approach to family education. Suggests some useful methodological strategies. Helpful for educators and professors of Jewish education.

Waxman, Chaim. "The Contemporary American Jewish Family." In *American Jews In Tradition*. Chaim Waxman, ed. Philadelphia: Temple University Press, 1983.

Good summary of recent sociological and demographic studies.

*Your Child*. New York: Family Education Committee of the United Synagogue of America Commission on Jewish Education.

Published quarterly, this newsletter presents articles taken from synagogue bulletins and from current secular and religious publications addressing every aspect of family life. Very helpful for the Jewish parents, as well as religious school principals and family educators

## Curricular Materials for Jewish Education

*Authority and Independence In Jewish Family Relationships*. Jerusalem: The Shalom Hartman Institute for Advanced Judaic Studies, August 1982.

This resource includes the following:
1. Excellent analysis of *kibbud* and *yirah* that shows their interaction and interpenetration (Judaism balances the two; both coexist harmoniously during the child's growth process).

2. Implication for educators

3. Provides texts for study dealing with obligations of parents to children and children to parents (Rabbinic, *Aggadah*, Rambam). Provides guided questions for texts. Excellent for adult education and parenting groups.

Baxter, Diane. *A Study Of the Child, the Family and the Culture From Which They Come.* Yehuda Ben David, ed. Jerusalem: Jewish Family Heritage Society Department of Development, World Zionist Organization in conjunction with the Los Angeles Bureau of Jewish Education, Department of Parent and Family Education.

This is a 14 week course of study for B'nai Mitzvah students and their families. The program provides detailed exercises, homework, didactic suggestions, a guide for interviewing, and worksheets. Topics include: Students autobiography, migration patterns, original names, oral history, problems of immigrants, bus trip, and suggestions for final project. The units are well planned and include activities which require parental involvement and which foster ties between generations through verbal exchange of their stories. Recommended for use in junior high day school, as well as afternoon and Sunday school settings.

Bayewitz, Passi Rosen, and Novek, Minda. *Shiloah: Discovering Jewish Identity Through Oral/Folk History.* New York: Institute for Jewish Life, Division of Council of Jewish Federations and Welfare Funds, 1976.

Excellent collection of successful programs which have utilized Jewish oral/folk history. Includes program ideas from other ethnic groups, as well as an update on projects throughout North America. The second section deals with methodology, organizational guidelines and suggestions, interviewing, communications, media, technology, funding, and resources. Useful for schools planning to undertake programs in the areas of family history and history of community.

Benson, Paulette, and Altschuler, Joanne. *The Jewish Family: Past, Present, and Future.* Denver: Alternatives in Religious Education, Inc., 1979.

A well thought out 10-14 hour course for use from junior high school through adult. Can be used as a mini-course or for a whole semester for youth groups, family retreats, Hebrew High School, summer camp. Excellent Leader Guide provides rationale, activities, quizzes, and bibliography. Topics include:

1. What is family?

2. Jewish families in the past (brief historical survey)

3. Jewish family today (differences between Jewish and non-Jewish families plus discussion of values which characterize Jewish families)

4. Contemporary family patterns

5. Problem areas

6. Students' vision of their ideal family

*B'nai Mitzvah — The Value Of the Individual.* Jerusalem: Ministry of Education and WZO David Schoen Institute for Creative Jewish Education, 1984.

Twelve chapters, for students of Bar Mitzvah age. Attempts to deal with the uniqueness of each individual and the effect of one's true understanding of world beliefs on moral judgments and daily practice of the individual. The course emphasizes the idea that active Jewish life involves constant choice and internalized commitments to Jewish values. Highly recommended. Helps the modern student see his/her path to self-definition within Judaism. Excellent Teachers Guide.

Bogan, Roz, and Katz, Betsy. *Teaching the Jewish Family In the Middle Grades.* Chicago: Board of Jewish Education of Metropolitan Chicago, 1982.

Four units geared for afternoon school. Topics: Family In Jewish Writings (Biblical), The Family and Jewish Tradition (Middle Ages and the *Shtetl*), The Jewish Family Today, The

Jewish Family Of the Future. Each unit has goals and behavioral objectives. A clear connection between the goals and the topics is not always established. No model lessons or student materials are included. However, an excellent selection of source material is provided for the teacher. Contains a good article showing how to teach the Abraham and Sarah story as a source for Jewish values.

*Changing: As a Jewish Individual In Society.* Jerusalem: Ministry of Education and WZO David Schoen Institute for Creative Jewish Education, 1984.

The focus here is on the student maturing within his/her social surroundings, on family, community, and on the responsibility of conscious choices. Deals with child's responsibility to parents and parents' to child. Asserts that assuming responsibility is the key to change and maturation. Examples of ethical dilemmas are provided from the tradition. Recommended for all denominations. Helps students understand Bar/Bat Mitzvah in terms relevant to their experience. Excellent Teachers Guide is provided.

Derovan, David Jay. *All In the Family.* Series II. New York: National Commission on Torah Education, February 1974.

Sourcebook with cartoons prepared for teen-age convention. Biblical and Talmudic sources are provided, as well as questions to facilitate discussion. Not a curriculum. Topics included: Man and women, dating ethics, parents and kids, family prayer, divorce, old people, children vs. parents, interpersonal relations. Presents traditional point of view. Useful for ideas.

*Education for Interdependence In the Jewish Family.* Part II. Jerusalem: Shalom Hartman Institute for Advanced Judaic Studies, 1982.

Contains Educators Guide and Sources. Focuses on approach of Jewish tradition to structuring parent child relationships:

1. Parent as socializer

2. Parent as person with real needs

3. Parent as educator

Each study-unit contains Rabbinic text with questions. Can be useful as self-study, or for parent and family education.

Feldman, David M. *The Jewish Family Relationship*. United Synagogue Youth Convention Source Book. New York: United Synagogue of America Youth Commission, United Synagogue Youth, 1975.

Excellent compilation of sources geared to high school students. Guide book does not provide significant pedagogic suggestions for discussion of texts. Topics include:

1. Sources for family from Bible through Middle Ages

2. *Sh'lom Bayit* – Sources for *kibbud av va'em* (parents and children), modern problems — e.g., generation gap, permissiveness, conflicts, honor vs. obeying, understanding one's parents, "The Jewish Mother," Grandparents, siblings, and peers

3. *Sh'lom Bayit* – Husband and wife — marriage, procreation, and companionship; modern issues – feminism, living together

Goodman, Robert. *A Teachers Guide To Jewish Holidays*. Denver: Alternatives in Religious Education, Inc., 1983.

A comprehensive overview of the Jewish holidays. For every major and minor holiday, the book includes: An extensive vocabulary list with definitions; a complete historic overview; dozens of activities at every grade level, including a section of family strategies; and a comprehensive resource list of books, films and filmstrips, records and tapes, games and dittos. An overall bibliography on the Jewish holidays completes the book. Useful for teachers of every age group.

Hardan, David, ed. *Methodical Guide To My Parents' House*. Jerusalem: Center for Programming, Department of

Development and Services, World Zionist Organization and the Cultural Department World Jewish Congress, 1981.

> Contains guide to the Claude Vigee story that appears in *My Parents' House I* as an example of how to use the various testimonies in the series. Text analysis with questions, description of sources used by Vigee, historical background of Alsace. Teaches how to interview family members. Provides guidelines for writing a personal family story. Also contains background for other testimonies. Contains suggestions for using this material in history, literature, and family heritage programs.

Lassman, Sheila King. *Parents and Children*. London: Michael Goulston Educational Foundation, 1975. (Duke Street House, 416 Oxford Street, London, England)

> Material produced in England for teen-agers, school, youth clubs, camp, or retreats. Uses literature, advertisements, cartoons, songs, poems, role play, case study, and some Jewish sources to deal with: the nature of parents, when parents are deserving of honor, communication, relationships, admitting wrong. Graphically quite attractive, minimal Jewish sources. Trivializes the *Akedah* account.

Marcus, Audrey Friedman, et al. *A Family Education Unit On Bar and Bat Mitzvah*. Denver: Alternatives in Religious Education, Inc., 1983.

> Fourteen to eighteen hour course for pre-Bar/Bat Mitzvah students and their families. History and tradition surrounding Bar Mitzvah, projects to help participants clarify values and determine the kind of celebration they want. Leader Guide by Kerry M. Olitzky. Good for parent education and family retreats.

Marx, Tzvi. *Study Kit Authority and Independence In Parent-Child Relations*. Hagi Ben Hartzi, ed. Jerusalem: Shalom Hartman Institute, June 1980.

> Study guide for high school students which serves as a companion to Hartman Institute units on Authority and Independence. Written in Hebrew, this kit is appropriate for day schools and Hebrew colleges.

*My Parents House I.* Jerusalem: The Center for Programming, Dept. of Development and Services, WZO and World Jewish Congress, 1984.

Selections from four testimonies written about their families by Jews from different Diaspora and Israeli communities: "A Family In Bischwiller" by Claude Vigee, "My Father's House" by Yigal Allon, "My Father Nachman Syrkin" by Marie Syrkin, and selected chapters by Albert Memmi.

*My Parents House II.* Jerusalem: The Center for Programming, Dept. of Development and Services, WZO and World Jewish Congress, 1984.

Contains four testimonies of personal and family histories which reflect different experiences in the Diaspora and Israel: "My Parents' House In Berlin" by Gershom Scholem; "Grandfather's House In Rosh Pina" by Menachem Ben Arieh; "In Another Petakh Tikvah" by Yehuda Raab, Esther Raab, and Ehud Ben Ezer; "A Family In Aleppo" by Amnon Shamosh.

Prushansky, Shmuel. *Guide to Composing An Ancestral Tree.* Jerusalem: The Society for the Jewish Family Heritage, Department of Development and Services WZO, n.d.

Contains clear diagrams and suggestions for sources, graphic presentations, methods for numbering, handling names, surnames, and dates. Gives elementary guidelines for family research. Extremely useful for students and teachers undertaking initial family genealogical research.

Stipelman, Sylvia, assisted by Bettman, Batia, and Pinchuk, Phyllis. *My Family.* Montreal: Educational Resource Center, 1973.

The unit in this student workbook concentrates on the oral history of families utilizing family traditions (stories, songs, recipes, and individual immigration stories) to teach social studies concepts, such as human geography, interviewing and charting skills, tolerance for other life styles, respect for elders, and empathy for the immigrants' situation. Parental involvement is encouraged by writing them into the program with special pages that provide clear instructions for helping students. These pages also clarify the goals of each unit. A bibliography is provided for parents. The chapter on Jewish values, intended to show the source of Jewish values, talks about the sources more than studies them. Values chosen are not specifically Jewish (respect for life) or are not tied to family life. Despite the lack of creativity in this chapter, the unit is highly recommended for use in day schools of all denominations for immigration and family heritage units.

*Yalkut Bar Mitzvah.* Jerusalem: Shalom Hartman Institute and Joint Program for Jewish Education of the State of Israel, Ministry of Education, The Jewish Agency for Israel and WZO, 1981.

Study of the traditional Jewish sources regarding the relationship between parents and children. Topics include: Parents as symbols, as real people; honor and fear; differential pattern of relationship; authority and independence; parental obligations to children.

## Program Aids

Appelman, Harlene Winnick. *CAJE Network Newsletter for Family Educators.* June 1985, November 1985, November 1986, February 1987. (Harlene Winnick Appelman, 6600 West Maple Rd., West Bloomfield, MI 48033)

Excellent newsletter containing articles about current issues. The February 1987 issue focuses on Bar/Bat Mitzvah programming with articles by Shirley Barish, Saundra Gruenberg, Sue Kitter, Sharon Morton, Jo Kay, Barbara Wachs, and Sally Weber.

Appelman, Harlene Winnick. *Hashofar Congregational Family Newsletter.* (Congregation Shaarey Zedek, 27375 Bell Road, P.O. Box 2056, Southfield, MI 48086)

The Spring 1985 issue, devoted to family ritual, contains a condensation of an article called "Family Rituals Are Important To Family Health" (from *New Family Process,* September 1984) about the long-term effects of ritual on family. Contains many new rituals and suggestions for creating original family rituals. The November 1985 issue is devoted to grandparenting, family history, and heirlooms. Both issues are useful as examples of material to be shared in congregational bulletins, and are good sources for discussions in parenting groups. Lists successful programs and useful techniques.

Arian, Philip. *Akiba and Rachel*. Philadelphia: Chomsky Educational Resource Center, Gratz College, 1969.

A play written as a response to problems of intermarriage for ages 12-13. Good for classroom and workshops.

Baker, Andrew, and Goodman, Lois. *Working With the Intermarried: A Practical Guide for Jewish Community Workshops*. New York: William Petschek National Jewish Family Center, American Jewish Committee, 1986.

This publication clearly outlines the steps necessary to offer a workshop for the intermarried. It includes everything from designing the workshop and identifying participants to the procedures and publicity. The bulk of the booklet outlines the content of the six sessions, lists the behavioral objects, reports on ideas to be highlighted, and provides sample questions for discussion. The useful appendixes contain administrative guidelines, a sample letter of invitation, a day-by-day program outline, and an evaluation form. While this program is ideal for a camp setting, it is replicable in other venues as well. The publication is worthwhile for those involved in Family Life Education programs and Outreach.

Bar-Din, Ilana. *Leaving Home: Family In Transition*. Direct Cinema, P.O.Box 69587, Los Angeles, CA 90069, 1981. (film, 28 min.)

Portrait of the Bar-Din family, parents and four daughters, ending one part of their lives and beginning another. Two of the daughters are about to leave home. Useful film for family life series particularly for those discussion groups that deal with these kinds of adjustments which parents and children have to make.

Bissell, Sherry H. "Family Education Days." *Pedagogic Reporter* 33, no. 3 (May 1982) :5.

> Each grade level at Temple Israel Torah School in Long Beach, California has a family program which is held from 9:30-12 on Sundays and which is coordinated with the curriculum. The program combines parallel learning and joint learning through learning centers and discussion groups. Contact: Sherry Bissell Blumberg, Hebrew Union College – Jewish Institute of Religion, One West 4th St., New York, NY 10012.

Blumberg, Sherry Bissell. "Family Education." In *The Jewish Principals Handbook*. Audrey Friedman Marcus and Raymond A. Zwerin, eds. Denver: Alternatives in Religious Education, Inc. 1983, 461-472.

> Provides a definition of family education and lists categories — e.g., celebrations, observances, workshops, *Sedarim*, joint learning, extended time programs, ongoing learning experiences, and family independent study. Suggestions for activities in each category are included. "How To" section includes: choosing a good program, organizing the Family Education program, problems and planning. Lists 72 resources prepared by Audrey Friedman Marcus based on the work of Cherie Koller Fox, Sylvan Wolf, and Sherry Bissell Blumberg for the CAJE Task Force on Family Education. Recommended for family educators, youth workers, and principals.

Bogot, Howard. *Family School*. Philadelphia: Chomsky Educational Resource Center, Gratz College, Division of Community Services, 1973.

> A plan by which a (Reform) Religious School can involve the entire family.

*The Book Of Songs and Blessings*. New York: United Jewish Appeal, 1982.

> A fine song book containing translations, as well as transliterations.

Braver, Joseph, ed. *Parent Education Program*. New York: United Synagogue of America, n.d.

An ongoing program offering study for parents of beginning students in religious school in content areas such as Bible, holidays, customs and rituals, prayers, and Hebrew. Includes some sessions on how to be a Jewish parent.

Brin, Ruth F. *The Shabbat Catalogue*. New York: KTAV Publishing House, 1978.

A resource of stories, arts and crafts, games and activities, readings and dialogues for children and adults for use at home by families who wish to enrich their Shabbat experience. The book's biggest weakness is a lack of general background for families with limited Shabbat experience. The stories and arts and crafts are a bit removed from the Shabbat theme.

Brinn, Ruth Esrig. *Let's Have a Party*. Rockville, MD: Kar-Ben Copies, 1981.

Good ideas for workshops and retreats.

Chanover, Hyman. *Family Guide for Hanukah*. Baltimore: Board of Jewish Education, 1983.

A guide that contains comprehensive background material, stories with questions for discussion, suggestions for after dinner activities, crafts and recipes. Helpful for all kinds of Chanukah programs and for providing background materials for family use.

Chanover, Hyman. *Family Guide for Shavuot*. Baltimore: Board of Jewish Education, 1981.

Good guide for families with school age children (including teen-agers). Contains historical background, practical suggestions — e.g., decorations, food ideas, and ceremony for festive meal. Also contains the entire Book of Ruth with a selection of commentaries. Good material for discussions. Useful for high school and Shavuot retreats.

Chanover, Hyman. *Family Guide for the High Holidays.* Baltimore: Board of Jewish Education, Parent and Family Department, 1981.

A guide for home celebration containing material for all the family — e.g., background of holiday, ceremony for festive meal, recipes, and art projects. The entire Book of Jonah and articles on repentance are included.

*Checkmate.* New York: Union of American Hebrew Congregations and United Synagogue Commission on Jewish Education, 1985.

A program about dating and intermarriage geared for teens and parents. Can be used in schools, youth groups, or camp settings. Contains an 11 minute VHS videocassette called *What Paul Told Sally.* A discussion manual features questions, role plays, and background materials, as well as quotations and sources on intermarriage.

*Chicken Soup: To Nourish Jewish Family Life.* Judith Bin Nun, Susan Wolfson, and Ron Wolfson, eds. Los Angeles: University of Judaism, 1979-1985. (Back issues available from Clejan Educational Resource Center, University of Judaism, 15600 Mulholland Drive, Los Angeles, CA 90077)

This magazine, no longer in print, helped parents introduce Jewish learning into the home. It provided activities for children ages 2-11 geared to the participation of the entire family and usually centered around a holiday. Back issues are highly recommended. Contains creative projects, background material, crafts, and recipes.

*Compass*, no. 22 (April/May 1973). Jack D. Spiro, ed. Union of American Hebrew Congregations.

This entire issue is devoted to parental involvement in Jewish education. Articles cover both family and parent education and contain many programmatic ideas. Includes a bibliography.

*Compass* 7, no. 2 (Spring 1984). Emily H. Feigenson, ed. Union of American Hebrew Congregations.

An entire issue devoted to Jewish Family Education. Contains articles and detailed programs for single parents, Family Education Day, parents as teachers, and evaluating sex bias in texts. Excellent description of goals and programming techniques.

Elkins, Dov Peretz. *Experiential Programs for Jewish Groups.* Rochester, NY: Growth Associates, 1979. (P.O. Box 18429, Rochester, NY 14618)

Thirty effective exercises to be used at family workshops and retreats.

Elkins, Dov Peretz. *Humanizing Jewish Life: Judaism and the Human Potential Movement.* New York: A.S. Barnes & Co., 1976.

This book describes how the author transformed his synagogue from a large impersonal institution into a community. Includes practical, concrete ideas, programs, and activities. Comprehensive descriptions of family learning activities are provided. For Rabbis, educators, and social workers.

Epstein, David, and Stutman, Suzanne Singer. *Torah With Love: A Guide To Strengthening Jewish Values Within the Family.* Englewood Cliffs, NJ: Prentice-Hall, 1986.

This book provides material for discussion of the weekly Torah portions at family meals. Most helpful for families trying to establish this as a tradition, as well as for leaders of youth services and teachers of Bible.

Epstein, Jane Geller. *The Jewish Working Parent: Determining Priorities.* New York: Family Education Committee of the United Synagogue of America Commission on Jewish Education, 1986.

This book provides advice for parents about Jewish parenting issues. Useful for parenting groups.

*Family Educators Kit*. New York: United Synagogue Commission on Jewish Education, n.d.

A compendium of materials helpful to family educators which have been produced by the Commission on Jewish Education of United Synagogue. The kit contains: An introductory cassette explaining the materials; Teachers Manuals for *Parent Education for Prospective Parents and Parents Of Young Children*, 1980, *Parent Education for Parents Of Juveniles*, 1973, and *Parent Education for Parents Of Adolescents*, 1976; trigger scripts *Frozen Family Frames* and *You Missed the Point* by Edya Arzt, n.d., covering the topics of aging parents; communication in marriage, abortion, and alcoholism; planning guides *So You're Having a Family Kallah* and *Your Child Newsletter*. In addition, sample copies of the newsletter *Your Child Newsletter* are included with subscription and ordering information. Particulary helpful for Conservative educators, but can be useful to other liberal groups as well.

Felder, Hannah. *There Ought to Be a Better Way*. New York: Women's League for Conservative Judaism, 1977.

A "trigger script" providing a good introduction to a discussion on Jewish parenting as it deals with attitudes of family members toward Jewish identity, community participation, and Jewish values.

Feinstein, Joseph N. "Between Jewish Parent and Child." *Alternatives Magazine* 5, no. 2 (Winter 1975): 31-32.

A rationale for a Family Education program for the 9th Grade students and parents of the Stephen S. Wise Temple in Los Angeles. Program details are not included, but the books, movies, newspaper articles, and field trips used to introduce the topics are listed.

"Focus On the Changing Family." *Genesis 2* 13, no. 5 (March 1982).

Contains articles about searching for roots, Jewish men and lesbians, caring for aging parents, etc. Good for insight into the lifestyle of many who are not affiliated with mainstream Jewish institutions.

Grazman, Marcia. *Tzedakah and the Jewish Home: A Family Education Program*. St. Louis, MO: Shaare Emeth Religious School. (11645 Ladue Road, St. Louis, MO 63141; also available from the CAJE Curriculum Bank, 15600 Mulholland Dr., Los Angeles, CA 90077)

Good example of detailed one day program which involves large groups of people and which provides activities for adults as well as students, both separate and jointly.

Green, Kathy. "Intergenerational Jewish Education." *Melton Journal*, no. 17 (Winter 1984).

A rationale for intergenerational Jewish education. Provides many possible programs and practical suggestions for recruitment, as well as a bibliography of stories, books, and articles. Useful for Family Educators and to introduce a Board of Trustees to the need for such programming.

Grishaver, Joel Lurie. *Being Torah: A First Book Of Torah Texts*. Los Angeles: Torah Aura Productions, 1985.

Innovative children's Bible complete with children's commentaries to stimulate discussion. Can be used for weekly Torah study at the table or in any other setting.

Grishaver, Joel Lurie. "Family Kallah: A Program Guide." *Alternatives Magazine* 4, no. 3 (Spring 1974): 26-29.

Identifies basic objectives and techniques of family *kallot* based on their use at North Shore Congregation Israel in Glencoe, Illinois. An outline for planning the family *kallah* and an example of a weekend *kallah* schedule is included. The outline is helpful for individuals inexperienced at planning such events.

Gruenberg, Sandra S. *Chanukah Family Education Institute*. White Plains, NY: The Solomon Schechter School of Westchester, 1985. (30 Dellwood Road, White Plains, NY 10605)

Program for parents of families of K-3 and their siblings which takes place on *Motza'ay Shabbat* and all day Sunday. Contains schedules, as well as content covered. A fine example of complete programming for *all* age groups in attendance.

Grunwald, Emily and Karyn. *Get Ready, Get Set, Play.* Miami, FL: Central Agency for Jewish Education, 1981. (4200 Biscayne Blvd., Miami, FL 33157)

A manual of early childhood readiness and primary games for teachers and parents for children between 3-10. This is a good resource for activities to be used at retreats and workshops.

Hahn, Linda K. "A Religious Rite Of Passage and Parent-Adolescent Relations: Family Life Education for Bar/Bat Mitzvah Students." *Family Perspective* 18, no. 4 (Fall 1984).

A rationale for a program which addresses the need to prevent the serious dysfunction or disruption which often occurs because of the tensions surrounding Bar/Bat Mitzvah. The program helps the students understand their changing relationship with their parents and develop new and more effective ways of coping. The workshops also help the students express their feelings and share their concerns with each other. Workshop topics are listed and some techniques demonstrated. Good example of this type of activity.

*Hanukah: A Family Learning Kit.* Tel Aviv: Everyman's University, 1982; distributed by Alternatives in Religious Education, Inc.

A set of attractively designed booklets which may be used by the entire family for workshops or used by individuals. Topics include: Home and synagogue ritual, games, riddles, history of the holiday, Chanukah around the world, military exploits, the *menorah*, stories of martyrdom and courage, party ideas, songs (booklet and cassette tape), quizzes, and poems, and a boxed game.

Holzer, Judy. *Hey Family Mitzvah.* Cleveland: B'nai Jeshurun, 1982. Also available from CAJE Curriculum Bank.

Detailed description of a series of lectures/workshops which coincide with the seventh grade program for the B'nai Mitzvah and their partners. Contains a discussion of program goals, successes, and failures.

*Home Start*. Developed by Board of Jewish Education of Baltimore. New York: Behrman House, 1985.

Seven Packets to be mailed to parents of children ages 4-6 preceding Jewish holidays. Each package contains a picture book and a play and learn magazine with stories, games, recipes, prayers, and blessings, plus a parents' handbook, and a cassette with songs of high quality. This "Cadillac" of preschool home programming fosters parent-child participation.

Isaacs, Ronald H. *The Jewish Instructional Games Book*. Cleveland: Bureau of Jewish Education, 1986; distributed by the Board of Jewish Education of Greater New York.

A comprehensive book that includes games for Shabbat and holidays, Hebrew language, and prayer. For use in Junior Congregation. Contains a special section with background reading for the teacher on the rationale and function of experiential gaming, as well as a bibliography and a list of resources. Many of the games are adaptable to a variety of situations. Particularly useful for planning for family programs and retreats.

*Jewish Activities for Parents With Infants and Toddlers*. Philadelphia: Chomsky Educational Resource Center, Gratz College, May 1986.

Designed to be used as a companion to the Reform Curriculum *To See the World Through Jewish Eyes*, this resource can also be used independently by parents. It is especially good for use with parenting groups in preschools and Jewish Centers.

"The Jewish Family." *Medium*, no. 20 (Fall 1979). Jewish Media Service.

Review of 19 films dealing with various family issues — e.g., becoming parents, men and women, families in Israel, single parents, between generations, etc. Very helpful for programming. See also *Medium*, no. 7, May/June 1975, "Marriage and Jewish Society," and *Medium*, no. 14, "The Jewish Woman," Winter 1977.

*The Jewish Family In Christian America.* New York: United
Synagogue of America, 1980.

A summary of conference presentations on the concerns
society presents to the Jew wishing to live a meaningful
Jewish life in a non-Jewish environment. Includes program
material. Good as background for Jewish identity programs.

*The Joys Of Parenting.* New York: William Petschek National
Family Center, American Jewish Committee, 1985.

Articles by five Jewish women and men of different ages,
occupations, life styles, and religious orientations that deal
with the challenges and satisfactions of child rearing.
Authors of the articles are Jonathan Groner, Linda Buch,
Avis Dimond Miller, David Singer, and Blu Greenberg.

Kass, Sonya, and Lublin, Abe. *Family Shabbat Services and
Melodies.* Chicago: Board of Education of Metropolitan
Chicago, 1983. (618 S. Michigan Avenue, Chicago, IL
60605)

A family Shabbat service and melodies kit based on the
Rabbinical Assembly *Siddur.* Contains traditional songs
and responses which are easy to sing and a list of all the
songs with composers and arrangers. Kit contains an
album booklet of prayers and melodies in Hebrew and a
cassette that includes 51 prayers and melodies. Useful to
prepare families at home before and after a family service
and retreat. Helpful for music teachers and summer camp
programming.

Katz, Paul, and Rappaport, Margery. *Aleph Bet Home Study
Programs.* Columbia, MD: Howard County Jewish Com-
munity School, 1983. (5885 Robert Oliver Place, Columbia,
MD 21045)

Home study kits include mini-magazines that teach
Hebrew letters and vowels, review sheets, games, stories,
and activities to be created and used at home. Useful for
involving parents in the process of teaching their children,
and also helps parents acquire some basic knowledge of
phonic reading of Hebrew.

Kelman, Vicki, ed. *Together: A Parent-Child Kit*. New York: Melton Research Center, 1984-85.

A monthly kit designed to encourage partnership between school and home (nine issues). The parent-child learning kits are tied to the Aleph Curriculum of the Melton Center, but can be used independently by others as well. While meant for 8-9 year olds, a lot of the material can be used by older and younger siblings. Topics included: Tishre holidays, gifts, *brachot*, Shabbat, Chanukah, communication, trees, Purim, Pesach, and Torah. Contains unique board games, stories, activities, recipes, and guides for discussions. Very creative and esthetically pleasing.

*Kivunim*, no. 2 (Summer 1985). Leslie Simon, ed. Family Education Issue. Board of Jewish Education of Metropolitan Chicago.

Contains articles on various forms of Family Education — e.g., workshops, social work settings, parental involvement in classes, homework, and publicity. The Family Education Council is described as well. Helpful for Bureau personnel.

Levine, Shlomo B. *The Singular Problem Of the Single Jewish Parent*. New York: United Synagogue Commission on Jewish Education, Family Education Committee, 1981.

Part of a series on parenting, this volume addresses the problems of continuity of ritual life in a single parent family, differing religious patterns of divorced parents, and ethical issues involving *lashon harah* and *kibbud av v'em* as related to the non-custodial parent. Supermoms and "bribing" are also covered. The text provides some excellent sources on the responsibilities of parents which do not change just because there is only one parent parenting. Sources deal with love, care, encouragement, roots, values, and support. Highly recommended for principals, youth workers, and family educators.

Lipschutz, Karen. "A Family Shabbat Experience." *Alternatives Magazine* 7, no. 3 (Fall 1976): 18-19.

The author explains how she organized a program centered around the concept of creation, arts and crafts, study, and worship at Leo Baeck School, Toronto, Canada.

Lubliner, Shira, and Freeman, Gordon. *Toldoteinu: A Program Of Parallel Family Education*. Walnut Creek, CA: Congregation B'nai Shalom Religious School, 1984-85. (74 Eckley Lane, Walnut Creek, CA 94596)

A five year plan of parallel education for high school students and their parents. Topics included: First year – Bible, Post Biblical Periods; Second year – Rabbinic Period; Third year – Spanish/Medieval; Fourth year – Eastern European; Fifth year – Modern Age In America and Israel. Syllabus for the first three years is available. Parents and students also meet for special programs dealing with Toldoteinu themes, lectures, panel discussions, concerts, and a film festival.

Lukinsky, Joseph. "Making the Seder a Personal Experience: A Workshop." *Melton Journal*, no. 15 (Winter 1983): 24.

Description and simulation of a workshop on making the *Seder* a personal experience. Helpful in planning workshops of this type.

Maisels, Stanley. "Parent Education At Congregation Solel." *Compass*, no. 23 (April/May 1973).

Describes a parent education program that took place during a particular school year. Shows what can be done when the congregation's primary concern is with the parents growing as Jews. Based on the principle that parents best help their children grow as knowledgeable and committed Jews if they grow in knowledge and commitment themselves.

*The Mishpachah (Family) Line Of the Day School Curriculum*. New York: United Synagogue of America Commission on Jewish Education, 1986.

Extensive suggestions for family activities to coordinate with the *Mitzvah*, Bible, and *Tefilah* tracks of the curriculum. Unpublished manuscript. Useful for all schools, not just day schools.

Monson, Rela Geffen. *The American Jewish Family: Values, Issues, and Communal Responses*. New York: National

Committee on Leadership Development, Council of Jewish Federations, 1987.

Originally produced for leadership training, these excellent case studies which reflect current family problems and accompanying relevant classical sources can be used for adult education, retreats, and courses on the Jewish family. The materials provided evoke discussions and role playing. Topics include: Intermarriage, dual career families, the ticking biological clock, parent-child role reversal, blended families, "professional volunteers," "sandwich generation."

Morton, Sharon. *Home Holiday Observance Program*. Glencoe, IL: Am Shalom. (840 Vernon Avenue, Glencoe, IL 60022)

Extensive holiday program that could serve as a model for those institutions thinking of undertaking such programs.

Olitzky, Kerry M.. "Across the Generations (A Family Shabbat Experience)." *Compass* 5, no. 2 (Winter/Spring 1981-82).

A program for 8th Graders, siblings, parents, and grand-parents which has as its goal to explain the basic Jewish attitude toward aging and the aged in contemporary American Jewish society. Uses textual sources, survey values chart, film, and discussion groups. Good program for promoting intergenerational interaction.

Olitzky, Kerry M. "How to Raise a Jewish Child." *Pedagogic Reporter* 34, no. 3 (May 1983): 11.

A report on a two part mini-series of discussion programs which is designed to help with issues that parents may be facing as their children grow. Session 1: Priorities in Jewish parenting; children's questions such as "why do people die?" Session 2: Focus on God and moral development. Religious and psychological implications are dealt with. A Rabbi, a social worker, and a clinical psychologist serve as resource people.

Packer, Barbara. "From Generation To Generation." *Our Child 18*, no. 1. New York: Family Education Committee of the United Synagogue.

Program honoring grandparents that can be adapted for any synagogue.

Pomerantz, Barbara. *Who Will Lead the Kiddush?*. New York: Union of American Hebrew Congregations, 1985.

The story of a young girl adjusting to the changes brought on by the divorce of her parents. Useful for single parent workshops, as well as to sensitize all students to the issues.

Quint, Helen, and Margolis, Daniel. *The Nitzanim Program: A Manual for Conducting Synagogue Services for Preschoolers*. Newton, MA: Bureau of Jewish Education, 1982. (333 Nahanton Street, Newton, MA 02159)

Comprehensive description of Shabbat services for children ages 2-6. The manual deals in detail with all aspects from recruitment to seat arrangement. Contains music, prayers, stories, dances, and suggestions for the High Holy Days as well. An excellent aid in planning meaningful activities for retreats for this age group.

Rauch, Eduardo. "Families Of Our Times: Challenges To Our Courage and Imagination." *Melton Journal*, no. 11 (Fall 1980).

Excellent article and review of current literature. The article poses dilemmas about "crises in family" that will encourage discussions — e.g., Where are we moving from? Which model of family (nuclear, single parent, patriarchal, extended)? If we could, would we revive the old model of family? What is the best model? Are there Jewish solutions to non-Jewish problems? Useful for study groups and retreats.

Reisman, Bernard. *Programs to Support the Resurgent Jewish Family*. New York: American Jewish Committee, 1977.

Reisman analyses ways the Jewish community has responded to the family in the recent past and the way the community may and should respond in the future. An excellent examination of the prevailing general societal forces, the special interests, and the historical perspectives of Jews, and the way these forces interact. The paper reflects a positive attitude to the future of the family. Reisman does not see modern societal changes as a reason for jettisoning the family, but as the rationale for assuring its continuity. Includes suggestions for programs for Jewish Centers. Could be used in a course on Jewish family or for parent education.

Reisman, Bernard, and Abraham, Harriet. *Jewish Families Together: A Model Weekend Retreat for Family Life Enhancement*. New York: William Petschek National Family Center, American Jewish Committee, Winter 1986.

This program, for intact Jewish families, has four objectives: togetherness, Jewish content, Family Life Education, and a support network. The publication summarizes the activities, discussions, and interactions from the weekend. Included are Family Scenarios and a Family Values Questionnaire. This is a valuable resource for anyone wishing to set up a family retreat. It provides specific administrative guidelines, along with sample letters, registration forms, and an evaluation form. The information in regard to scheduling allows enough flexibility for the creative program coordinator to plug into different content areas.

Reisman, Bernard, and Rosen, Gladys. *Single Parent Families At Camp: The Essence Of An Experience*. New York: William Petschek National Family Center, American Jewish Committee, 1983.

This publication summarizes the five day 1983 seminar sponsored by the American Jewish Committee and B'nai B'rith Camps for single parents and their children and gives concrete suggestions for its replication. An important section entitled "Afterward: The Summary Of An Experience" pinpoints the issues which came to the fore at camp and addresses specifically three elements of the retreat: single parent family status, the camp experience as paradigm, and Jewishness.

Robbins, Reuven. *Jewish Family Rituals*. Philadelphia: Chomsky Educational Resource Center, Gratz College, 1980.

> Family communication exercises based on Jewish topics, such as liturgy, Purim, family, Shabbat. Useful for ideas for retreats and for family initiated home activities.

Ruberg, Arthur. *Jewish Survival and Intermarriage*. Philadelphia: Chomsky Educational Resource Center, Gratz College, November 1980.

> Discussions and activities for ages 14-17. Useful for high school and Jewish identity programs.

Saypol, Judyth Robbins, and Wikler, Madeline. *Come Let Us Welcome Shabbat*, 1978; *My Very Own Chanukah*, 1978; *My Very Own Haggadah*, 1974; *My Very Own Megillah*, 1976; *My Very Own Rosh Hashanah*, 1978; *My Very Own Sukkot*, 1980. Rockville, MD: Kar-Ben Copies, Inc.

> Although these books were meant for family use at home to enrich home celebrations, they are fine resources for parents, teachers, and retreat leaders, and are also good sources of information for student reports. Each contains explanations, songs, prayers, recipes, and topics for discussions. Highly recommended for elementary grades. Based on a two year cycle. Have a clear statement of goals.

Schacter, Lisa. "Reflections On the Brit Mila Ceremony." *Conservative Judaism* 38, no. 4 (Summer 1986).

> An analysis of the *Brit Milah* liturgy with particular emphasis on the function of the biblical figures mentioned. The inclusion of these figures in the service conveys to the family assembled a message that is of particular interest to new parents, as well as to those studying and teaching life cycle.

Shafton, Sally. "The Shabbat Family." *Reconstructionist* 45, no. 5 (July 1979): 17-22.

> The story of the Shafton Family's Shabbat Torah discussions. Useful for parenting groups and holiday workshops.

Silk, Carol. *Kadimah Family Programming: Seudah Shleesheet*. Carl Wolkin, ed. New York: Department of Youth Activities, United Synagogue of America, n.d.

A detailed example of a successful monthly program for Bar/Bat Mitzvah age children and their families. Useful for others planning similar programs.

Simon, Leslie. *Outreach To Intermarrieds and Jews By Choice*. Philadelphia: Chomsky Educational Resource Center, Gratz College, 1985.

Workshop outlines for study groups and retreats.

*So You're Having a Family Kallah*. New York: United Synagogue Commission on Jewish Education, 1975.

Detailed guide dealing with the how, when, what, and where of *Kallot*. Includes sample letter, publicity, schedules, outline of service.

Spiro, Jack D. "Family Life In Jewish Education." *Dimensions In American Judaism* 5 (Summer 1971): 38-41.

After discussing the phenomenon of family breakdown and the process of creating other forms of family, the author discusses the Family Life Education program of the Union of American Hebrew Congregations. The goals and some of the program materials are described. The parent-child encounter session is mentioned as a method for communication building. This monograph is a good stimulus for considering the family problems of today. No bibliography. Useful for educators.

*Stepfamily Bulletin*. Yvonne Horn, ed. Stepfamily Association of America, 28 Allegheny Avenue, Suite 1307, Baltimore, MD 21204.

This newsletter of the Stepfamily Association of America provides material for the educator and is a source of articles for discussions. Published since 1981, the information it contains is current and useful.

•

Swarttz, Michael. "Bar and Bat Mitzvah Workshops." *Pedagogic Reporter* 35, no. 1 (1984).

Report on workshops held at the Germantown Jewish Center. Useful as a model for Bar/Bat Mitzvah Programs.

Syme, Daniel. "Promoting Family Education." *Compass*, no. 27, (March 1974): 7.

A list of modules and program suggestions that can be used in synagogues.

Tornberg, Robert E. "Dad and I." *Compass* 2, no. 3 (Summer 1979): 18-19.

A description of a program based on Indian Guides and Princesses from an idea conceived by Stanley Ferdman of the J.C.C. of St. Louis. The goal is to provide opportunities for fathers and young children to have regular, structured, quality time together. A tribe of 7-10 fathers and children attend weekly meetings for 1½ hours. Each such group chooses a name from one of the 12 tribes of Israel and makes shirts, banners, etc. Each meeting begins with a candle lighting ceremony, followed by the giving of *tzedakah* and an explanation of how it was earned. Once in six weeks there is a meeting of all the tribes together which is usually centered around a holiday theme. The weekly program also contains crafts, songs, and a friendship circle. Fathers and children plan the program that they will host.

*Vital Connections*. Foundation for Grandparenting, P.O. Box 97, Jay, NY 12941.

Useful journal for family educators. Contains information that could be reproduced in the synagogue bulletin.

Wachs, Saul P. *Shimu V'Rananu*. New York: United Synagogue, Commission on Jewish Education, n.d.

Thirteen cassettes which teach the correct *nusach* for all services of the year (weekday, holiday, and Shabbat). Useful for schools, youth groups, and camps. Coordinated with the Conservative prayerbook and the United Synagogue afternoon school curriculum, although it can also be used independently. Very helpful for home study and for preparing students to lead worship services as *Shelichei Tzibur.* A guide accompanies the tapes. Individual cassettes may be obtained.

"Winning the Jewish Home: A New Frontier In Jewish Education." *Pedagogic Reporter* 27, no. 3 (Spring 1977).

Four articles and a fine annotated bibliography of theory and programming ideas.

*Within Reach.* New York: Task Force On Family Education, Board of Jewish Education, 1984.

An account of a project sponsored by the Department of Early Childhood Education which provides cumulative layers of enriching Jewish experiences for children attending Jewish Early Childhood programs in synagogues and J.C.C.'s. The program was designed to help the sponsoring agency to be a "communal parent" for the young family. Funded with a grant, it makes use of an outreach worker and clusters of families. Useful for both synagogue, communal, and city-wide agencies planning to initiate such programs.

Wolfe, Michael. "Perspectives On Jewish Family Education." *Pedagogic Reporter* 35, no. 1 (January 1984).

The author advocates a curriculum of caring and sharing and suggests that Jewish educational institutions should be thinking of ways they can help families cope with the stresses and problems of living. One idea is for educational institutions to coordinate their efforts and to provide direct services.

Wolfson, Ron; Segal, Benjamin; and Tucker, Sandy. *Ramah Israel Family Seminars.* New York: National Ramah Commission, 1985.

Intergenerational family education in Israel. Each family is assigned projects to be fulfilled during trip — e.g., researching a different tribe of Israel when they visited the Chagall windows at Hadassah Hospital. Each family

reported about their assigned tribe. Good use of environment for family education.

Wolfson, Ron. *Shall You Teach Them Diligently?* Los Angeles:
University of Judaism, University Papers, 1983.

A rationale for Jewish Family Education. Useful for training
family educators.

Wolfson, Ron. *The Art Of Jewish Living: The Shabbat Seder.*
New York: The Federation of Jewish Men's Clubs and
The University of Judaism, 1985.

This book combines a "how to" approach to the ten steps
necessary for the Friday night Shabbat meal with the
answers to the questions that beginning learners usually
ask. Interspersed are sections dealing with concepts,
objects, and Jewish practice, along with reactions and
comments of different families to the various steps.
Although usually used as part of an adult education course,
the book can be effective for self-teaching as well. Clear
and attractively presented.

Portions of this bibliography were prepared for The Seniors
Jewish Education Program Louis A. Pincus Fund for Jewish
Education for the Diaspora World Zionist Organization, Depart-
ment of Education and Culture, and Melton Center for Jewish
Education for the Diaspora of the Hebrew University. Much
assistance was given by the Chomsky Resource Center of Gratz
College, Philadelphia, Pennsylvania.

# Contributors

Janice P. Alper
Principal
Kehillath Israel Congregation, Pacific Palisades, California
28605 Quailhill Drive
Rancho Palos Verdes, California 90274

Harlene Winnick Appelman
Coordinator
Jewish Experiences for Families
6600 West Maple Road
West Bloomfield, Michigan 48033

Judy Aronson
Director of Education
Shir Chadash – New Reform Congregation
17000 Ventura Boulevard
Encino, California 91316

Shirley Barish
Education Consultant
Southwest Council Union of American Hebrew
Congregations
5227 Dumfries
Houston, Texas 77096

Sherry Bissell Blumberg
Professor of Education
Hebrew Union College – Jewish Institute of Religion
One West 4th Street
New York, New York 10012

Maureen Carey-Back
Activities Therapy Supervisor
Philadelphia Geriatric Center
5301 Old York Road
Philadelphia, Pennsylvania 19141

Debra Cohn-Levine
Director of Education
The United Jewish Center Religious School
141 Deer Hill Avenue
Danbury, Connecticut 06810

Melissa Coopersmith
Coordinator of Community Education Programs
Philadelphia Geriatric Center
5301 Old York Road
Philadelphia, Pennsylvania 19141

Sandy Dashefsky
Director
Hamerkaz Teacher Resource Center
Commission on Jewish Education –
Greater Hartford Jewish Federation
26 Buena Vista Road
West Hartford, Connecticut 06107

Dr. Leo Davids, Associate Professor
Department of Sociology
York University
4700 Keele Street
Downsview, Ontario M3J 2R7
Canada

Arlene Eisenberg
Author
Writing Associates
144 West 80 Street
New York, New York 10024

Robin Eisenberg
Director of Education
Temple Beth El of Boca Raton
333 S.W. 4th Avenue
Boca Raton, Florida 33432

Miriam Feinberg
Early Childhood Consultant
Board of Jewish Education of Greater Washington
11710 Hunters Lane
Rockville, Maryland 20852

Deborah Fins
Assistant to the Director
Jewish Family Service of Worcester, Inc.
646 Salisbury Street
Worcester, Massachusetts 01609

Annette Fish
Chairperson of the Early Childhood Subcommittee
Congregation B'nai Jehudah
712 East 69th Street
Kansas City, Missouri 64131

Rabbi Dayle Friedman
Chaplain
Philadelphia Geriatric Center
5301 Old York Road
Philadelphia, Pennsylvania 19141

Patricia Singer Golden
Director of Holiday Workshop Department
Stephen S. Wise Temple
433 18th Street
Santa Monica, California 90402

Maralee Gordon
Former Bar/Bat Mitzvah Coordinator
Am Shalom, Glencoe, Illinois
370 Lincoln
Woodstock, Illinois 60098

Alan W. Harris
Certified Rehabilitation Counselor
Jewish Family Service of Worcester, Inc.
646 Salisbury Street
Worcester, Massachusetts 01609

Saundra Heller
Director
Stepping Stones – To a Jewish Me
Temple Emanuel
51 Grape Street
Denver, Colorado 80220

Dorothy C. Herman
Director of Education
Temple Beth Am
5950 North Kendall Drive
Miami, Florida 33156

Cynthia Himmelfarb
Executive Director
Jewish Family Service of Santa Clara County
14855 Oka Rd. #18
Los Gatos, California 95030

Frieda Hershman Huberman
Program Director
Temple Beth Am
1039 South La Cienega Boulevard
Los Angeles, California 90035

Carol K. Ingall
Executive Director
Bureau of Jewish Education of Rhode Island
130 Sessions Street
Providence, Rhode Island 02906

Dr. Leora Isaacs
Faculty Member and Co-Administrator
Temple Sholom Hebrew High School
Box 6007
Bridgewater, New Jersey 08807

Rabbi Ronald Isaacs
Temple Sholom
Box 6007
Bridgewater, New Jersey 08807

Esphira "Happy" Iscove
Supervisor
Parent Student Programming, Primary Department
Holy Blossom Temple
1950 Bathurst Street
Toronto, Ontario M5P 3K9
Canada

Sharon Katz
Youth Activities Director
Congregation B'nai Jehudah
712 East 69th Street
Kansas City, Missouri 64131

Jo Kay
Teacher
Temple Emanuel of East Meadow
123 Merrick Avenue
East Meadow, New York 11554

Cherie Koller-Fox
Director
Harvard Hillel Children's School
89 Abbotsford
Brookline, Massachusetts 02146

Dr. Michael Korman
Director
Solomon Schechter School of Queens
76-16 Parsons Boulevard
Flushing, New York 11366

Karen Lebow
Consultant, Parent and Family Education
Jewish Family Life Education
Bureau of Jewish Education
6505 Wilshire Boulevard
Los Angeles, Calfornia 90048

Rabbi David Lieb
Temple Beth El
1435 West 7th Street
San Pedro, California 90732

Nachama Skolnik Moskowitz
Director of Education
Temple Israel
2004 East 22 Place
Tulsa, Oklahoma 74114

Dr. Judy Press
Director
Hamerkaz East and Suburban School Services
Commission on Jewish Education –
Greater Hartford Jewish Federation
26 Buena Vista Road
West Hartford, Connecticut 06107

Susan Rachlin
Family Education Coordinator
Board of Jewish Education
426 West 58th Street
New York, New York 10019

Fradya Rembaum
Assistant Director
Council on Jewish Life
Jewish Federation Council of Greater Los Angeles
6505 Wilshire Boulevard
Los Angeles, California 90048

Rabbi Nathan H. Rose
Director of Education
Temple Beth El
139 South Winton Road
Rochester, New York 14610

Ira H. Schweitzer
NFTY and Kutz Camp Program Director
National Federation of Temple Youth
838 Fifth Avenue
New York, New York 10021

Alan Shapiro
Jewish Family Life Education Coordinator
Jewish Family Service of Rochester, Inc.
441 East Avenue
Rochester, New York 14607

Marilyn E. Stoumen
Certified Social Worker in Family Life Education
Jewish Family and Community Service
2710 West Devon
Chicago, Illinois 60659

Robert E. Tornberg
Director of Education
Congregation B'nai Jehudah
712 East 69th Street
Kansas City, Missouri 64131

Union of American Hebrew Congregations
Department of Education
838 Fifth Avenue
New York, New York 10021

Barbara Eidelman Wachs
Coordinator of Community Service Activities
and Faculty Member Judaic Studies Department
Akiba Hebrew Academy
223 North Highland Avenue
Merion Station, Pennsylvania 19066

Sally Weber
Program Director
Adat Ari-El
5540 Laurel Canyon Boulevard
North Hollywood, California 91607

# Index Of Chapters
# By Subject

## Israel

## Jews In Other Lands

## Life Cycle

## Mitzvot

## Values